30
BEFORE
30

MARINA SHIFRIN

HOW I MADE A MESS OF MY 20s, AND YOU CAN TOO

The names and identifying characteristics of some persons described in this book have been changed, as have other details of events depicted in the book.

Printed in the United States of America. For information, address St. Martin's Press, 175 Fifth Avenue, New York, N.Y. 10010.

www.wednesdaybooks.com
www.stmartins.com

All images courtesy of the author

Designed by Anna Gorovoy

The Library of Congress Cataloging-in-Publication Data is available upon request.

ISBN 978-1-250-12971-0 (trade paperback)
ISBN 978-1-250-12972-7 (ebook)

Our books may be purchased in bulk for promotional, educational, or business use. Please contact your local bookseller or the Macmillan Corporate and Premium Sales Department at 1-800-221-7945, extension 5442, or by email at MacmillanSpecialMarkets@macmillan.com.

First Edition: July 2018

10 9 8 7 6 5 4 3 2 1

For Vladimir and Olga

CONTENTS

ACKNOWLEDGMENTS

This book would not exist if it weren't for three very special people: thank you to my editor, Sara Goodman, who has only said "Yes" to me. Sara, you've made my wildest dreams come true, and I will continue to show my appreciation through overly emotional emails. I'm extremely grateful for Anthony Mattero, my literary agent, who took a discarded baby idea and brought it into the light of day. Anthony, you are so good at what you do it's maddening. Oh my goodness, I have the largest amount of gratitude for Tim Honigman, my friend and manager, who is constantly demanding that I write, even when I don't wanna. Tim, thank you for feeding me, calling me babe, and holding my hand through this insane industry.

I have to thank Vladimir and Olga Shifrin: you two are my heart and soul, and every word in this book is dedicated to you. Everything is dedicated to you. To my little brother, Sanya, thank you for handing me the reins when it comes to capitalizing off the insanity that is our family. To my big sister, Lena, and brother-in law, Emil, thank you for having real jobs and for giving Vladimir three big 'n' bouncy grandchildren to distract from the fact that I have very little interest in doing the same.

Thank you to my family in Moscow: Olga, Ilya, Sopha, Aunt Tanya, Uncle Zhenya, Tanya, Denis, and little Anya, for giving me a home in my homeland and for stuffing me full of mushrooms.

I have to extend an extremely warm and grateful thank-you to my writer friends and the readers of my first draft: Katie Mathewson, Daniel Shar, Amy Dallas, Rebecca Grodner, and Ellington Wells (even though Ellington only read half the draft before getting distracted).

Thank you to Lucas, Soo, Michael G., Meredith, Clare, Tessa, Moshe, Guy, Dan, Ryan, Kyle, Sal, Disha, Barbie, Uncle Alan, Uncle Mark, Uncle Fima, Ben C., Ben L., Mariam, Lauren, Otto, Erez, Kevin, Mike, and Carl for letting me share their names and our stories—from my perspective.

I want to thank Daniel Jones, the editor of Modern Love, for being the first person to publish my writing. Daniel, you got me into this mess, and I am so appreciative.

Thank you to Roe Conn for giving me the encouragement needed to ditch my shadow career.

Thank you to Bettiann and Kelvin for always asking how the book was coming and for sharing Sam.

There is not enough paper on this earth for me to properly thank my real-kind-of-love Sam, so I'll say this: Thank you for chapter 19. This book would not be complete without you, and neither would I.

30
BEFORE
30

A LITTLE INTRO, IF I MAY...

I am moments away from turning thirty, and as I look back on my sloppy, sexy, sometimes sweet twenties, one thought runs through my head: "*I dominated.*" I don't have this kind of confidence with anything, mind you. I spend most of my time harshly judging my social skills, eyebrows, and internet consumption. But, when it comes to my twenties, I straight-up murdered them.

In the past nine years, I pursued my childhood dream of becoming a comedian. I moved to New York, then to Los Angeles. Kissed so, so many people. I lived in Asia and learned how to say, "I have one son," in perfect Mandarin. I bought a car and crashed it. I found the man of my dreams and turned him into my boyfriend—he's sitting next to me playing on his phone right now. I quit my day job in pursuit of my dream job. I went viral. I met, and accidentally flirted with, my childhood hero. I voted. I told all my crushes that I had a crush on them. I adopted a dog. I had some good one-night stands and some terrible ones. I got in shape and found some style. I took art classes. I surfed. I was wild and stupid, but in a constructive and educational way. I did a lot.

I'm not saying all of this to brag; I'm saying all of this because I want you to dominate your twenties too. It's hard at this age—no one takes you seriously, you're broke, and you no longer have the gentle and encouraging hand of teachers or parents guiding your every move. Speaking of teachers and parents, I've been very lucky on both counts, especially with the latter. My goofy, hilarious, kind, persistent parents are the reason I've accomplished each and every goal on this list. I've been absurdly privileged to come from a home of loud cheerleaders, harsh critics, and loving people. Vladimir and Olga Shifrin will always be funnier and more impressive than I am, but I have the upper hand when it comes to writing in English so you'll have to get their stories through me.

My parents moved to America in the early nineties in search of better opportunities than the ones they had in Russia. I am reminded of this at every moment possible. "See this cheese, Marina?" my father would ask, shaking a jar of parmesan in my face. "No such cheese in Russia. You're lucky to have such cheeses."

Even if I wanted to take my citizenship for granted, it was not allowed. To this day, I can't look at jumbo shrimp, Levi's jeans, or strollers without seeing escaped oppression, pain, and suffering.

Aside from the superior cheese selection in America, I was constantly reminded of something else: my unalienable right to pursue happiness. I was encouraged to go after anything I wanted, as long as what I wanted wasn't hurting people or getting tattoos. (For better or worse, I've done both.) Other than that, the only caveat to my pursuit of happiness was that I had to work for it. According to Vladimir Shifrin, "In America, work plus creativity plus work equals whatever you want." Sure, America was (and is) imperfect—devastatingly so at times—but it's still a million times better than Russia. This mentality is so deeply ingrained in my soul it seeps into my every action.

Being an immigrant is akin to surviving a near-death experience—minus the excitement. You constantly feel like you were given a second shot at life, and you want that shot to amount to something spectacular. I shudder to think I was a few lost documents away from brutal Soviet oppression—or at least that's what my parents tell me. I am currently crammed into window seat 43A on Aeroflot flight 107 heading to Moscow to find out what life in Russia would've been like.

When my family moved to the United States, we settled on Devon Avenue in Chicago. My dad worked a full-time job at a tiny jewelry shop and two part-time jobs at other jewelry stores in the Chicagoland area. When he wasn't working, he was studying English. The first phrase he learned was, "There are five eggs on the table. Do you want an egg?" Eight years later my dad became the boss of his own tiny jewelry shop and bought a four-bedroom house in the suburbs. Our house was a few blocks from where Chicago Bulls MVP and nineties hero Michael Jordan lived. If that's not the American Dream, I don't know what is.

Watching what my parents went through, the struggles they faced and all they've achieved, eliminated any excuse I could ever have for *not* achieving success in America. All I needed to do was define what "success" meant for me.

Turns out, this was a lot harder than it seems.

I woke up one day, a little hungover, and found that I was profoundly disillusioned with my life. The one I had built for myself. The night prior to this revelation, I was at my friend Tessa's apartment loaded up on wine and complaining about work. Like most people our age, Tessa and I were disappointed with where the tuition dollars, hours of studying, and countless job interviews had gotten us. Tessa was a textile manufacturer's bitch in Manhattan and I was a hardly paid financial blogger in Brooklyn. She wanted to be a fashion designer, and I wanted to be a stand-up comedian—we'd both missed the mark.

It wasn't until I was sitting on Tessa's floor that I realized I'd not only failed to achieve *any* successes, but I'd also developed a minor drinking problem in the process. I'd known how to say, "There are five eggs on the table. Do you want an egg?" for over twenty years and it got me nowhere. What was I doing with my life?

On this night, the too-much-wine night, our cynicism led us to an idea: a list of thirty things to complete by the time we each turned thirty. No rules. No impossibilities. Only a timeline.

We became intoxicated with the idea of having a hobby that would add some dimension to our stagnant lives. We spent the entire night yelling goals at each other, our excitement growing with each one. Drive a cab. Have a drink in every borough. Buy real furniture. Get published in *The New York Times*. Be on the *Today Show*. Eat at every dollar dumpling spot in Chinatown. In the end, the only goal we had in common was "Quit Shitty Job."

The next morning, I woke up, faced with my mind-numbingly boring job, and made a decision: I was going to actually stick to my list. I didn't want this thing to disappear into a drunken Brooklyn night like many of our other "genius ideas."

My 30 before 30 list was the restart button I was looking for. I desperately wanted to prove to my parents that moving to America was a good choice and that I was taking advantage of the opportunities for which they worked so hard. I didn't want to be another lost twentysomething, wasting my youth and smooth skin on a bad job and recurring existential crises. My father didn't work himself to the bone so that I could curl up into an anxious ball every time I was confronted with my difficult-to-pursue dreams. Coming up with, and sticking to, my 30 before 30 list gave me some much-needed focus. It gave me a second chance at doing my twenties right and conquering my own version of the American Dream.

Slowly, I began valuing The List over everything else. It became more important than work, relationships, and gut instincts. I found that completing one goal led me to the next, which led to the next. I climbed it like a ladder, pounding my chest every time I got a little higher. I began to gain attention from people, first a couple hundred, then a thousand, and eventually millions—thanks to the great and terrifying equalizer that is the internet.

Emails from strangers asking for my advice on everything from romance to business flooded my inbox. My instinctual reaction was to tell them to ask someone more experienced, but I realized that my inexperience was what was making people comfortable enough to come to me. I'm not a guru of knowledge and sanity; I'm stressed, insecure, and sometimes shrewd, but mostly obsessed with finding ways to become a better/cooler/smarter person. I'm not an enlightened twenty-nine-year-old (there's no such thing); I'm just a shmuck who figured out, finally, how to negotiate a decent salary, pack a suitcase in under thirty minutes, compose a direct email, ask a guy out, and wash my bras.

On paper, I shouldn't have anything interesting to say about my life. My parents are still married. Aside from a few slippers (and unintelligible Russian curses) thrown in my direction, I was never abused. I grew up in the quiet, middle-class suburbs where the biggest obstacle kids face is whether to get on Ritalin, antidepressants, or both. I like to drink, but not enough to miss work. I've had a pretty fucking idyllic life. But thanks to The List, I've carved out a little bit of a name for myself, grown into a somewhat happy person, and squeezed out every perk my twenties had to offer.

I've had a lot of incredible opportunities, and it wouldn't be fair to keep them to myself. That's why I want you to read this book. I worked hard on it and I wrote it for you. Especially if "you" are: a young woman, a friend of mine, a follower of mine, an emotionally progressive frat boy, an entitled overachiever, a lawyer who wants to be more creative, an old man who wants a different perspective, a doctor who's super inventive but a little depressed, an immigrant with beautiful handwriting, a programmer who likes to bake, an accountant who dreams of being a wedding planner, my dad, an Instagram celebrity, an unemployed administrative assistant, a comedian, an unfulfilled graphic designer, a teacher with a penchant for organizing, a parent with a college kid, a parent without a college kid, a college kid, rich, poor, or a person who is about to go on vacation and forgot the book you were reading so now you're standing in the airport wanting to read something funny and uplifting.

This book will teach you how to take advantage of your twenties while simultaneously coming to terms with the fact that they are ending. I want every young person on earth to know it's okay to have high, possibly unrealistic, expectations of yourself and that it's also okay to pursue those expectations like the obsessive fool that you are. Throughout all the successes and failures of pursuing the goals on my 30 before 30 list, I found there is no defined pathway to success. There's what works for you and what doesn't.

So take that motorcycle riding class, construct a healthy relationship with failure, buy a one-way ticket to Japan, muster up the courage to tell someone you're in love with them, or ask for a promotion—I'll be here, cheering you on.

These stories will show you that you don't have to be extraordinary to accomplish your biggest, dreamiest goals. I mean, just look at me: I am an average-looking, sometimes overweight Russian girl from the suburbs, and I've maintained your attention for this long. Anything is possible!

NOTES

MARINA'S 30 BEFORE 30 LIST!

10·13·201

1. QUIT SHITTY JOB
2. FIND A JOB I LOVE
3. ADOPT A DOG
4. BUY real FURNITURE
5. SELL A PAINTING
6. LIVE IN A DIFFERENT COUNTRY
7. MOVE BACK TO NEW YORK
8. TAKE A WRITING CLASS
9. BECOME A MUSE
10. FLY FIRST CLASS
11. LEARN HOW TO DRESS MY BODY
12. GO TO A NUDE BEACH
13. DONATE HAIR
14. COOK A FIVE-COURSE MEAL
15. RIDE BIKE ACROSS BROOKLYN BRIDGE

The order of accomplishments has been changed

NOTES

16. HAVE A DRAMATIC AIRPORT REUNION
17. SUBMIT AN ESSAY TO THE NYT
18. DO A LATE-NIGHT SET
19. WATCH ALL THREE GODFATHER MOVIES
20. GO TO INDIA
21. EAT A MEAL ALONE
22. TAKE A CITY BUS TOUR
23. LEARN TO DRINK
24. TELL A STORY AT THE MOTH
25. BECOME FAMOUS
26. BECOME A GOOD HOST
27. MEET ROE CONN
28. FALL IN LOVE (FOR REAL)
29. VISIT RUSSIA
30. WRITE A BOOK

to reflect their "order of appearance" in my life.

GO TO A NUDE BEACH

When I was in the sixth grade, I used to smell like beef jerky. The smell, I'm sure, came from the thick leather jacket I wore every . . . single . . . day. Even during muggy Midwestern summers. I told everybody that I wore the jacket to be more like my idol Michael Jackson (which, now that I think about it, seems more embarrassing than the actual reason).

The real reason I wore a leather jacket every day was because I was embarrassed about my arms. More specifically: the jet-black hair poking through my skin like puberty weeds. The stiff leather of my jacket prevented me from mindlessly pushing up my sleeves and revealing my secret.

There were times when it was hard to hide my condition from the outside world. Gym, for example. I'd change into the required T-shirt and shorts, then proceed to walk around with my hands interlocked behind my back. I was awful at dodgeball.

My hairy arms are a gift from my dad, a furry little European man who has enough chest hair to cause a PETA rally. I used to bury my Polly Pocket in his hair, pretending like she was lost in a haunted forest. I also got his thin wrists, short temper, skinny legs, and big chest—our body type is bullfrog, our demeanor is bulldog. My mom, on the other hand, is a taller gentile with bare legs, arms, and god knows what else. It was always her objective to be as hairless as possible. I once walked in on her shaving the thin, wispy hair on her forearms. "Are you shaving your arms?" I asked. "No." She answered while parting a sea of shaving cream with a pink plastic razor.

My embarrassment about my arms spread to the rest of my body in the seventh grade. I was at my most-beautiful-friend Clare's house when I learned there were a lot of parts to your body and that you should hate most of them. I knew Clare was my most beautiful friend because my mother told me that every chance she got. "You know who is the most beautiful girl in your grade?" My mother told me while flipping through my yearbook. "Clare," she followed, not waiting for a response.

One day Clare and I were in her den, watching TV, when she got up to use the bathroom. As she passed a full-length mirror, she moaned, "God, I fucking hate my thighs. They're too big." (She was one of the only twelve-year-olds in my grade who sounded natural when she swore. I always sounded clumsy, like I was trying to pronounce a foreign word. I still do. I once called someone a "fulcker" because I got nervous in the middle of saying it.) Clare's declaration was the first time I learned that body parts could be "too big." I came home and examined my own body. My feet were tiny, my ankles were thin, my legs slender, and my thighs were not big. Then I got to my stomach. At the time, I liked to squeeze my gut between my hands until there was a vertical crease from the belly button down. "It looks like a lady's butt!" I'd scream as my parents shrieked with laughter. I'd jump on their bed and pretend to belly dance by flopping my stomach from left to right. I can still see the two of them curled over, in the fetal position, gasping for air. I stood at the mirror squeezing my fat. Just like that, my funniest weapon turned into my greatest enemy. Woof.

Contrary to what a man with shaggy hair and deep eye-sockets once said, no one's body is a "wonderland." We're all skin burritos, filled with organs, blood, and bile, John Mayer. *All* bodies are gross. Sure, there are anomalies (I've seen Kate Upton, RuPaul, and Cher—those three will always have better bodies than all of us combined), but I am talking about you and me here. We're just normal humans. Normal humans who don't have a team of professionals coating us in makeup so that it seems like we're somehow lovelier than the rest of the world.

Maintaining and projecting a body that's considered to be a "wonderland" is an unreasonable standard and also a waste of time. I realized my body wasn't that big of a deal at twenty-three, when I got naked on a beach for the first time.

My obsession with nude beaches had started ten years earlier, when my dogmatic commitment to keeping my body fully covered at all times reached a snag. My sister was getting married and decided to have a sort of a familymoon in the middle of the summer on a beach in a hot, hot desert country known to most people as Israel.

"Why does Lena hate me?" I whined at my father as he delicately folded a white linen suit into his suitcase. "I can't go to the Middle East! It's dangerous, and even worse: hot!"

He walked over to a drawer of Speedos and pulled two out. My mom came into the room to run defense. "Не качайся на папе! Он не для этого повесился," she grumbled while ushering me out. This directly translates to, "Stop swinging on your father, that's not why he hanged himself!" I heard it a lot as a child.

"Am I fat?" I asked my mom as she headed downstairs.

Mom and I both striking our most flattering poses.

"Yes! But don't worry, Marina," she tried to console me, "you are just in your ugly face." My mom meant to say, "ugly phase," but it was too difficult for her to pronounce with a Russian accent.

No matter how much I petitioned to move the wedding somewhere cooler, the location remained in Israel.

When we got off the plane in Eilat, I noticed something I'd never noticed before: bodies. Half-naked, toned, glistening, adult bodies. These were nothing like the bloated Midwestern bodies I'd grown accustomed to seeing on the edges of Lake Michigan. These were exotic, sea-bodies, sporting G-string bikinis, Speedos, and the kind of lightness that comes with not obsessing over what you look like.

My confidence had been demolished by the hordes of Russian women buzzing around my teen years. Women who, during holidays, squeezed themselves into a pair of Spanx only to shimmy into their tightest discount T.J. Maxx dress. They looked like sparkly sausages. These women would then wrap themselves in the largest, gaudiest fur coats their husbands could afford. They spent their nights huddled in doorways, chain smoking and complaining about how chubby their daughters were getting. I, of course, was one of those chubby daughters. I'd developed the bad habit of snacking on mayonnaise sandwiches, and it was beginning to show.

"Ты поправилась!" those same women would exclaim when they saw me, which directly translates to "You've gotten better!" This compliment never quite made sense to me, but I accepted it all the same. "Спасибо!" was my go-to response. I loved being noticed by adults. I loved being noticed.

Years later I'd learn that while "Ты поправилась" does indeed mean "You've gotten better," it also means "You've gotten fatter." I was blushing and thanking people who were calling me fat.

I wish I'd seen the Israeli beach bodies as an invitation to embrace my own, but they felt like reminders to stay covered up.

My sister's familymoon forced me out of my bulky sweatshirts and into beach attire. Our first morning in Eilat, I stood naked in my parents' hotel bathroom, avoiding eye contact with the wall-to-wall mirrors. My stomach had grown so rapidly that I had four lightning-bolt-shaped stretchmarks all pointing toward my belly button—ones I still have today.

My entire family was already at the beach, or as my dad calls it, "the bitch." Russians take vacation bitch culture very seriously. Starting at six a.m., they race (in hordes) to the hotel's meticulously aligned plastic lounge chairs—channeling Soviet-era grocery store intensity. They drag said chairs by twos, elbowing other Russians as they go, to the most ideal spots on the beach: next to trees, under umbrellas, near the bar. They line up their spoils and repeat this process until there are enough chairs for the entire family—and some extra because, "You never know who we'll run into." To claim a plastic village as one's own, Russians will take every available towel, including hand and face, from their hotel rooms and drape each one across the lounge chairs they've gathered. It creates a terrycloth chain of protection. The towels are then topped with knock-off Gucci sunglasses to finalize the newly erected territory.

Back in my parents' bathroom I shoved my tubby body into a bathing suit. The stretchy nylon fabric groaned against my girth. I then took a second bathing suit, with a completely different cut and color, and squeezed myself into that one too. Voilà! Spanx. I sucked in my stomach until my ribs were almost visible. *Not so bad*, I thought. I searched for a towel to cover myself for the walk to the water, but gave up quickly after realizing they were all at the bitch.

I scurried to where my entire family, plus gaggles of gorgeous Middle Eastern men, were smoking breakfast cigarettes. My father was the first one to see me. He slid his sunglasses off his face. "Why are you wearing two bathing suits?" he asked. A valid question, considering normal people don't layer bathing suits. My chest tightened. Busted.

"Are you saying I'm fat?" I screamed, before jumping into the pool to hide my body. "Are you saying I'm fat?" became my family's favorite response to any and every question. One that's still used today.

My interest in going to a nude beach didn't come until later in the trip, when I was on a scuba-diving excursion with my uncle, twelve-year-old cousin, and brother-in-law of five minutes. It happened while we were submerged underwater; the boys were off trying to do somersaults while I was screaming into my mask to see if anyone could hear me.

I noticed that my uncle, cousin, and brother-in-law had stopped goofing around and were mesmerized by something above them. I flipped onto my back, and then I saw it: a topless woman doing the breast stroke through the Red Sea. They were my first stranger-boobs, and they were magnificent. The way they floated in the water, two yolks, converging and diverging. All four of us drifted there staring. It's a fond family memory, for different reasons, obviously, but still. I decided, right then, that I too wanted to be unapologetically naked like a foreigner. I wanted to have the grace and confidence of this empowered mermaid, to be as self-assured in my own skin as she was in hers. I wanted to peel off my double-layer bathing suit and float through the water, bare chested, without a care in the world.

Ten years after first spotting this woman, I was in Chile visiting my college friend Ben when the opportunity to get naked at a beach presented itself. Ben, a tall, sometimes serious, usually silly man with six-pack abs and broad shoulders, was my co–resident assistant in college. We were assigned to the floor with all international students and loved our jobs *almost* as much as we loved hanging out with each other. Because we were RAs our social lives involved little more than resident assistant safety trainings, bulletin boards, and weekly meetings. Most of my college memories are comprised of sitting on Ben's bed, eating pre-sleep Gardetto's, watching him do pre-sleep crunches.

Ben was also the first person to see me do "stand-up." I made him sit on my bed as I performed stand-up into a hairbrush. I told him jokes until he was on the floor, in a fit of giggles, and then spent two years asking him if he thought I was funny enough to do real stand-up.

I got into Santiago, Chile, early in the morning and immediately crawled into bed at Ben's hostel where his Chilean boyfriend, Francisco, slept. Francisco was the most beautiful person I'd seen up close. He looked like an E! host and had four names, each sounding more exotic than the previous one. But he went by Pancho, which is how I will reluctantly be referring to him for the remainder of this story.

"Hello, I am Pancho, you are nice"—his brow furrowed—"you are nice to—" He looked at Ben for help. Not happening. "You are nice to meet you?" He attempted to correct himself and concluded with, "A*i*, fuck it!" Which became our slogan for the trip.

We spent the Fourth of July in a cabin on a beach called Playa Luna, Chile's most popular (and only) nude beach. Ben's friends Jill and Matias tagged along for the trip. Matias was from Chile, while Jill was from the States, which meant they were in the most exciting of relationships: one with an expiration date. It's a shame too; they clearly loved each other. Their effervescent connection almost made me regret being single, but I quickly remembered how much fun it is to make out with strangers at three a.m.

That night, in the cabin, we drank hot wine, played cards,

and ate hot dogs. The couples would take turns sneaking into corners to kiss, while I talked *at* whoever was stuck babysitting me. When I drink, I become a conversational vampire—sucking all the energy out of discussions, growing stronger and louder as I do it. "The thing people don't understand about Search Engine Optimization . . ." I droned on until everyone fell asleep, each cuddling their loved one, and one person cuddling her empty family-sized bag of chips.

In the morning, I woke up to a small tremor, my first. I played it cool by screaming "EARTHQUAKE" and crawling under the nearest table. The outburst got a few grumbles, but no one else woke up. My heart was racing too fast to go back to bed, so I headed out to the balcony. The cold, gray beach was quiet and empty. Too dreary to be peaceful, too foreign to be boring.

Once everyone was awake and had had enough weak coffee to stave off any potential hangovers, we went for a wander on the beach. We found weird rocks and picked up tiny crabs. We hugged and took photos. I practiced Spanish with Pancho, and he practiced English with me. It was a listless kind of wander. The kind you only get to indulge in when you're an independent, responsibility-free beta-adult.

We got to a particularly secluded part of the beach when Jill stopped dead in her tracks, turned to the group, and said, "You wanna do it? You guys want to get naked?"

A jolt of adrenaline coursed through my chip-and-alcohol-filled body. I pulled Jill aside, "I'm not, um. My situation isn't taken care of," I whispered. (This is one of the last times I referred to my pubic hair as my situation. It's pubic hair on my vagina. Every woman past college-age, nay, past high-school-age, should be able to confidentially refer to her vagina as a "vagina," or whatever the equivalent is in her native tongue. Situation, Lady Parts, Down There, Hoo-ha—it's too cutesy. Just this past week, I heard a forty-year-old woman refer to her vagina as her "Suzie." Stop it.)

"Uh, yeah . . . neither is mine," Jill responded. I'd just assumed that pretty girls always had perfectly manicured pubic areas. Not the dark and tangled web us Russian girls occasionally sport. Jill's confused response made me realize how stupid my comment was. As if unkempt pubic hair and being naked are mutually exclusive. Can you imagine?

"So, let's do it?" Jill repeated.

I hesitated. Again, I was on a beach, but this time my body was ten years older. The stretchmarks were still there but they had faded from pink to white. Now they curved, like large quotation marks, around my belly button, which made it feel ironic. Yes, I wanted to be the woman with the egg-yolk breasts, swimming through the Red Sea. But I also assumed that there would be more time to build up my confidence, maybe do some crunches before disrobing in public.

Pancho, who had been planning his wedding to Ben (they broke up a year later), walked over when he noticed I was grappling with something. He took my hands, looked deep into my eyes, and said, "A*i*, fuck it?"

I looked around. I didn't expect my crowning moment of body clarity would be as the fifth wheel on an empty beach in the middle of a Chilean winter, but I also knew there wouldn't be many opportunities to get naked in public later on. "Fuck it," I told the group.

Matias and Jill cheered, while Ben grew uncharacteristically quiet. "I'm getting over a cold, so I should probably bow out of this one," he told us. I couldn't believe it. The only person I knew who was built like a Grecian statue was bowing out of getting naked.

"But you're the one who put all of this together," I said as I waved an upturned palm across the empty water, "You brought us to a nude beach."

"Well, I think you guys should definitely get naked. Pancho and I will guard the clothes." Pancho walked over to some rocks and obediently sat down.

"What are we? In summer camp? Who's going to take a hoodie from Target and my saggy underwear?" I snarked. Ben pressed his lips together. I'd seen that look when we were RAs. It was the look he'd get before he'd yell at our residents. Something he hated doing, but was goddamn great at. I backed down. I was a guest, after all. Besides, what kind of decent person strong-arms someone into getting naked against his will? "Okay, you snooze you lose, loser," I grumbled.

Ben later admitted that he was feeling a little insecure about an innocuous rash he'd gotten on his upper thighs. *See?* Even hot people have body issues. It's a shame though, I would've really liked to have seen his penis.

Jill took off her green long-sleeve shirt, revealing a flat tummy and perfectly sized breasts tucked away in a very cute bra. I suddenly felt trapped in my momentary expression of carefreeness. I didn't want to get naked with these two conventionally hot and fit people. Matias took off his pants. It started and it wasn't going to stop. Jill removed her pants. I was trapped. I sighed, turned my back to the group, and began wriggling out of my sweatshirt. I tore off my clothes so quickly, you would've thought they were on fire. I didn't want anyone to see my body bending and jiggling out of all the layers I'd worn. My worst angle is a ninety-degree one. When I'm bent over, my breasts look like udders. So do everyone's, though.

The winter air hit my pale skin, and I braced for the stares I assumed would accompany nudity. But instead of looking at my stretchmarks and hair, Matias and Jill ran off hand in hand toward the beach. I looked over to Ben and Pancho, who were playing with the settings on my camera. No one was looking at me. Of course. Of course, nobody was looking at me. Because couples don't care what your body looks like. Most people don't.

"Ben, take a picture," Jill called over her shoulder. She turned back to Matias and me, "Let's grab butts!" And so, we grabbed butts.

Sometimes I think about all those trips to beaches I'd missed out on. I think about how I spent years meticulously shielding my body from any kind of light, air, or touch, and I get sad for my younger self. What a waste of a good and functioning body.

That day on the freezing beach, with someone else's buttocks in my hands, I learned to coexist with my body. I even started taking care of it. Nothing fancy: some light exercise, eating decent things, sometimes. Not vacuum sealing myself in leather during the summers. You know, simple stuff. My life improved immensely after that. I had more time to think about other things, easier to control things, like my career.

As time goes on, our responsibilities increase, our skin becomes less taut, wrinkles creep into the corners of our eyes—and listen, all of that's great! It's going to help you get that promotion/respect/footing you want because you'll look all stately and stuff. It's not, however, going to make nakedness any easier. Your body will continue to change as you get older—constantly forcing you to get used to the new version.

That's why I cannot emphasize this enough: *Your twenties are for being naked as much as possible.* So please, take off your clothes. Now.

Playa Luna, Horcón, Chile.

RIDE BIKE ACROSS BROOKLYN BRIDGE

There is no better way to greet a city than from the seat of a bike. You become intimately connected to the streets as they vibrate through the rubber wheels, up the metal frame, and into your vagina—or, if you're a man, your male vagina.

But it took me a long time to learn the beauty of owning a bike.

My first bike in New York was a shitty beach cruiser that couldn't go up hills. I had to get off and push it like a stalled car. In fact, it didn't take flat surfaces that well either. I was always showing up to places drenched in sweat and smelling of onions.* "What's that smell?" I'd say, deflecting attention from that fact that it was my own armpits. I almost immediately got a biking ticket and rarely got through a ride without slamming my shins into the pedals. The cruiser was heavy and awkward, which made me feel heavy and awkward when I was on it. I hated that bike.

All I wanted was to blissfully ride through the city, maybe

---

* At least I'd graduated from beef jerky.

even in a dress, like the girls in the yogurt commercials. I wanted to torpedo across the Brooklyn Bridge, with nothing but the East River surrounding me. Plus, bridge bikers are exceptionally cool. Fearless. Unlike the joggers, who are clearly there to show off, or the tourists who are clogging up the flow, bikers have somewhere to be—so much so that they risk the intactness of their skulls to get there.

And, my god, did I love that bridge; the squat men selling icy water bottles at each end, how it lights up like a menorah at night, the arches that meet at a point. I used to have this theory that if I had a first-date kiss on the Brooklyn Bridge, I'd most likely marry that person.* (My understanding of love, at the time, was sophomoric at best.) I spent years luring guys toward the bridge like a slutty siren centering her prey, but something always got in the way—most of the time it was my inability to stop talking.

I wanted to ride my bike across the bridge because it would symbolize a unique kind of city mastery, a trust between myself and New York. A trust built on knowing the roads, potholes, cracks, and how to ride a damn bike without closing my eyes. As the months went on, it became clear that my beach cruiser was not going to *cruise* anywhere, especially not over that bridge.

But I never got rid of that bike because it had been free and I am an immigrant. It's a cultural taboo, in our community, to throw anything away. "If you can use it, it is to be cherished," my mother told me while writing "sleeping pills" on an empty

---

* If you're wondering, I *did* end up having a first kiss on that bridge. It was with a comedian friend named Kyle. He'd moved to Brooklyn and we decided to celebrate with whiskey. I, drunk-girl, demanded that we end the night on the bridge. As soon as we set foot onto the wooden slats, I swung my body into Kyle's and proceeded to kiss his mouth. Kyle kissed me back and then violently threw up all our celebratory whiskey. We are not married.

bottle of aspirin. Despite the fact that the bike was essentially useless, I still grew attached to it; but that's probably because of the guy who gave it to me.

Erez and I met on Fourth Avenue and President Street in Brooklyn. I was grabbing a coffee with my friend Mariam, who was roommates with my most recent ex-boyfriend, Mike.

Earlier that morning, Mike and I had still been a couple. However, our relationship quickly ended after I drank too much at a work event and locked lips with a greasy magazine editor in the office next door. Because I cannot live with shame, I trudged to Mike's house first thing in the morning and woke him up with news of my infidelity. Mariam happened to walk into her living room moments after he broke up with me. I stood on their porch, with a plastic bag of my things, and asked Mike for a goodbye hug because I'm a social-etiquette-idiot. He obliged. It was the stingiest, coldest hug to ever take place on that porch, I'm sure of it. The last thing I saw was Mariam mouthing, *What the fuck?* And then the door shut.

I hadn't gotten more than a few steps out of the apartment before Mariam texted me, demanding we get coffee. Twenty minutes later, we were sitting in the corner of Root Hill Cafe where I tearfully told Mariam about my infidelity.

When I finished, Mariam laughed. Directly chuckled into my face. "Who cares, you weren't right for each other anyway," she told me. Why is it that when you break up with someone, all these people come out of the woodwork like clairvoyant gnomes? "I *knew* this would happen," they say while filing their toenails.

After coffee, we stepped out into the street, toward the Union R station, and someone yelled, "HEY!" At this point, I had been in New York for over a year and knew better than to turn around when some guy was yelling at me, but this particular dude was persistent. "Hey!" This time it was closer. I turned around to see a guy running toward us. He had these huge nostrils that looked like they could each fit two slender fingers inside and lollipop curls that bounced as he jogged over. His lips were full, large even, and nestled in a bed of stubble. I was taken with how handsome he was.

"You kind of ruined everything," he said. Mariam and I exchanged confused looks. He rested his hands on his knees to catch his breath. "I was going to come over, introduce myself, and maybe ask for your number and you just . . . left," he told us between breaths.

I don't know if it was my absolute obliviousness to the male gaze, or because New York is packed with young, horny people who have disproportionate amounts of confidence (due to alcohol and lack of sleep), but I was very good at attracting strange, emotionally unavailable men. "Do you soak your nipples in beer every night?" a friend asked me after a LensCrafters model–looking guy followed us off the bus to ask for my number.

The embers from my most recent relationship were still hot enough to blow back to life, but I couldn't pass up a good opportunity to flirt. "I guess you'll have to be faster next time," I told him. My snide comment worked, and he handed me a small business card. All it said was "Erez: Expert" with a phone number at the bottom.

I only waited a week after my breakup before calling Erez; my relationship metabolism was very strong at the time. We made plans to meet for ice cream on a Saturday and then he promptly stood me up. *He'd better be in a car accident,* I thought as I wriggled out of my roommate's dress. Two days later Erez texted. He *was* in a car accident and was *so sorry,* could he make it up to me? The accident, while only a fender-bender, gave me enough guilt to let him stand me up for the rest of our semi-relationship.

Once a month for about four months, Erez would delicately fold up my heart and then stomp on it. He'd disappear, come back, and mend my heart so that it'd be in proper shape to stomp on again. When he wasn't standing me up, he was the most confusing and romantic partner. He introduced me to musicians, artists, and home-cooked meals. He'd hold my hand in convenience stores and proudly kiss me in front of his friends. He would swipe flowers from planters and give them to me.

"Hey," he'd softly say as he tucked the dog-urine-soaked flower behind my ear, "I'm not your boyfriend, okay?"

"Of course," I told him, my voice rising to an unnatural octave. Maybe if I were as relaxed about our relationship as he was he'd want to give more of himself to me.

"You're incredible," he'd tell me as I blacked out with elation.

Another thing Erez introduced me to was his red fixed-gear bike. He brought it everywhere with him. I wanted him to love me as much as he did that bicycle.

At this point, I hadn't been on a bike since middle school, but maybe if I, too, had a bike, it'd be easier to force a connection with Erez. We could ride across the Brooklyn Bridge, holding hands as we pedaled, kiss in the middle, and he'd fall in love with me because that bridge is magic. Perhaps I'd even let go of the handlebars and let out a scream of jubilation.

When I told Erez I was thinking of getting a bike, he was nothing but supportive. We began sizing up bikes on the street to see if we could imagine my little body riding on top. He'd position me next to a faded blue commuter and squint his eyes. "Nah." We'd move on.

The most dangerous people are those who get wrapped up in your plans, but cannot help you execute them. Their inability to commit slows you down until you're barely moving . . . like a broken cruiser. But isn't that just a part of the endless cycle of dating? Hurt. Love. Love Hurts. Hurt Loves.

BOYS N' BIKES
(what does his bike say about him?)
BMX
Can't take you out on fancy dates because of his exorbitant medical bills (or because he's a middle schooler)
CRUISER
all about sun, surfing, and sex, bruh
(or is a jewish city gal who got a good deal ($0) on this bike.)
FOLDING BIKE
nerdy xenophile who kinda wishes he were born in a different country but will work hard to fit into your life
FIXED GEAR
Smells of sweat and pickles, has 1-10 tattoos and an unquenchable thirst for PBR (might also be a Latino teen)
PENNY FARTHING
loves attention, hates intact bones
ROAD
Can crush your head with his thighs - in a good way. Loves: craft beer, tan lines, and the movie "Top Gun."

One night, after disappearing for two weeks, Erez asked me out to dinner. I was so jazzed to hear from him that I ignored the disappearance. I spent a night of babysitting money on a nice bottle of wine.

By the time we killed the bottle and were done making out, it was eleven p.m. and nearly every restaurant in the neighborhood was done serving food—except for Blue Ribbon. I'd never been because the dim lighting and gaunt servers led me to believe I could not afford a meal there. I was not wrong.

"Steak or lobster?" Erez asked, glancing through the menu. "Never mind, let's do both!"

I quickly opened the menu to peek at how much that would cost: sixty-two dollars. Then calmly closed it. Sixty-two motherfucking dollars. I could buy sixty-five bagels with that kind of cash or take twenty-seven trips on the subway or afford thirteen bottles of shit-wine. I looked over at Erez, and he gave me a roguish smile. His attention span said, "I hate you," but his actions, well, they also said, "I hate you." But his lips, that smile, they were killer. Seriously.

When the food came out, Erez began to tell me a beautiful story about his mother, and I sighed directly after putting a piece of steak in my mouth. I breathed in and that was it. No out. The steak was lodged in my throat. It was 12:47 a.m. on Saturday, March 12. I remember all this because I later wrote it down as the precise time death was at my door.

Like most young and desperate-to-be classy ladies, I grew embarrassed about the choking. I didn't want to make a scene, so instead, I watched Erez's mouth move and thought about what a lovely restaurant we chose for me to die in. I'm not sure if it was because my lips were turning blue, or because I hadn't spoken in ten seconds, but Erez grew alarmed. "Is everything okay?" he asked, moving his face closer to mine. He had such a nice face.

The corners of the room began to sparkle and the sound

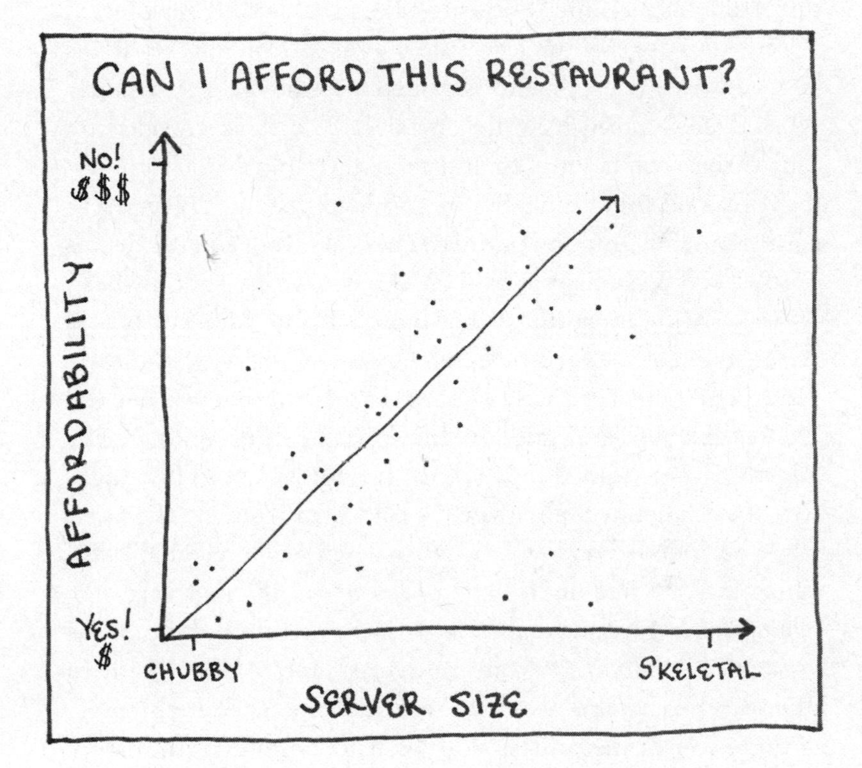
CAN I AFFORD THIS RESTAURANT?
AFFORDABILITY
No!
$$$
YES!
$
CHUBBY
SKELETAL
SERVER SIZE

dropped out. *Enough.* A disappearing-act pseudo-boyfriend was not about to be the last person I saw before kicking it. Not wanting to ruin our sixty-two-dollar-plus-tax spread by Heimliching on it, I directed my attention to the couple next to us. They were splitting cake, or was it ice cream? It was probably ice cream. Who eats cake on a date? Regardless, I decided to use their table to free the steak from my throat. As I stood up, my esophagus widened and the food reluctantly dislodged. No self-Heimlich needed. The steak traveled up my throat into my mouth and then my napkin.

Erez said something, but he sounded distant. Oxygen was still funneling into my brain and my ears were ringing. It was probably "What happened?" or "Are you okay?" but my head wasn't taking in words at that moment. I nodded softly and Erez stared at me for a beat before continuing with his story. It happened in a span of twenty seconds, all that was needed to realize this non-relationship–relationship could be the death of me. I folded my napkin and put it next to my thigh.

"I can't see you anymore," I told Erez a few weeks later. "Or be friends with you, because when we're friends, I still answer your late-night calls." *You know, the flattering ones that result in touching and kissing?* Erez's affection for me was strongest at night. "No more drunk texts. I don't want to know when you're near my apartment or if something reminds you of me, unless you want to be in a relationship. If not, please don't contact me anymore," I concluded. I felt empowered and exposed waiting for a response.

"You're so mature," Erez sighed. He kissed me on the cheek, gave a little smile, and left. It was over. I no longer had to wrack my brain for the perfect joke, or demeanor, or outfit to trick him into thinking I was an easy breezy lady who was cool with his monthly disappearances. I was truthful with what I wanted, and he didn't want the same thing—it was a relief to know where we stood. No more Erez in my life.

He texted me the next day.

Erez: I have a surprise for you
Me: I don't want it.
Erez: Yes, you do. I promise.
Me: No.
Erez: I'll bring it over and I'll leave you alone forever. Scout's honor.

Men are dense creatures and need women to explain things slowly and thoroughly, multiple times, before they get it straight. Have you seen a rom-com? It's true. If we *were* in a rom-com, this exchange would be cute. He'd come over, bring me the surprise (something unique and sentimental), and then kiss me. The camera would pan above us as the credits rolled, implying that we figured our shit out and were in love.

Instead, Erez brought me a bike. The very same bike that couldn't make it across my beloved Brooklyn Bridge. It was a white beach cruiser with a lock around the body. A lock that didn't have a key—it became the most symbolic gift anyone has ever given me.

Erez handed the bike off and stood there waiting for a reaction. I didn't know what to say. "Maybe we can ride together sometime," he suggested. I surveyed his dreamy face. His nose looked like it was shaped out of clay. His lips were the color of raspberries. I wanted to bite them off so that he'd never kiss another person again. But I didn't. Instead, I thanked him for the bike and awkwardly carried it inside, tripping over the heavy body.

Like most hobbies, mine was sparked as an attempt to impress someone I was attracted to, but eventually it morphed into its own thing. My fantasies of first kisses and magical moments faded away and my focus shifted to riding across the bridge. Every morning for six months, I'd ride to work in DUMBO,* lock my bike up, and shout, "I'm gonna ride you!" at the bridge.

But by the time I moved on to a different job in the further-away borough of Manhattan, my free bike had grown heavier and even more unwieldy. I'd pack the basket with all my things, get on the seat, and ride to the first hill, where I'd promptly get off and walk the bike the rest of the way. Eventually, that bike was banished to the corner of my living room, repurposed as a bra-drying rack.

Four years passed and my thirtieth birthday began to peek out over the horizon. As the rays of aging began to tickle my toes, I revisited my 30 before 30 list, desperate to accomplish the goals I'd set for myself as a young lady. Riding a bike seemed like the easiest one to complete, even though the Brooklyn Bridge was now 2,801 miles from my apartment in Hollywood. I bought a flight out, determined to whittle down my list.

DUMBO was nearly unrecognizable. The streets were the same, but everything else was different. It's surreal to know where you're going while simultaneously not recognizing anything around you. What used to be a semi-abandoned startup mecca had turned into a bustling scene, equipped with Starbucks and a Shake Shack.

I made it to Henry Street, where a militant line of blue Citi bikes sat waiting. The year I left New York, the city launched

---

* For those of you not familiar with trendy New York real estate circa mid-2000s, DUMBO (which stands for "Down Under the Manhattan Bridge Overpass") is a manufacturing district, turned arts district, turned tech district, turned Brooklyn's most expensive neighborhood. My first post-college job was at 18 Jay Street.

the largest bicycle share program in America; everyone was given the opportunity to ride a heavy, bright blue bike in exchange for their balls. So, I folded up my balls, put them in the credit card slot, and was handed a bike in return.

The bike made me look like a dingus, but it didn't matter. I'd been through so much at that point—most of it described in the following chapters—that I didn't care what I was projecting out into the world.

It was a crisp, unremarkable August day which provided a nice breeze for the first athletic activity I'd done in months. As I pedaled down the pathway designated for bikers, I cautiously watched out for tourist-toes. I rode through families in matching shirts and dumbfounded gawkers. An Italian dad gave me a high-five and yelled "*Ciao!*" when I crossed over to the Manhattan side. The ride felt sluggish and relaxing, a feeling I'd never attributed to New York City before, but LA had softened me . . . possibly for the better.

I wasn't a fearless bicyclist tearing a path through her city, but an awkward tourist in everyone's way. The thing is, there was nothing I could do; New York eats Midwestern girls for breakfast. It digests us, the acid working away at our sunny predispositions, hardening our souls and soles. Some girls become barnacles who feed off the art and culture, absorbing it into their porous brains, growing bigger in ego, until they've taken everything, contributed nothing, and disappeared from the city. Other girls stick it out. They shed their Midwestern skin only to reluctantly put it back on during holiday visits and whenever they get a little drunk. They become women, call themselves New Yorkers, and vow to never love another city. (The city will never love you back, but that's okay.) I thought that riding my bike across the Brooklyn Bridge would mean I'd developed the sort of agility needed to be a true and courageous New Yorker, but here I was, on a bike that didn't belong to me in a city I'd moved away from.

As I neared the end of the bridge, I lifted my feet off the pedals and rested them on the body of the bike. The gentle decline carried me down the concrete pathway and into Manhattan. I passed the brightly colored umbrella clump of vendors and smiled for floating smartphones. Brooklyn sat behind me and endless opportunities lay ahead. I got to City Hall Park, clicked my bike back into a Citi station, and walked off in search of some coffee and dumplings.

Symbolic gestures will very rarely satisfy your desires. Pathways will change, people will flake, and sometimes you move out of the city you so love. But the beauty of accomplishing a goal you set for yourself is that it doesn't matter how or why you accomplish it—the process feels good regardless. I wanted you to know that. Well, *that* and also not to trust a guy who only has "Expert" written on his business card.

BECOME A MUSE

Freshly out of college, without the first clue about how to pursue a creative career, I turned to creative dudes; men who unabashedly called themselves artists. Maybe if I was their muse, the one who inspired them to make art, then that would be good enough—I'd contribute to the world in my own bass-ackward way.

The desire to be a muse is not unique to me; it's the narrative of many angsty, unremarkable kids who want to be *seen* instead of simply noticed. As much as it goes against my hard-won sense of self, there *is* value in letting someone else define you. It's definitely easier than trying to define yourself.

I was unexceptional as a young person. It wasn't until my junior year that I was *seen*, and that's largely due to the fact that I got my first boyfriend—Otto, a kid from the rival high school. We met in the summer, when the Chicago suburbs become sticky atriums filled with boredom and boners. My friends and I got kicked out of our hang-out park by restless suburban police, so we headed to the park on the other side of the Interstate, where the rival high schoolers hung out. The two groups united through mutual connections, and we sat in a circle talking, picking grass, and toying with hypotheticals. People slowly retired one by one, until Otto and I were the only ones left. We were destined to be together by process of elimination. Otto was weird in a hot kinda way; I was weird in a raised-by-bears kinda way.

Shortly after that night in the park, Otto burned me a copy of Wilco's *Yankee Hotel Foxtrot*, deeming us "official." It was the first time a boy gave me a tangible thing, and I treasured it with all of my delicate girl-heart. I would've worn that CD around my neck if I weren't so worried about it getting scratched.

Otto was a dweeb's dream. The summer we met, the sun had turned his skin the color of a UPS truck, and his thick chestnut curls had flecks of blond. He was good-looking, yet slightly socially strange, which threw his confidence in my favor. He also seemed so calm. Not many sixteen-year-olds are relaxed. I was an anxiety-filled capsule, ready to burst at any moment, but not Otto. Unlike most teenagers, he knew what he wanted to do with the rest of his life: music.

Teenagers who know which direction to face have this untouchable nature. The light hits them in all the right ways. I wanted, so badly, to have the same sense of purpose and depth that Otto did, but I was a sixteen-year-old who wasn't very good at anything. I watched as my friends and peers slowly started finding little morsels of passion lying around classrooms and summer jobs. I found nothing. I was good at fighting with my parents and making myself invisible to classmates—neither of which could be turned into a professional career. I wanted to be more creative, or passionate, or unique, but I didn't know how. My solution? Outsource my narrative to a guitar-slinging boyfriend. I was convinced that if Otto used me as his inspiration, my existence would have more meaning than it currently had.

Our relationship was your typical inexperienced teen romance in that we spent most of the time trying to figure out what to do with our angular, greasy bodies. At that point, my sexual résumé was pithy at best.

My first erotic experience was with Ben, a pale noodle, who had watery, puppy-dog eyes. We were walking through our high school hallway—Ben a little ahead of me—when he reached behind to grab my hand, but miscalculated and brushed against my vagina instead. I immediately tried to figure out what base that was. Bunting and tripping my way to first, baby.

Next up: an attempted first kiss with my best friend Kevin. When we were done, I had to wipe saliva from the bridge of my nose—it was gross and I wanted to do it again immediately. Shortly after that sloppy kiss, Kevin told me he had secured his very first girlfriend, a girl who was cute, bubbly, and most importantly: not me. "That's so great!" I told him as my vaginal muscles slammed shut.

Aside from my failed kiss and Ben's vagina-grab, I hadn't done much else. My eight-year-old brother, Sanya, on the other hand, was more educated on the subject than I'm comfortable with—I found this out during lunch one day.

"Jordan and Dana had sex," he told me while casually eating soup.

"Shut up, Sanya, you don't even know what sex is," I replied.

"Yeah, he put, um, his penis into her wah-gina," my soft-skinned, doughy baby brother informed me. Game point. Even the eight-year-olds were doing it.

One night, at one of the three parties I attended during my high school career, Otto found an empty room and we 69ed. Arguably one of the most acrobatic and advanced sexual things you can do with someone. The whole maneuver is absurd, like when newlyweds smash cake into each other's faces. How are you supposed to enjoy someone caking all over your face when you're too busy trying to cake on theirs? I spent

--EXPERIENCE------------

BEN (2003)
Responsible for maintaining vibrant AIM conversations without speaking in the halls. Partook in naughty hand-holding.

KEVIN (2004)
Dedicated 7 years of unrequited love towards kevin and all related properties
Gave away first kiss to kevin.

--SKILLS-------------

none.

the whole time thinking: *Is this right? Is this it? Is my face supposed to be so close to his butthole?* Going from an awkward first kiss to 69ing is like trying your first cigarette and following it with LSD. But there I was, nose to cheeks. He was on a different level, and it was up to me to figure out how to climb.

I wanted things to work with Otto so that I could be his muse. So that he would write about me, to help define who I was. I wanted him to think of me as worthy and interesting enough to inspire his creativity. I was willing to do anything, including *that* stuff. Unfortunately, an imbalance of hunger in a relationship causes the bond to quickly corrode.

As it happens with feeble-baby dating, Otto told me he wanted to "talk." I hadn't even had a chance to brainstorm more than a couple of song titles (*I Sea You; Miss Marina; Hurricane Marina; When the Acne Clears*), and this jerk was laying the groundwork for my first breakup.

I got into my car (read: my mom's Nissan Quest minivan) right as the first song off *Yankee Hotel Foxtrot* came on. I'd been playing his CD nonstop, and it had just restarted.

"*I am trying to break your heart, but still I'd be lying if I said it wasn't easy, I am trying to break your heart,*" the lyrics droned.

I pulled my mom's minivan up behind his mom's minivan and checked my makeup in the driver's seat visor. I made sure there wasn't any eyeliner on my lower lids so that if I were to cry, it wouldn't run, because, how gauche, you know? I got into his mom's minivan and blankly stared out the windshield as he sweetly and softly ended our relationship. It stung but I didn't cry, at least not in front of Otto. I saved it for my minivan, where Wilco was there to provide a soundtrack to my sadness.

The breakup with Otto didn't come as a surprise to me. I knew he was going to break up with me shortly after we met. My first clue was that we were both sixteen, all sixteen-year-olds break up. (Unless they're religious, then they get married so that they can have awkward teenage sex, tons of babies, and possibly a reality TV show marketed toward stay-at-home moms.) I was also tipped off by my parents.

"Marina, he's too attractive for you," my mother told me, while clicking through photos of Otto on my digital camera.

My dad grabbed the camera and scrolled through too. "I agree with Mom, this is not going to end happy for you." It's nice that my always-bickering, polar-opposite parents can come together in a show of unity over my underwhelming looks. They were right. Two weeks later, he started dating my friend Kathleen, a wispy girl with a good singing voice and a spiritual vibe. She soon had a burned copy of *Yankee Hotel Foxtrot* of her very own. Honestly, their relationship helped me move past him quickly. We were children, after all, and there are plenty of other 69s in the sea.

If we lived in any other era, this would've been the end of the Otto story. But the pesky internet kept him in my orbit. Whenever I was bored at my startup job and needed a break from wondering when Erez would call next, I'd go online. I watched as Otto grew from flaky teen with lofty ambitions into a talented musician with an actually good band. Meanwhile, I'd grown from listless and angry into listless and lost. I spent my days writing credit card reviews for a small website and my nights envisioning creative ways to kill myself in the office.

It was one of those tech startups that keeps their employees slightly drunk so that they don't notice they're being taken advantage of. "Here's the beer fridge!" my boss loudly yelled when he gave me my first office tour. "You get free drinks and lunches." He reached inside the fridge to get me a drink. "But we can't pay you anything to start," he whispered to the glass bottles.

I was in the beginning stages of entering my shadow-career. Meaning my job had the potential to be fulfilling, but wasn't exactly what I wanted to be doing with my life. I was writing, yes, but it was about the inanest subject matter on earth. Shadow-careers* are easy to get trapped in because they bring you as close as possible to your dream job without the risk of failure. Failing at a job you don't care about does not carry the breath-stealing pain of failing at your dream job. Otto, on the other hand, was pursuing the same dream he had when he was a kid, and it was spectacular to watch.

I've always been drawn to people who are unapologetically passionate. I never had the balls to be that person. That's why when Otto messaged me asking for a place to crash while touring, I jumped at the opportunity. Real musicians staying on *my* couch? I couldn't wait to share this story with everyone at work. "Yeah, I'm probably going to be busy this weekend," I told our graphic designer, "my ex-boyfriend's band is staying at my place." She didn't respond because she had her headphones in, but I'm sure she would've at least been intrigued had she heard me.

When Otto arrived at my apartment, I was surprised to see he was almost the exact same size as when we dated in high school. His outline had filled in, but it made him that much cuter. I learned that he had a long-term girlfriend and a completely lackadaisical attitude toward the responsibilities of being an adult—I felt a nostalgic draw toward him. *This man knows how to live*, I thought.

Although Otto only crashed on my couch for a night, I would go on to attend nearly every show his band had. I followed them around like a little duck. Watching the five of

---

* I first came across the "shadow" concept in Julia Cameron's book *The Artist's Way*: "Very often audacity, not talent, makes one person an artist and another a shadow artist—hiding in the shadows, afraid to step out and expose the dream to the light, fearful that it will disintegrate to the touch." Unfortunately, I've never gotten past the first two chapters because I have the attention span of a housefly.

them, night after night, performing with such gusto—it put me in a trance. Their psychedelic sound had catchy lyrics and an undercurrent of melancholy impossible not to adore. As I watched Otto on stage, I began to develop feelings for him, except this time those feelings largely consisted of jealousy.

When Otto left New York, we kept in touch via postcards. He wrote from every city he performed in, and I delicately placed all his updates in a box of letters near my bed. I'd collected nearly eight postcards when he sent me one that said, "It will be so grand to hang out in Brooklyn." With this addendum: "Also notably my girlfriend broke up with me."

A sensational thrill of implication ran down my spine. On a confidence scale of perfect-fitting jeans to vodka, having an ex semi-hit on you with goddamn pen and paper is pretty high up there.

When Otto was back in town we grabbed catch-up drinks. There are few things more socially gratifying than getting a drink with someone you knew before you were allowed to drink. I was *on* that night: charming, coy, confident. God, I love tipsy flirting—you fool yourself into feeling like the best version of you. After shutting down the bar at Union Hall, we stumbled into the early morning mist and began dancing under the streetlights. "Do you hear that?" I asked.

Otto listened for a moment. "No," he admitted.

"I know, it's weird," I told him. The city was uncharacteristically quiet, most likely due to Hurricane Irene fitfully coursing through the Bahamas (rumored to be on her way to New York). Irene created this odd, unfamiliar tension in the Brooklyn air. I shivered. "Let's go home," I said, hooking my arm through his.

But he didn't move, instead, he turned to me and said, "Hey, I love you." Just like that. Like he had remembered a fact that he wanted to share with me, "*Hydrogen is the first element on the periodic table, and, hey, I love you.*"

Breaking Bad News with Baby Animals

It will be so grand
to hangout in Brooklyn
again. The stationary life is pretty
great. I feel bad for the ~~people~~
nomadic Souix Indians. What
an eternally lonely life. You
cannot communicate much with
smoke signals.

— Otto

Marina Shifrin
660 Degraw St Apt#1
Brooklyn, NY 11217

#2

Breaking Bad News with Baby Animals

Marina—
I decided to write you a second card because
I did not answer any of your numerous questions.
To sum up the trip in one word would be "spicy."
My word might be "nom" as in "nom, nom, nom."
Your word should be dance, or joke or paraglide.
I'm confused where you stayed in Chile.
Beach? cold beach? city? cold city? with one
friend? a cold friend? did you buy anything
fun? I bought a money belt and cymbals!
I'm moving away from Urbana, IL to HP for a little,
probably move to Chicago (Logan Square) in November.
Also notably my girlfriend broke up with me because
I'm never around. Justified. And I'm moving away
sooo. OK. Borderline homeless (will never be found again!)
no one to "tie me down." I'm becoming a drifter! Neat!

— Otto

Marina Shifrin
660 Degraw St
Brooklyn, NY, 11217

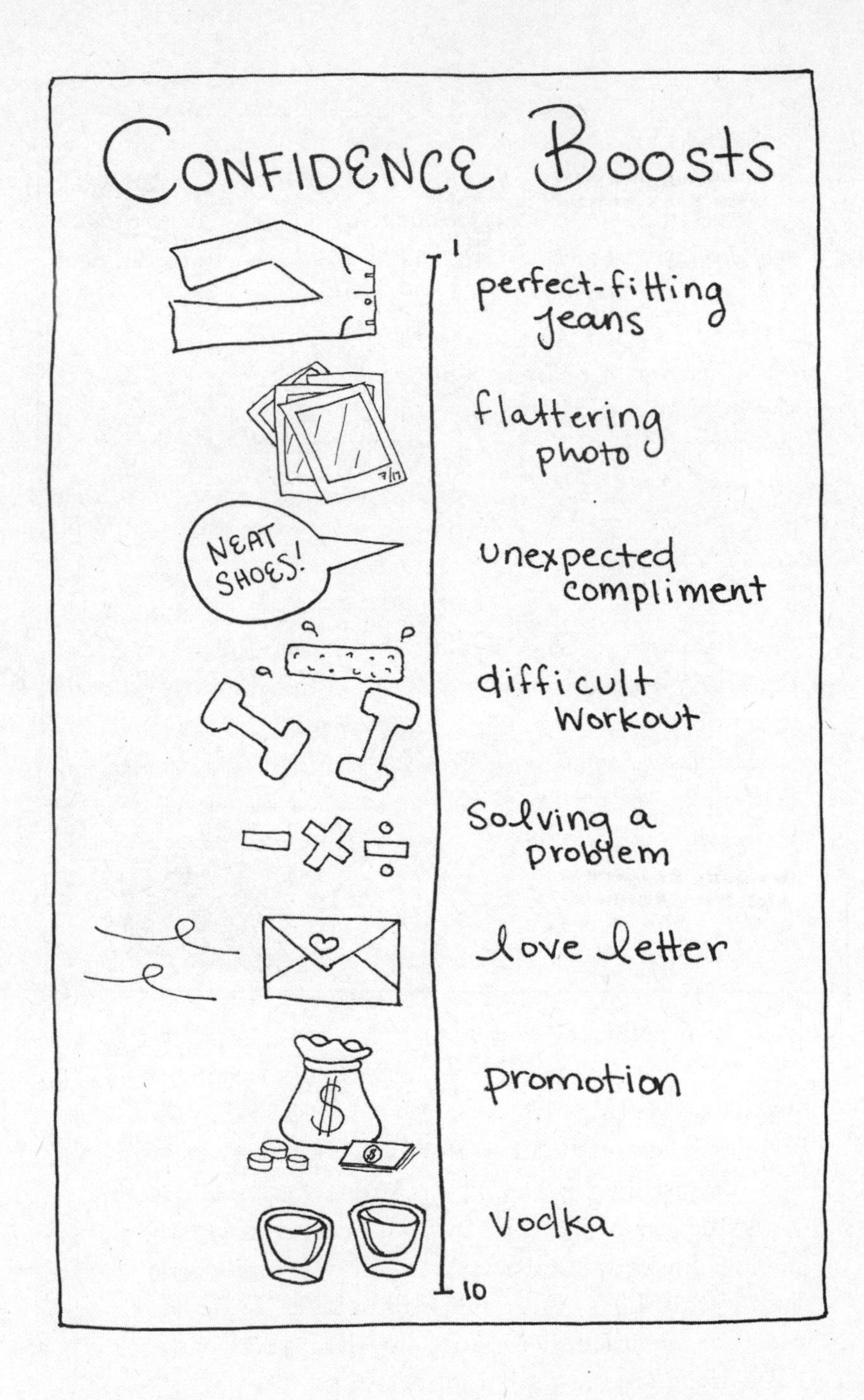
Confidence Boosts
1
perfect-fitting jeans
7/17
flattering photo
NEAT SHOES!
unexpected compliment
difficult workout
solving a problem
love letter
promotion
vodka
10

I had bagged my first adult "I love you," and the person who said it was my high school boyfriend. I was back in Chicago, in his green minivan, only this time I wasn't getting dumped, I was getting six years of insecurities reversed. I didn't know what to say back, but it didn't matter because he leaned in and kissed me. We went back to my apartment and that night, we 66ed.

When we woke up in a hungover haze, Otto repeated it again, "I love you," and this time he followed it with, "We should be together." He was a rootless musician who was coming out of a serious relationship, but I believed him. I believed in a world in which my first boyfriend would become my last boyfriend. My emotions got wrapped up in the narrative weight that story held. I didn't say anything right then, because, I felt, it wouldn't be a respectable business practice—when given an offer, especially if it's a good one, it's important to "take a night" before giving your decision. I told Otto I needed time to think about it. "Of course," he said. He kissed me the way you kiss someone you've known for years. It was tender and familiar. I became a sixteen-year-old who was being noticed for the first time. "I'll be back tonight," Otto said. "This is good. We are good."

I waited until he was safely out of the apartment before throwing myself back into bed. It smelled like *band*, I loved it. A new smell for my bored nostrils. My proclivity for sleeping with creatives made me mistakenly feel connected to art itself; as if sharing my bed with a hairy guy and his sensitive soul would eventually rub off on me. It made me feel eclectic and interesting; empty and dangerously addictive feelings.

While I was too precious with my career to take any risks, my love life was on the opposite end of the spectrum. "Yes, let's do this. Let's be together and in love," I planned to tell him. For me, it is easier to lose love than it is to live with the curiosity of an unexplored relationship.

As I was melting into my bed, the Hurricane Irene headlines went from a murmur to a scream. The first hints of love diluted my brain cells while New York was bracing for The Big One. I spent the day cleaning my apartment, cooking perishables, and redoing my eyeliner. I wanted everything to look nice for when Otto returned . . . but Otto never came back.

Instead, he retreated to Maine with his band to avoid the storm. He told me he loved me and then immediately left me, during a hurricane, in an apartment made of cardboard and wishful thinking.

I tried to ignore the fact that Otto was sitting under the stars, in the safety of Maine, while I was watching my roommate Rob frantically fill our bathtub with ice and bratwursts. "In case the power goes out," he told me as he stood over the brat bath. I spent that night drinking emergency reserve alcohol and refreshing my email. I got bored, straightened my hair, and shot a music video for my parents. In it, I danced around the apartment while blaring "Hello" by Martin Solveig & Dragonette. I posted the video to YouTube and fell asleep around two a.m.

I woke up to a soggy but intact city. Irene had stood me up, just like Otto. I reached under my bed, grabbed my computer, checked my emails, and found one from him. The subject line said, "Song response, I'll sing it when I see you!" I devoured the email so fast it gave me heartburn. Inside was an mp3 and lyrics to a song he'd written about me. I was a muse.

As the headlines faded to punchlines, Otto and his band came back to finish their East Coast tour. Attending a show knowing that I'd be going home with someone on stage was electrifying. "Maybe he'll sing the song he wrote about me," I told Rob while pouring whiskey into a half-empty Coke bottle. By the time I got to the Knitting Factory, the band was on their second song and I was D-runk. Two syllables. One capital.

I circled Otto's sweaty body, waiting for a moment to

steal him away and tell him, "Yes, I love you too." He seemed cagey, but then again, he was performing. I filled my time with more drinks and wild dancing across the semi-empty venue. When Otto finally got off stage and came over, he was treated to my wilted "We should be together" drunk girl speech. He told me that it wasn't the right time to have this discussion, which felt like a rejection. I pushed harder and my proclamation of love turned into more of a slurred growl. Then, I vaguely remember standing at a cab, hissing: "Are you in or are you out?" as his band members awkwardly slunk away from Hurricane Marina. If you ever need to ask someone if he's your boyfriend through gritted teeth and a snarl, the answer is most likely "no" and, if it's not, it should be.

"I'm going to stay with the band tonight." Otto's eyes dropped to the ground. That was my last mental snapshot of him. He looked so ashamed. Later, the soberer version of me would realize it wasn't shame, but embarrassment. I came home, turned on *Yankee Hotel Foxtrot*, and cried until I woke up Rob.

The next day I got an email from Otto, with the following statement:

> I want to be in this band, follow through this dream, and try as hard as I can to make it work.
>
> I want to show you that I care about you and that I treasure you.
>
> I do not want either of these dreams to impede upon each other.

I stopped reading after the first line. He chose the band. I don't blame him—it *was* a better decision. It turns out, the artist never chooses the muse over the music.

Wanting someone to define who you are through *their* art, romantically known as "being a muse," is not worth the effort. If you want the nuances of your character brought to the surface of the world, you either have to do it on your own, or get over yourself. Because in the end, it is better to be the artist than the muse. From that day forward, I became the boss of the words written about me.

When it came time to put this story into writing, I dug up Otto's song, read the lyrics with a clear head, and laughed at myself. Written there, plain as day, was Otto's breakup note. It wasn't a love song, it was, well, I don't even know what the fuck it was. He clearly had a change of heart while he was in Maine, and I was too blinded by my own narcissism to see what he was saying. "You're an idiot," I whispered to myself while scanning through the email. I printed out the lyrics, grabbed a red pen, and translated them into my own words. That way, if I ever got carried away by a cute guy with a guitar again, I would be reminded of the truth hiding behind his pretty words.

Hopefully Holding

no thank you to any real commitment

The answer my darling,
Is that I love you too much to keep ya,
I'm a traveling bard, without a place to call my own

So, um, I'm actually homeless right now

can I stay with you while I'm in New York?

I'd always want you back x 2
and back you'd come,
hopefully holding my heart
you remind of a girl,
of which I never met another

remember when we 69ed? that was tight!

she was 16 and sweet to me, I loved her.
now we have grown,
and I have no place to keep ya
It's between holding on
and holding you back

honestly? I'm doing you a favor

I'd always want you back x 2
and back you'd come,
hopefully holding my heart

but still can I crash with you when I'm in New York? We can do stuff...

here's the thing, you're not the only broad in my life

you may think that
I am just another lover
having told just four girls
that I'd never want another
I make no sense when it comes to love but love to tie you down
and sing

random question: are you into kinky stuff?

let's keep things open even though I already made it clear I'm not that into you

I'd always want you back x 2
and back you'd come,
hopefully holding my heart
The answer my darling,
Is that I love you too much to keep ya,
I'll come back a million times
hopefully still holding your heart
come back to me
hopefully holding
my heart

I'd take the couch too!

4

TAKE A WRITING CLASS

I am sprinting through New York. The audible *thwap, thwap, thwap* of my breasts knocking together is the only sound louder than my breathing. I'm wearing one of my loose bras, and it's causing my boobs to bounce around like enormous pink pinballs. I have three types of bras: loose bras, tight bras, and sports bras.

My loose bras are my favorite, but they do very little for my chest (other than make sure my nipples stay hidden from sight). My tight bras dig into my ribcage creating looseleaf lines across my sides, but they hold my tits up like the trophies that they are. My sports bras sit unused in the back of my closet.

I'm running because I'm late for my very first writing class—one I signed up for in a fit of anger. Otto left me with the realization that I was kind of a boring person and it made me furious. That's the reality of growing up in the suburbs with parents who are happily married—you have a higher chance of being a dull adult. Sure, I have the immigrant thing, which is kind of different, but it only gets me so far. After

My 3
TYPES OF
Bras
loose
•hanging out at home
•6+ dates
•work at your soul-sucking job.
tight
•job interviews
•first dates
•not much else
SPORTS
self-explanatory
• dancing
•putting over loose bras to make them tight again
•transforming your juggs into a sack of potatoes.

the Admitting You've Never Been Back to Your Mother Country conversation, there's really nowhere else to go. An easy way to counteract a bland existence is to move to a major metropolitan city, but after a while, that also gets very formulaic. Even city girls get trapped in the cycle of sameness.

"I'm in a rut," I whined over drinks with my close friend Rebecca. "My job sucks. My apartment is too small. I have no money. Everything blows. I need to do something more interesting with my life. Like start taking stand-up more seriously—become an actual stand-up comedian."

Satisfaction—much like allergies and smiling—just doesn't exist in Russian culture. Part of me is thankful because my unquenchable drive for more increases the likelihood of success. The other part of me is fucking exhausted from always being frustrated with everything.

"You always get like this after you end a relationship," Rebecca said as she fished a weird speck out of her beer. Her mom is a psychologist and her dad, a lawyer. That combination of personalities produced a small person with measured words and a blunt demeanor who absorbs all my anxieties and spits out the best advice. She has a talent for making me feel unimpressive and stupid when I deserve to feel unimpressive and stupid. If you can swing it, I highly suggest you find a Rebecca for yourself.

"You date a guy, it doesn't work. You get sad, you make a life change. You get bored again, so you date a guy, it doesn't work . . ." She trailed off.

She was right. Otto created a hole in my life, and it was more than just a romantic one—it was existential too. His profession of love and subsequent take-back made me determined to prove myself as the artist and not the muse—so I put in my two weeks' notice at the credit card review shadow-job and decided to pursue comedy full-time. As my dad always

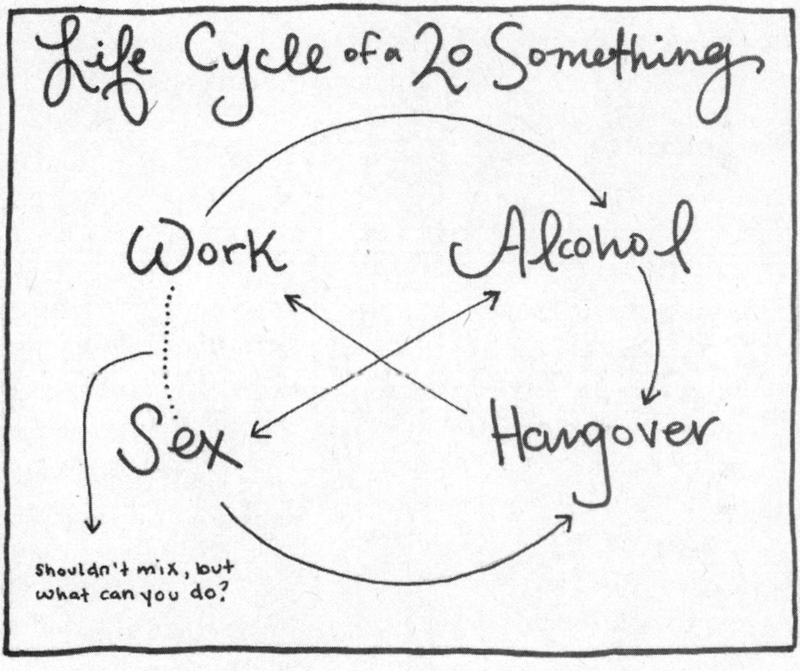

Life Cycle of a 20 Something

Work

Alcohol

Sex

Hangover

shouldn't mix, but
what can you do?

QUALITIES of a REBECCA

smarter than you

likes whiskey + dancing

blunt

knows the past you

masculine energy feminine soul

opposite on the attention spectrum

better at stuff than you

calm

opposite on the emotion spectrum

different taste in men

weirdo

says, "Success is the best form of revenge." And revenge was the fuel I needed to get out of bed in the morning.

I quit on a Friday—and asked for my job back the following Monday, after a total of two days pursuing the life of an artist. Surely a record. My two days as an artist involved crying, an unsuccessful, desperate job search, and little else. Monday morning, I marched into my boss's office and said, "Upon further consideration, I will not be quitting after all," and sat down at my desk like nothing had happened. My boss didn't even dispute me because he was shocked into submission. It has since come to my attention that normal human professionals do not act this way. But after a breakup—even a small one—I become a revolving door of bad decisions.

Signing up for a writing class was my take-two way of easing into a creative career. I wanted to learn the kind of writing that would maybe expose a little too much of my soul. I didn't know what to do with this writing, but the nice thing about learning how to eloquently communicate via written word is it's a skill that everyone needs. Whether it's to convince employers to hire you or for the ever-popular reason of getting people to fall in love with you—it always proves useful. Plus, adding classes to your repertoire makes your résumé look more impressive than it is.

So, I'm running in this loose bra, right? Sweat's trickling down my back and into my butt crack. My stomach is in knots because it is the first day of my Creative Writing 101 class. Row after row of fabric shops blur past me as I beeline toward an innocuous brown building in New York's Fashion District.

I get there on time, by the way. The classroom is unimpressive. White walls. Gray desks. Quiet lumps of human staring at their phones. I join the lumps and take out a small notepad half-filled with my grocery lists, jokes, and people I've slept with. *If you can keep track of everyone you've slept with, then you're not a promiscuous person* is my sexual mantra. I flip past the list of names to a fresh sheet of paper and wait patiently. I don't know it at the time, but this class is going to change the trajectory of my writing career.

The thing no one tells you about adult classes is that the affordable ones are filled with foreigners (hey, me too!) and broken women (hey, me too!). My class was no exception; most of the people were working on their English or getting over a breakup. I've since taken many classes in different types of institutions and found that city colleges are my favorite. The majority of students in city or community colleges are so damn happy to be there that you catch a little bit of their happiness. A lot of them are ebullient immigrants who have an unquenchable thirst for knowledge. I am particularly drawn to these people because: 1) They remind me of my own clumsy-tongued family, and 2) You will not find a more hopeful, motivated, smart, and fascinating group of people. If you ever feel down on life, hang out with an immigrant for a day—they'll check your privilege so hard you won't know where to turn.

Initially, learning how to be creative in a classroom felt counterintuitive. "You can't learn art in a room, man," I told Rebecca, who is an English teacher by profession.

"Yeah, but you can get better at it," she shot back. I buttoned my lip and signed up for the class.

I chose this particular writing class because it promised to "guide you surely and safely into the writing life" and because my teacher, David Yastrow, was very adorable. He looked like the wispy love child of Ira Glass and Woody Allen. In fact, he had such a 1930s shtetl face that my parents congratulated me when they saw his photo. "Is he married?" my mom asked.

David began the first class with a roll call. It felt warm and familiar. When he got to my name, I said "I'm here" with more certainty than I had in a long while. Two people were missing. *Who, in New York, has $66.66 to spare on a writing class?* I wondered.

We started our time together with a simple bell chart on the whiteboard. It had five points that added up to a narrative arc, which, I now know, is at the heart and soul of every good story. That arc made writing seem devastatingly simple. Like a math problem: 1+2=story.

After he'd finished going through the details of a narrative arc, David told us a story about a girl. "I was once in love with a girl named Astrid," he said, before launching into a diary-like spiel about how Astrid was the one who inspired him to write. It was the first of many times that he exposed his romantic history on an intimate level. David liked to wrench open his ribcage and let us peek in at his heart. Like Otto, David was a musician. His words were dipped in wine, his stories sounded like lyrics, resulting in an overtly saccharine class. I was learning more about his ex-girlfriends than about sentence structure, but his honesty and openness were so endearing to me that my crush grew deeper with each class. But that's mostly because I was twenty-three years old and attracted to any man who talked about love.

Not every lesson unraveled into the David Yastrow and His Exes Show—sometimes he'd go over the basics of writing. One of our more straightforward weekly assignments was to write about our day, any day from that week. Getting homework when you've aged out of school is kind of like getting adult braces—inconvenient, but it could lead to an uptick in confidence.

Although I loved the assignment, I had zero motivation to write about my days, especially because they were so boring. I wanted to improve as a person, I really did. I wanted to try to be a real writer—but I also wanted to have a nightcap at my

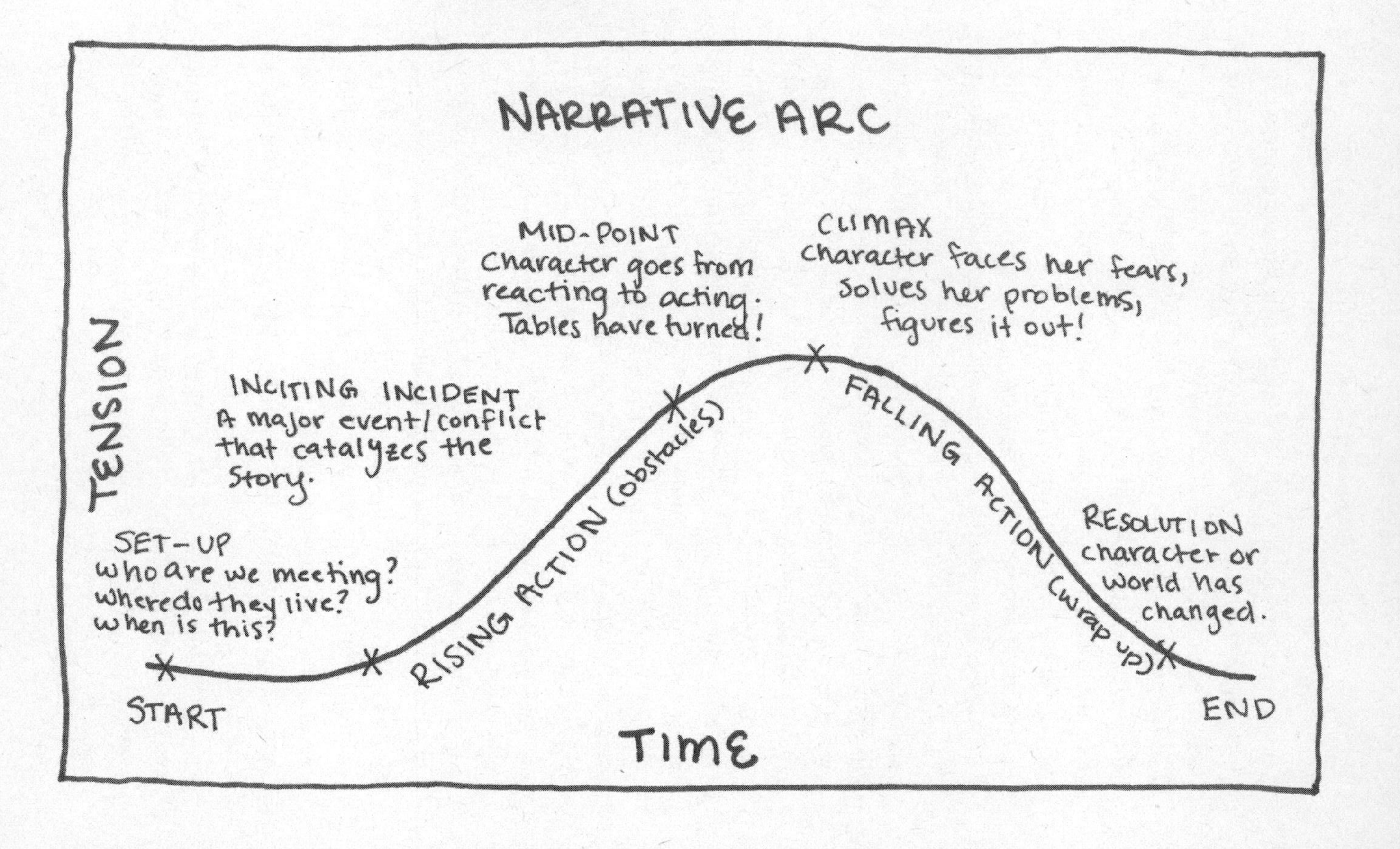
NARRATIVE ARC
TENSION
SET-UP
who are we meeting?
where do they live?
when is this?
INCITING INCIDENT
A major event/conflict
that catalyzes the
story.
MID-POINT
Character goes from
reacting to acting.
Tables have turned!
CLIMAX
character faces her fears,
solves her problems,
figures it out!
RISING ACTION (obstacles)
FALLING ACTION (wrap up)
RESOLUTION
character or
world has
changed.
START
END
TIME

neighborhood dive, or spend the weekend playing cards in Prospect Park, or go out with the cute guitarist from Bushwick. Anything but homework.

In high school and college, I was motivated by the superfluous competition created by assigning letter grades to everything. It didn't matter what was absorbed, as long as my GPA was higher than my intellectual nemesis Joe Schein's. But, adult classes are strictly for bettering yourself, which is a difficult concept to grasp when you're used to a different kind of reward structure.

In school, I spent a long time beating myself up because other people wrote better, faster, and funnier than me. I tried to mimic my smarter, more successful peers, but noticed that my process didn't fit into their mold. It turns out that "process is messy."* It's just throwing noodles at a wall and seeing what sticks. You can't be upset that your wall or your throwing technique looks different than the person next to you—that's what makes creating so fun: there's no correct process! (Same goes for losing weight.) The only piece of writing advice that has ever helped me was simply "finish what you're writing."

The night before class, I still hadn't finished my assignment. I opened my computer to write and, after an hour of nothing, decided to read a few pages of a book. When I'm having grand troubles with writing, a good book will often give me the right amount of inspiration. Inspiration, procrastination—either way, for me, the work eventually gets done, even if I have to force it.

During that particular week, I was getting my inspiration from Jonathan Ames's *What's Not to Love?*—a book I found on a stoop in Williamsburg. I like to read the first couple pages of stoop-books, to gauge whether to keep the book. When I found Ames's book, I read the first few pages and

---

* As Austin Kleon so smartly points out in his book *Show Your Work!*

then proceeded to polish off the entire first chapter, standing there, at a stranger's doorstep.

Ames's writing was uncivilized and interesting. He painted a perverted picture of being a young writer in New York, and I kept getting lost in that picture. So lost, in fact, that when I sat down to read a chapter the night before class, I ended up finishing the whole book.

In the epilogue, Jonathan Ames talks about giving up on three years of sobriety due to a wine-soaked dessert in Florence. He does a breathtaking job describing what it's like to tumble off the wagon and succumb to his dipsomania. Even the term he uses to describe alcoholism has an enviable elegance: *dipsomania*. Dip. So? Mania. A great word, fun to say, with underlying darkness. Ames leaves the reader with a final vow to "get back on the water wagon." I shut the book, craving a glass of whiskey.

The homework was still unfinished, so I grabbed my laptop and woke up my foster dog, John. "What if I let you decide where we go tonight?" I whispered into his floppy ear. He didn't seem to mind the assignment, although he was perturbed I'd asked him so late in the evening. We stepped out into the street and he immediately sniffed out a pathway toward one of my favorite neighborhood bars, Mission Delores. Everyone who hung out there was a musician, writer, or disillusioned with life—I loved it. Mission Delores made me feel close to the creative world without actually needing to be a part of it.

I let John off his leash and he scurried toward a group of people crowded around a man. The man's oval face and downturned nose were familiar, but the rest of his face was obscured under a newsboy cap. He crouched down to pet John, spilling a little of his beer as he knelt. I got a better look, only to realize it was—I kid you not—Jonathan Ames. Jonathan Ames with a beer. The book I was reading just moments before—the one that inspired me to go on the hunt for some fun—came to life in front of me. I watched him rub John's face for a moment before I got up the courage to walk over. It was too unbelievable of an opportunity to pass up.

"Um, Mister Ames?" my mouth turned to mush, "You're never going to believe this, but I was literally *just* reading your book. I love it. I can't believe you're here. I love you," I blurted.

"Oh, that's nice," Jonathan Ames replied, tugging on John's ear. "What's his name?"

"John," I said, realizing that they shared the same name *and* I'd just told Jonathan Ames that I loved him.

"Don't get a boner, ha," I said, immediately regretting my choice. I was referencing an essay from his book in which he mentions getting an erection while petting a golden retriever. I later realized that the essay had been written ten years earlier and my comment had zero context.

Jonathan stood up, and I scooped up John. It is then that I noticed he was standing awfully close to a perky-breasted young girl who I recognized as the bartender's girlfriend; not only had I accidentally walked into a potentially salacious situation, but I'd also said the word *boner.*

"Can I buy you guys beers?" My impulse after doing anything awkward is to buy alcohol for the people I did it in front of.

At the bar, I ordered two beers and quickly realized that the bartender and his cronies were planning on smashing Jonathan Ames's skull in. "No one treats my boy like that. My fist, his face . . ." said a man who looked like a hamburger. My breath caught in my chest. My new mission for the night was to protect that beautiful bald head, with all of its dirty thoughts and penchant for prose.

Before I could pay for the beers, Jonathan came up. "You don't have to pay for me," he told me, while waving a twenty in the air. He smelled of alcohol and talent.

"Jonathan, that girl?" I said, pointing to Perky Breasts. "She has a boyfriend."

The speed with which I went from reading about his life to inserting myself into it was wild. In his novel, Ames constantly mentions that he'd often black out while drinking, which will explain my actions in a minute. Jonathan let the information sink in for a moment before frantically scanning the bar for the bartender, "Oh no, no. Where is he? I didn't mean to . . . didn't know he . . ."

"Wait here, I'm going to call you cab." I went back to the bar and tore a small sheet of paper from my notebook. On it, I wrote: "Thank you for letting me pick your brain over coffee. See you next Monday," with my email and phone number, then called for a cab before walking back over to Ames.

I patted his chest and slipped the note into the breast pocket of his blazer. "It's going to be okay, Jonathan." I was a double-agent, saving my new favorite author from peril while being a manipulative sneak. *This is how I'm going to get my start*, I thought. We stood at the curb waiting. "Do you have tips for someone who wants to be a writer?" I asked to break the silence.

He thought about it for a moment, slightly swaying in his drunken stupor. "I guess, just pray," he told me.

It was hard to tell if he was being genuine or ironic, but it didn't matter because the cab pulled up and he got in. I shut the door and leaned into the window, but before I could say anything he looked up at me, his eyes giant and tired, "Please don't write about this," he pleaded. My heart fluttered. *He thinks I'm a writer.*

I walked to the bar where I'd left John to guard my laptop and sat down to do my assignment. I typed "Just Pray" at the top of my Word document and began to write.

The most valuable thing I learned during Creative Writing 101 was that everyone has a story to tell. "If you believe you are special and interesting, others will too," David told us in class one day. I took out a deep green pen and wrote this sentence in the middle of my notebook.

At that time, my age group had the dark mark of narcissism, entitlement, and unrealistic expectations hanging over our heads. Anyone in their twenties who carried any sort of confidence or wanted to do something besides mundane office work was considered to be a (pause for eye roll) *millennial.* Sitting in a class where the teacher told you to believe that you are a little bit special built a thin layer of protection against the growing despondence about my generation. I began to think that maybe, just maybe, I *was* a tiny bit interesting.

At the end of the six weeks, during which I missed only one class,* David came in with a single sheet of paper. "I'm going to read to you a story that has all the concepts we've discussed in class. It's a nonfiction essay published in the Modern Love section of *The New York Times,*" he said. This was typical; he'd often start out with a piece of writing that perfectly encapsulated the lesson of the day. The atypical

---

* During the second to last week of class, Rebecca's dad passed away unexpectedly. His death set off a sort of soul-searing sorrow I'd never experienced before. On my walk to class the day after his death, Rebecca called to ask if I could do the eulogy. A "funny one," she specified. I'd never been to a funeral, to say nothing of being asked to perform at one. "Of course," I told her. Moments later, I ran into David in the hallway and burst into tears. He empathetically sent me home for the day. "If you have any eulogy writing advice, it'd be greatly appreciated," I told him. He sent me this response: "I'd say be careful to make it more about the person who died than about you. When talking about one's feelings about death or about the person, it's hard to write without making it about yourself. So, find that balance if you can, between talking about yourself and talking about the person. I also always suggest telling stories. In fact, I'd argue that the best memorial services and funerals really take place after official ceremonies when everyone goes out drinking telling stories about the person who died." I learned a lot about confidence and story structure in that class, but David's advice on how to write a eulogy resulted in the one of the most meaningful things I've ever written.

6 · 7 · 2012

"Speak in your actual voice, everyone is interesting."

NON-FICTION

Opinion (op-ed) / Personal Essays

1. Try to be convincing (story)
2. Writing / Telling stories within your piece (traditional vs. non-traditiona

AUDACITY

BE BOLD, BRAV

→ Don't argue the obvious.

3. Be open to the ideas of your ow delusion (++ contradiction)
4. Brutal honesty is risky

* An opinion you hold which is controversial:
You should not be allowed to get married before the age of 25.

RHETORIC: How to convince people

• story • emotion • re-definition

Don't convince people by making rational arguments PERSONAL as much about YOU as possible.

* IF you believe you are special and interesting others will too.

NON-FICTION WRITING

YOU

Perspective experience character

VOICE

· people should seek discomfort: once people have gotten to a stable place in life they are no longer changing and growing.

Boldness x Braveness ⟹ fascinated by feelings

· combine opinion with emotional stories

thing about this particular essay was that it was written by David himself. Sure, he had told us stories, but he'd never read his own writing.

A hum of excitement rippled through the room. I shifted in my seat uncomfortably. Earnest people performing their own work is a nightmare. Poetry readings, interpretive dance recitals, they all give me an inexplicable amount of stress. "No one cares!" I scream in my head. I am, in fact, a monster.

David read his story with a sort of poetic cadence. Slow and calculated, he made sure we heard all his words clearly. David's essay was an ode to a young musician he'd met when he first moved to New York. He was captivated by her talent, modesty, and beauty. I guess you could say she was his muse, but this muse was clearly uninterested in David. Parts of his essay dissected her lyrics, *her* words, while other parts dissected her as a person, her gummy smile and childlike hands. As the story progresses, David becomes more and more set on getting her to notice him. Because they are both musicians, he decides to demonstrate his love by crafting a handmade musical instrument. At the end of the piece, David is left alone, standing in a line of other suckers who have fallen for the young musician girl. All of them holding a present.

As soon as he was done reading, four words popped into my head, words that have launched numerous creative careers and continue to inspire successful individuals to this very day. Those four words were: I can do that. That night I came home, pulled up David's essay on my computer, and read it again to make sure I didn't miss any subtle nuances. It was sweet, cheesy, but not at all ground-breaking. As the last pangs of my crush faded, I shut my laptop and whispered: "I can do *that*."

ADOPT A DOG

John came to me in a pet adoption newsletter I signed up for after four glasses of wine–induced loneliness. I cannot recommend getting a dog as a young, unemployed city-dweller, but I do know that if you end up getting one, you'll love that dog more than you thought was possible.

My mother was skeptical of my new life change. "You can't have a dog. You're not even married!" Olga yelled over the phone. My mom is a sniper; she can sneak my relationship status into just about any conversation.

"It's like having a baby," my dad chimed in. "A baby that never grows up, Marina."

I hate the pet-mom comparison—I cannot stand it when people add "hyphen mom" to anything. Dog-mom. Cat-mom. Plant-mom. It's too much pressure to be the mother of a cactus. I didn't push the thing out of my vagina. I'm not going to put it through college or criticize its taste in men—I'm not its mother. You're not either! "Mother" is a remarkable title, and should be treated with reverence, not callously assigned to anyone lording their power over a defenseless creature.

John celebrating moving into our new apartment.

"A dog is nothing like having a baby," I told my dad. "You can't breastfeed a dog in public—"

"That's girl's stuff!!!" Vladimir interrupted. He calls anything from periods to imaginary scenarios in which I breastfeed a dog Girl's Stuff. I vividly remember waking up one morning to him swinging my bra like a lasso, screaming, "Why is this Girl's Stuff lying on the stairs!?"

But here's the thing about Girl's Stuff. As you get older—around your mid-to-late-twenties—it begins to whisper in your ear, "Wouldn't it be great to have something to keep alive, you beautiful Goddess?" You begin with plants, then you get more plants, then your house is covered in greenery—most of it dead—then your Girl's Stuff starts asking for more. "Something easier to kill," it hisses. One night, when you're vulnerable, you sign up for a newsletter and stumble upon a courtesy post for Randall, a man in the middle of such a nasty divorce that he can't get through a sentence without his voice quivering.

John, his dog of eleven years, was a big obstacle in Randall's apartment hunt. He needed someone to take John in for a few weeks while he looked for a place. When Randall came over to my apartment to drop off John, he looked haggard. I'd never met him before, but I could tell the divorce was taking its toll on his skin and posture. Randall was about half my size and a little shifty, like he was on the brink of offering you drugs or bursting into tears.

"He's a hunting dog," Randall told me as he pulled John out of his carrier. He held John in his arms like a football before continuing to describe his beloved dog to me. "John likes to burrow." Randall gave a big, sad sigh before continuing, "And he's built for catching small animals." He lifted John by the tail and his wiener-body dangled in the air. "See?" Randall pointed to his spine, "It splits here, so he's designed to be pulled out by his tail. You know, from badgers' burrows and stuff." John hung motionless in the air.

He's going to snap this dog in half, and this block is too loud for anyone to hear my screams, I thought.

"Don't do that, please," I said, louder than intended. Randall placed the dog on the ground and John joyfully wagged his entire body, like a little snake. "He burrows in bed sheets, and make sure to keep him away from stuffed animals," Randall continued.

"Ha, well, my roommate and I are both in our twenties, so . . ." I responded.

"No stuffed animals. Good," Randall said. This isn't true. I have a stuffed Dalmatian, Lucky, who I can't fall asleep without. I talk to Lucky more than anyone else—including Siri. There was no way I was going to let a stuffed-animal murderer, no matter how cute, sleep in my bed. Yes, I was protecting Lucky, but also: John's spongy foot pads were covered in the piss and filth of New York's gag-inducing streets.

Not wanting to spend my afternoon making small talk with a devastated divorcé, I inched toward the door until Randall got the hint and John and I were left with only each other.

Small dogs are not usually my bag, but John had a boxy face and big velvet ears that I liked to curl between my fingers. He loved me fiercely and immediately. Aside from my dad, I'd never had a man express such loyalty. I was addicted. His attachment to me proved to be a problem for my male roommate, really any man who tried to get near; I loved John all the more for it. My protector.

Behind every dog with behavioral issues, there's a narcissist who loves being the only one the dog responds to. The smaller the dog, the bigger the emotional needs of the owner, is my theory.

John spent the first night crying at the foot of my bed. He stopped around two a.m., because I brought him, and his poo-

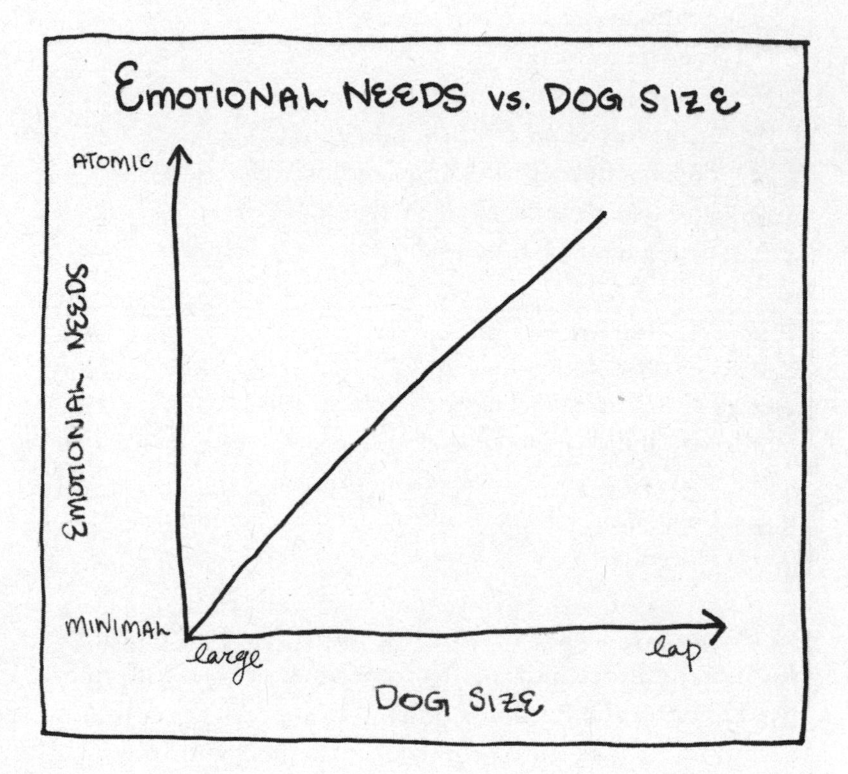
EMOTIONAL NEEDS VS. DOG SIZE
ATOMIC
EMOTIONAL NEEDS
MINIMAL
large
lap
DOG SIZE

pee foot pads, into bed. Lucky moved onto the shelf, where he stayed for the rest of my affair with John.

It only took me a couple of weeks to pick up on John's other quirks:

John's Likes

- Throwing up on clean sheets
- Peeing on trash bags
- Rolling in his own urine
- Attacking other Dachshunds
- Shitting himself when my landlord, Herb, comes into the apartment
- Eating tennis balls

John's Dislikes

- Sleeping alone
- Stuffed animals bigger than him
- My landlord, Herb
- Men
- Small dogs
- His collar

Eventually, a few weeks turned into a few months, and a few months turned into an offer for me to keep John full-time. By that point, I'd become completely dependent on John's attention, so I accepted—partially thrilled with my luck and partially disappointed in Randall's decision to abandon his dog.

John and I became the Queens of Brooklyn (he was neutered). We'd wander the streets for hours; sipping on iced coffees, smelling buttholes, sitting on benches, peeing on trash bags, attracting men who liked other men.

We always disagreed on the amount of time it took to effectively smell another dog's anus. I thought it was twenty

John in my bed.

seconds, John thought it was until I used all of my weight to pull his sausage body in the opposite direction. I can still hear the sound of his nails scraping against the cement as he was dragged away from his beloved butts. He was the greatest slinky, bendy addition to my life. I cared more about his well-being than my own. He trained me to take pauses throughout the day, step away from my stresses, wake up early, drink less, and rub his belly. I even began to make plans in the park (in nature!) so that he could come. John upped my fresh air intake and my skin reflected that. He made me more attentive, sensitive to the surrounding world. I even became more thoughtful about the men I dated, choosing wisely who I brought around.

John boosted me from an insecure and sloppy girl to an insecure and sloppy woman. The careless tides of my early twenties were slipping away. He was my new focus and I was happy to stop worrying about myself for a moment.

John was with me when I got my first real, decent boyfriend in New York. He was with me when I moved into a new apartment. And when I decided to look for a more creative job. He was the first one to learn that I got an offer to work at an animation company and the first to celebrate when I accepted. John was even allowed to go to work with me. New York was opening up in ways I'd never imagined. I felt everything settling, becoming more manageable, coming together—which everyone knows is what life feels like right before it all comes crashing down. Hard.

The night before my first day on the new job, I took my bedsheets to the laundromat; I reserved bedsheet washes for special occasions and wanted to feel extra clean in the morning. I came home, made the bed—which takes forever when you're single—and lifted John into it for the night. In the morning, I woke up in a pile of John's vomit. "Damnit, John!" I yelled, shooting out of bed. He wagged his tail as if nothing had happened. His chickpea brain already erased the memory.

Initially, I thought John's stomach was upset because he was picking up on my first-day jitters, but now I know it was his warning shot; a prediction of trouble to come. A prediction that would result in my giving John back to Randall, proving that I was still a little girl dealing with little girl's stuff. Not prepared for any real responsibility.

6

DONATE HAIR

I believe that if you have too much of something you should share it—a controversial opinion in my family. My parents came from a Communist country where the whole "sharing" thing didn't quite work out. In fact, it was a catastrophe. Tired of the living conditions, they clawed their way out of Russia and headed to the land of life, liberty, and the "great music band, 'Bee Gees.'"

In America, my parents started looking out for themselves; family first. Period. Their move proved that life is indeed better when you don't have to share. My dad immediately began making more money and upgraded almost every facet of our lives. Then my parents took this no-share way of thinking and passed it down to me. I was raised with a lone-wolf mentality. "Look out for yourself, no one else will," my mom sang as she rocked me to sleep at night. "Trust no one!" my dad yelled at my soccer games.

The thing is, my parents earned the right not to share; they came from a rough country that didn't play by the rules of basic human rights. I came from Michael Stars, BMWs, and tween Xanax fever dreams. I'd faced about as much adversity as a palm tree. So my life was too cushy not to share.

After college, the itch to give back to the world began to travel down my spine and into my soul, but I had a low paying job and was barely covering rent. My hair was my only possession of monetary value.

I never quite understood anyone's attachment to their hair—unless it's for religious reasons, then I understand it even less. Hair is not necessary for daily functioning; it's the only thing that grows back, and people with short hair *always* look cooler. Of anything to cut off my body, hair would always be my first pick. I'd cut off my ring finger second, because I spend too much time wondering what to put on it. My left foot comes third, and I'd always keep my hands because I need them to write.

I guess it's not fair of me to judge how others relate to their hair because I've always had a lot of it. Too much of it, really. The thickness of each strand carries the historic weight of my ancestors, whose hair protected them against their greatest enemy: the cold. My ponytail boasts the girth of one baby arm. It weighs down my head and ruins my posture. I'm going to be a hunchback one day but, like, so is everyone else in Generation Laptop.

When my brother was a toddler, I used to demand he play with my hair, because he was younger and weaker, making it easy to bully him. I go into a trance-like state when someone is running their fingers through my hair. This is particularly weird considering I don't like to be touched; hand-holding makes me gag, I hate sharing beds, and massages are a nightmare. But if a stranger came up behind me and started stroking my locks, I'd stand there motionless, letting the tingles travel up and down my spine. I even started perusing Craigslist to see if I could hire someone to come into my home and play with my hair—little-brother style.

Please stop thinking this is a sexual thing. It is not. I don't think.

One time when my brother was braiding my hair, he asked if we could play Barber Shop. "Sure. Why not?" I was amused that he was taking my abuse of his baby-brained naiveté to a new and innovative level. As he used his fingers to "cut" my hair, he got into character. "Trimmies here, trimmies there!" Then he got bored and ran off.

I didn't pay much attention to where he went because four-year-old boys are not very linear humans: they're eating string-cheese one minute and peeing off your parents' deck the next. Moments later, he came running back.

"Bar-bar is back!" he yelled.

"Okay, Barber. Can I have—" there was a distinct snip, and I felt the tension in my hair slack. I turned around in time to watch him run off with a fistful of my freshly cut hair.

"Mom!" I screamed at the top of my lungs. She didn't respond because she was in the backyard ashing her cigarette into an empty orange juice carton. When Olga was on her cigarette breaks, everything went to shit for ten minutes. For example: my brother would run around with scissors positioned directly under his jugular while I ran after him, attempting to catalyze his death. My mother, oblivious to the madness inside the house, stood on the deck, shifting her weight from left to right, smoking with her eyes closed.

I went into the bathroom to survey the damage, bringing my head close to the mirror as I dug through my knotted tresses. Regardless of how hard I looked, I couldn't find where my brother had made his cut. My mane just engulfed the six-inch missing piece—like in a sci-fi movie. There was too much hair. That's why giving it away never seemed like a big deal to me. Anyone who has long hair should be donating it. But as with anything, there is a right and wrong way to do it.

The process of donating your hair, although a simple one,

takes a lot of time. There are different rules for different places—you can't just send a toddler with a fistful of his sister's hair to a hospital's doorstep and expect a bald kid to get a tear-jerking wig. So here is a good umbrella of rules to operate under:

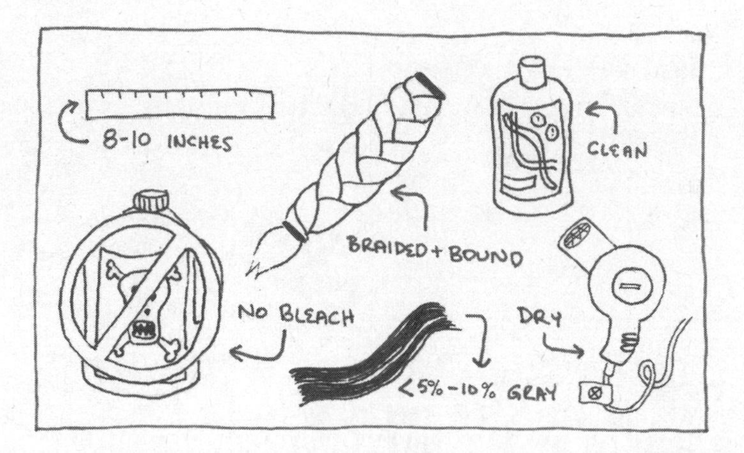

My hair was basically unusable for seven years due to horrendous self-dye jobs and self-haircuts. I was twenty-three the first time it was in good enough shape to donate.

One Friday, my boyfriend Carl brought me sunflowers during my lunch break at my new job. Sunflowers are my favorite flower. They're so happy and robust, plus they produce snacks; I like me a flower I can also eat. It was the first time Carl brought me flowers, and I couldn't help but get carried away. I pressed the bouquet to my chest, absorbing the warm glow of a nice gesture. Carl gave me a kiss on the cheek before disappearing into the madness of Times Square. Back in my office, I grabbed a pair of scissors and stood over the trash can, shearing off stem after stem until there was a lighter, more manageable, bouquet. The act of snipping the stems made me realize that I was feeling heavy lately, emotionally and literally. My body was plump with the diet of a new

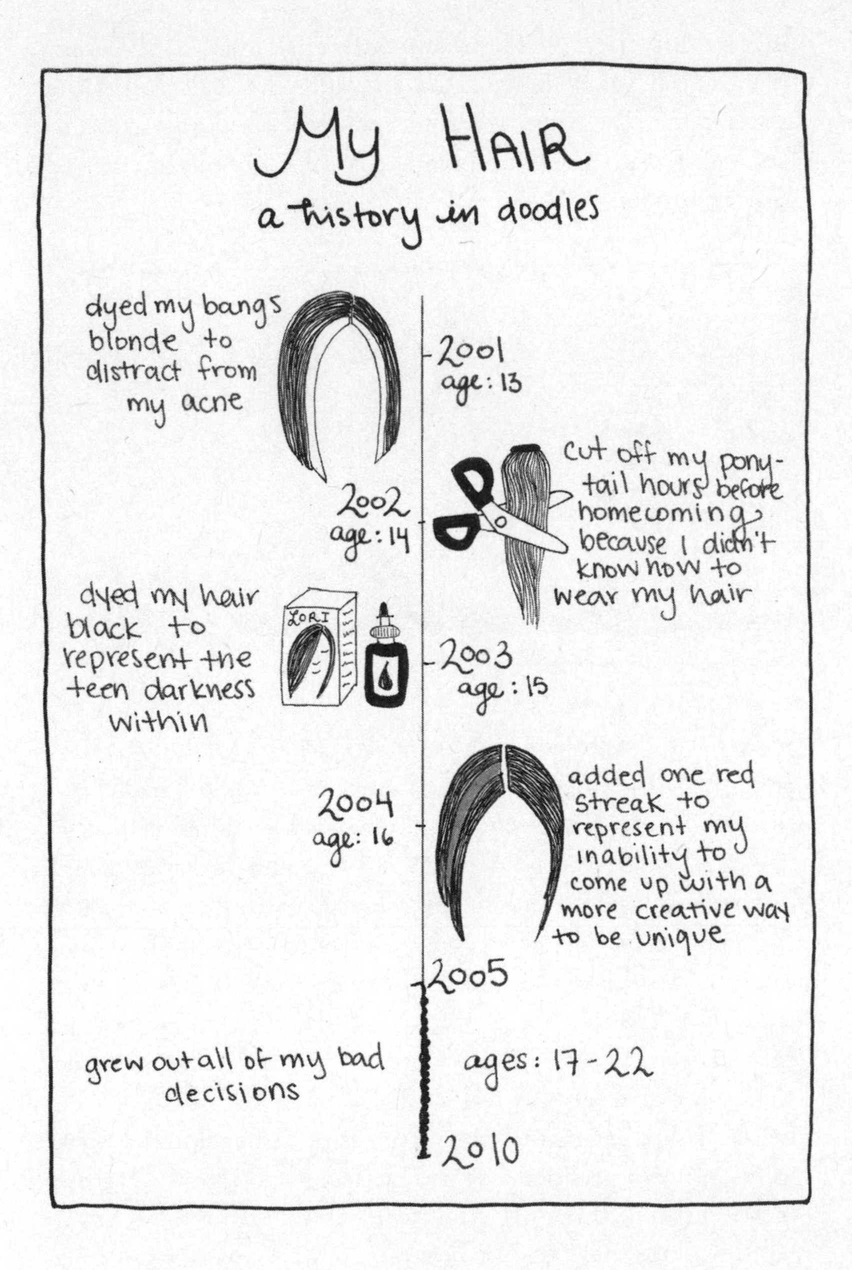
My Hair
a history in doodles
dyed my bangs blonde to distract from my acne
2001
age: 13
2002
age: 14
cut off my pony-tail hours before homecoming because I didn't know how to wear my hair
LORI
dyed my hair black to represent the teen darkness within
2003
age: 15
2004
age: 16
added one red streak to represent my inability to come up with a more creative way to be unique
2005
grew out all of my bad decisions
ages: 17-22
2010

relationship, and my soul sagged heavy with the stress of a new job. I put the scissors away and began to look at hair salons near my apartment. I wanted a change, and my hair was ready for one.

I spent my post-college years taking too much from the world. It was time to give back, to restore a little balance to my twenties. While my parents do not agree with what they call my "Communist" beliefs, they have grown accustomed to my unending desire for societal symmetry and my instinct to give away anything that was gifted to me, like good hair.

I went to a woman named Lisa in Brooklyn because she was the only one who would take me on such short notice. She twisted my hair into one thick braid, and cut it off. Snip. No *America's Next Top Model* makeover tears or anything exciting like that. She handed me the braid and charged extra for an "intensive" haircut. The whole experience proved that donating hair is possibly the easiest thing one can do to improve the world and that's why everyone should be doing it.

Had I done more research, I would've learned that many salons offer discounts for hair donation cuts, that a large percentage of hair is rejected due to the volume of donations and the state of the hair, and that some recipients are charged on a sliding scale depending on their family's income.

I'd later find that the best way to donate hair is to sell it on eBay and give your proceeds to a charity of your choosing. Money will always be the most useful thing you can give, and if you don't have any of it, the internet has plenty of ways for you to make some. Selling your hair online is clearly the superior way to help out—it's cheaper and creepier, which makes for a more interesting story. What is life if not a vessel for you to fill with good stories.

7

HAVE A DRAMATIC AIRPORT REUNION

I treat rom-coms like masturbation; something for when I'm alone and a little drunk, and never to be spoken about with my friends. My shame of rom-coms stems from a forever-fear of being considered basic. People don't even use that insult anymore, yet I avoid the label like a shelter dog avoids a vacuum.

That being said, I go weak in the knees for a good airport scene. Especially pre-9/11 ones when the main character breezes past security. "I need to tell her I love her!" he screams over his shoulder as a smiley guard nods in understanding.

"Go get her," the guard yells back. The nineties were a time when it was still socially acceptable to *get* a woman. Retrieve her, like groceries or gas. This scene has been used so many times, it's now an ouroboros: difficult to tell where the cliché begins and the romanticism ends.

At the peak of my rom-com consumption, my brain was plastic and malleable, forming ideas around concepts hand-fed to me on pop-culture crackers. I left the nineties with a young understanding of what love looked like: a dramatic proclamation—preferably involving an airport. This understanding grew its own pulsating heartbeat as my brain filed away more and more movies: *When Harry Met Sally*, *Cruel Intentions*, *The Wedding Singer*, *Sleepless in Seattle*—they all cast airports as settings for the breeding ground of love. I was sixteen when *Garden State* came out. That scene when Zach Braff, a struggling actor, misses his flight to tell Natalie Portman that he loves her? Please. I know plenty of struggling actors and not a single one of them would squander a plane ticket. It's impossible to find even a sliver of reality in most romantic comedies. But I didn't think like that at the time, I thought: this is what I want.

Watching those movies over and over again created a deep desire to have an airport scene of my very own. I hopped from long-distance relationship to long-distance relationship, hoping that one day we'd get to the point where an airport greeting was on the table. To me, there was no greater marker of love than going all the way to the airport to pick up someone. I never dated anyone long enough to experience such a thing . . . until Carl came into my life.

Carl was—you guessed it—a musician. We had been introduced to each other years earlier by his sister, Barbie, whom I worked for as a Resident Assistant in Missouri. Carl and I reconnected after he invited me to his show at Pete's Candy Store, a small bar in Williamsburg, Brooklyn. Pete's Candy Store usually booked acts with words like *folk* and *rustic* in their bios, and Carl was no exception. It was a long and narrow space with a tiny stage nestled in the back. A cacophonous coffin, really. Small but cavernous, warm and dark. It felt like stepping inside a rotting heart.

Carl was easy to spot. He had the same round face, striking eyes, and dark hair as his older sister. He sat at the bar with a PBR and shot of whiskey—a boilermaker, I believe it's called. I'd never seen anyone consume two different drinks at once and found it incredibly adult. It was like seeing your

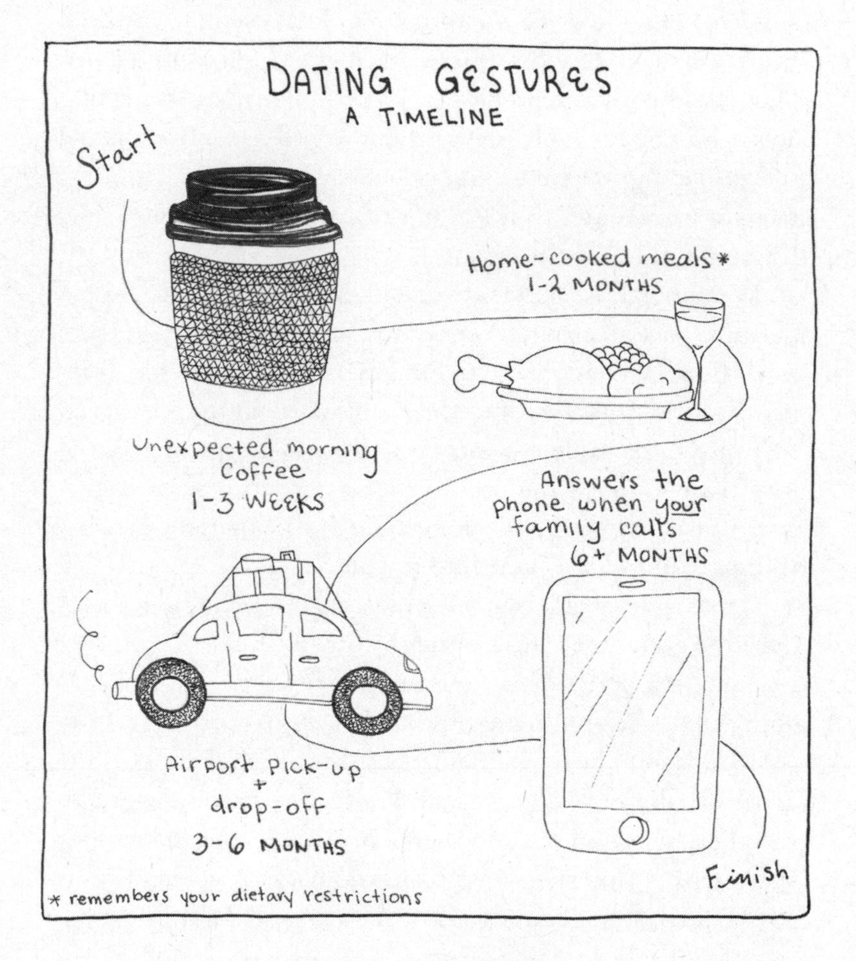
DATING GESTURES
A TIMELINE
Start
Home-cooked meals*
1-2 MONTHS
Unexpected morning
Coffee
1-3 WEEKS
Answers the
phone when your
family calls
6+ MONTHS
Airport Pick-up
+
drop-off
3-6 MONTHS
Finish
* remembers your dietary restrictions

high school crush smoking a cigarette and holding a cigar at the same time: confusing, yet cool. It was evident that he'd lost a lot of the boyish weight from the photos Barbie proudly displayed around her apartment. New York had made him hungry, both metaphorically and physically. That hunger took a tubby boy from the Midwest and chiseled him into the starving artist who was about to insert himself into my life.

When Carl got on stage and sang, his voice filled the rotting heart with beauty and optimism. He crooned about Missouri, oysters, beer, family, breakups, money—all the while occasionally glancing my way. After his set, he got off stage, and I urgently offered to buy him a PBR and whiskey.

We sat at the bar and turned our backs to everyone, creating a mini-chamber of nervous laughter, and first date–like chemistry. He asked me over for pizza the next week and so began our relationship.

One evening, shortly after Carl and I started dating, he grabbed my shirt and asked if it was expensive.

"Not really, it was like nine bucks," I told him, confused.

"Can I rip it off of you?" he asked.

I nodded my head yes and he proceeded to tear my shirt in half before throwing me onto his bed. It was the politest and sexiest thing to ever happen to me. I am from the suburbs. During high school, I had a mustache and questionable hygiene. In college, I loved "rules *and* studying." Having my shirt torn off by hot musicians was never an option on my sex menu. But when you live in a city that never sleeps, people need to find something—or someone, rather—to fill all that free time.

Carl and I had been dating on and off for nine months when a work opportunity to go to Taiwan on a six-week training session came up. I immediately asked Carl if he'd greet me at the airport when I returned.

"I'll see," he told me. "Don't know if I'll be able to." John F. Kennedy Airport is a trek, it's even more of a trek when you're poor. You really gotta love someone to make that journey, only to immediately turn around and journey back home.

"Is this one of those things where you pretend you can't come but then you show up at the last minute?" I asked.

"I'll see," Carl repeated with a laugh. He kissed my nose and got up to get ready for his day job as a dog walker.

The night before my trip, I went out for drinks with some friends. "You're not coming back, are you?" Rebecca said, studying my face.

"What are you talking about? I have a ticket back," I told her.

"Yeah, but you're not going to *really* come back."

"You're bein—"

"What are you guys talking about?" Carl asked as he slid next to me with a PBR.

"Nothing," Rebecca quickly answered. "You aren't," she silently mouthed at me. I rolled my eyes.

By my fourth week in Taiwan, it became clear that Rebecca was right. Living in an Asian country awoke a discomfort I hadn't felt in a long while. A discomfort that would provide the disruption needed for my sedentary life.

"Are you sure?" Carl asked over Skype.

"Not really, but when else will I have an opportunity to live abroad?"

"Never. It's wild. You're wild."

"You should move with me. You could teach!" I told him. In my mind, Carl would move to Taiwan with me, we'd spend a few years saving up and exploring, then return a little richer, a little more stable than we currently were. Money was a difficult subject in our relationship; Carl didn't care about it while I was fixated on it, constantly worrying about how little I had and how to get more. Carl had slightly less than what he needed, and he didn't mind. If it were up to him, he'd live out of a van, off of nature, and play music all day. It drove me crazy and made me hate myself for feeling that way.

"I don't want to be a teacher," he rapidly replied. "I'm a musician." Our conversation ended there. If we were truly meant to be together, I wouldn't be moving to Taiwan in the first place.

Carl silently lay in his bed in Bushwick, while I sat at a desk in Taipei and began to cry. Our inability to compromise meant we were going to break up, and now there was a set date: October 29, the day I was moving to Asia.

The weekend before my return to the States, my coworkers took me out to karaoke to celebrate my impending move. Going to karaoke with Asian people is a sport of strength and endurance.

I thought I *knew* karaoke. In college, the karaoke kids shared a space with the comedy nerds. Tuesdays were for stand-up and Fridays were for singing. There were many parallels between the two groups: we took our performances seriously, we drank heavily, and a few in the crew actually had enough talent to go pro one day. A couple of the stand-ups crossed into the karaoke crowd. Ryan, for example, had an off-brand Frank Sinatra kinda voice and would sing his songs to the front row. Then there was Dan, the host of the comedy nights. Dan knew the song binder better than his own jokes. Kyle, the heartthrob of the comedy scene, would often default to funny monologues in the musical breaks. Pants, the three-hundred-pound tattooed and sober bartender, sang Bon Jovi's "I'll Be There for You" without fail. He was magic.

I didn't usually participate in karaoke because my mom made me promise to never sing in public. I once got grounded for singing too loud in the shower. "Stop singing! You're scaring your little brother," my mother's muffled voice came from the door. I sang "Flagpole Sitta" even louder because teens like to do the opposite of what they're asked. My parents took away my driver's license for two weeks.

When my Taiwanese coworkers insisted on karaoke, warm memories of my college weekends flooded to mind. The stage, the little monitor, the bar filled with alt-y kids who wanted to know, if only for a moment, what it felt like to be a star. That's what I was expecting.

The actual place you do karaoke in Asia is in a small room with black walls and pleather couches. When you sit down, your thigh grease slides around on other people's thigh grease. Two microphones with brightly colored foam caps and an old TV filled with mostly Taiwanese and Chinese songs sit at the front. The decor is minimal. (I think there was a flower painting in our room, but it was dark, so my eyes couldn't really focus.) The monitor not only plays lyrics, but a music video accompanying each song. All the videos start the same, with some sort of screensaver-like nature landscape. After a series of cross-dissolves, you are treated to a woman, usually blond or Asian, prancing through fields, reading books on benches, or laughing at the sky. They all kind of look like tampon commercials with Chinese subtitles.

Unlike karaoke in America, where there are endless distractions between you and the bar, in Asia you order bottles of alcohol that are brought to your room. Bottles. This was at a time when I drank as if all the alcohol would run out one day, possibly *that* day.

I don't exactly remember what we drank that night, it was probably whiskey and most likely a Johnny Walker type. I do remember that Cathy, a boyish thirty-year-old, was egging me on. Every office has one, an egger, the person who always wants another round. I was happy to see that Asia was no different when it came to office culture. Cathy, who identified as a straight woman, looked like Justin Bieber and was dating a woman. She was a bowl of anomalies and spoke pretty good English, making it easier for me to barter with her.

"Too much, Cathy," I told her.

"You're a big girl, you need more!" she responded. Cathy's favorite thing to do was make fun of my weight. I was five-foot-two and about 125 pounds at the time. In Taiwan, this was considered obese. Martti, Cathy's best friend and partner in mischief, came over to make sure I was drinking. Martti spoke the least English of the crew, but was one of my favorites. Even through the language barrier, I could tell he was charming. The way he leaned in to listen intently to what you had to say. The way his eyebrows pointed upward with concern when he could sense sadness. Everything about him screamed sweetie. It also didn't hurt that he had defined features and a gentle yet masculine air about him.

Cathy poured me a fourth glass of whiskey when Meggie, a mousy project manager, put on Aqua's "Barbie Girl." She placed the mic to her mouth and made a sound I'd never heard before. Like a witch who'd had her throat replaced with a garbage disposal. I took a big sip of my drink before getting up to sing with her . . . and everyone else who went up for the rest of night.

At the end of the ordeal, I was so smashed that I tried to get Cathy to go home with me.* "You're crazy," she said. "Go-ah, home." She put her cigarette in her mouth and shoved me toward the street. I shrugged and began to look for a cab, my brain slowly turning off on the way home.

I woke up in my room, still in my dress, with a hangover so bad that my face changed shape. My shoes were sitting next to my bed and I was proud of myself for remembering to take

---

* I'm always hitting on women when I'm drunk. Taiwan was the first place I succeeded in getting one to go home with me. Sadly, not on that night, and not with Cathy. She was so cute!

them off—a sign that I don't have a problem. Even my purse made it back with me. Right as my body began to relax a little bit, I noticed there was one small thing missing: my underwear.

They weren't hard to find. I spotted them balled up under one of the shiny, gold curtains separating my hotel room from the balcony. *Hm. That's weird*, I thought. I grabbed my underwear, threw them in a different corner, and went to check my phone. There was a text from Martti. All it said was:

Sorry 2 leave. C u work.

Everything came crashing back into my skull. His chest, my hand on it. My face on his, too close to tell who he was. My skirt pulled over my hips. His hand disappearing. Carl's beard. How long he hugged me before I left for Taiwan. Carl. My job. Carl. Oh my god, my job. I had to get ready for work.

I ran into the bathroom, toppled into the shower, and quickly washed the night off. I tumbled out, went to the sink to brush my teeth, and caught my reflection in the mirror. *What did you do?* I burst into tears and called Carl.

"Hello?" Carl's confused voice came over the line. I was making an international call on my Samsung e1105t burner phone, purchased for emergencies. It turns out admitting that you're a piece of shit is not an emergency, but is expensive.

"IkissedsomeoneandI'msosorryandsoashamed," I wailed into the receiver. That was a lie. We did more than kiss, but I couldn't bring myself to tell Carl.

"Oh, Marina," Carl said. There was a long pause. "I have to get ready for my show."

"Okay," I told him. A click and the phone went dead. It

was a selfish move. We could've quietly broken up, let the doomed relationship fizzle out on its own, but no, I had to go and be honest with him. Honesty is *not* the best policy.

Disappointing someone you love is the worst feeling, especially when you're too far away to fix it. We were still together. I still had a boyfriend. A boyfriend I'd cheated on. What a nasty word, *cheated.* In an astonishing attempt to soothe my shame, I immediately called Carl's sister Barbie to tell her what happened. Yes, counterintuitive, but my anxiety of people *discovering* that I did something awful is greater than the shame of them knowing. Barbie sounded baffled and sympathetic.

"It's okay. I'm sure he'll understand," she said. "Weren't you two going to break up anyway?" I sobbed louder.

At work, I couldn't even look up from my computer. I simply sat in my cubicle and cried. Martti came over, but when he saw my face, his whole body dropped and he slunk away.

Carl eventually came on Gchat after he got back from his show and if I really hated myself, I could probably still find that conversation. I remember distinctly asking him if he was still planning to meet me at the airport. I don't know was all he sent.

The bathroom was my only savior. In it, shielded from the wandering eyes of my coworkers, I faced the mirror again. My eyes were the color of wine, giving a demonic glow to my face. I slapped my cheeks a bit, smiled enthusiastically, stretching my lips as wide as possible. I don't know what it is about smiling like a juggalo, but it usually helps clear the redness in my face. It doesn't make me feel better, or stop the moisture from gathering in my eyes, it just helps with the redness.

An idea to salvage the remaining moments of my relationship popped into my head. I bolted to my desk and sat down.

HOW TO CRY AT WORK

I CRY ALL THE TIME. I HATE THAT IT'S CONSIDERED A SIGN OF WEAKNESS IN PROFESSIONAL ENVIRONMENTS. HERE'S HOW YOU CAN BECOME A STEALTH-MASTER AT DISCREETLY CRYING AT WORK WITH MY 4-STEP PLAN!

1.

KEEP A PAIR OF SUNGLASSES AT YOUR DESK. IF IT'S A SHORT CRY, POP THOSE BABIES ON AND PRETEND LIKE YOU FORGOT TO TAKE THEM OFF. IF IT'S A LONG CRY, POP THEM ON AS YOU HEAD TO THE BATHROOM LEST YOU RUN INTO YOUR BOSS, OR A COWORKER YOU UNINTENTIONALLY MADE OUT WITH THE NIGHT BEFORE.

2.

CRY IN A BATHROOM STALL ON A DIFFERENT FLOOR (OR WING), SOMEWHERE NO ONE WILL RECOGNIZE YOUR PUFFY FACE.

3.

TAKE 3 RAPID, DEEP BREATHS, EACH ONE FASTER THAN THE PREVIOUS. SHAKE YOUR HANDS OUT LIKE A JAZZ DANCER ABOUT TO GET IN A MUSICAL FIGHT (OR LIKE A 70s MAN WHO SEES A HOT LADY) TRUST ME, IT JUST WORKS.

4.

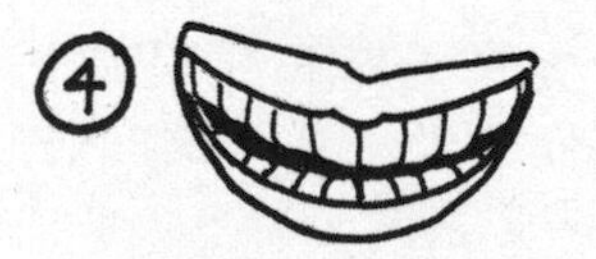

SMILE AS WIDE AND FRENZIED AS YOU CAN. SMILE UNTIL YOUR NECK HURTS AND YOUR EYES DISAPPEAR BEHIND YOUR CHEEKS.

Something drastic needed to be done, something to make me feel better. It was my turn to *get* the guy.

My plan was to write one hundred emails to Carl; each one listing something that I loved about him. It is important to note that Carl was not ignoring me, nor was he not talking to me—he was simply sleeping as it was the middle of the night in Brooklyn. I look back at those emails, gathering dust in the archives of my inbox and cringe. So hard.

It took me two hours and twenty minutes of projecting all of my guilt into Carl's inbox before he Gchatted me. I had made it to 97: "You threw me a fake birthday party when I was sad."

Carl: I'm over it
no need to dwell on things in the past tomorrow will be better ;)
Me: Well I am still not over it but like I said, all I care about is you.
Carl: I just feel like we are in our 20s why the fuck not kiss whoever you want?

I couldn't decide which one was worse, being faux-ignored or being dismissed. That's the difficult thing about messing up as an adult: you often don't get the punishment that is necessary to move on. Carl moved on quickly, but I fell into a self-humiliation spiral. It took a long time to realize that he was right. Why the fuck not kiss whoever I want? Hooking up with the wrong people is exactly what your twenties are tailor-made for.

Back at the hotel room, I immediately hopped in the shower again. I used my mint green loofah in an attempt to wash off the stench of shame. It didn't work. It's hard to feel fully clean in hotel showers anyway; it's difficult for me to shake the image of businessmen peeing in the drain. I got out, wrapped myself in a pure white robe, grabbed my computer, and crawled into bed. Although I didn't know how to feel better, I did know how to numb my mind with YouTube videos.

The doorbell unexpectedly rang, distracting me from my mission. I hadn't heard that sound since the time a hotel employee came in to explain how to use the toilet—there were thirteen buttons on it, none of which I understood. "This one here, sprinkles here," the poor employee explained while pointing to his ass. "This one here, do this." He began to act out what can only be described as the YMCA. I missed the last three buttons because I was too preoccupied trying to figure out how much to tip him for the impromptu bathroom charades.

I cautiously looked through the peephole and was greeted by Martti's bulbous head. My chest constricted. I wanted to tell him to leave, that I didn't want to see him, that he ruined my relationship and the rest of my trip, but he didn't speak English and I didn't speak Mandarin. That's the crazy thing about humans. We are truly animals. One animal relayed to the other animal that they wanted to rub bodies, which hurt the third animal. No words needed. We all understood each other's mistakes. I tightened the belt on my robe and let him in. He immediately hugged my damp body and I felt absolutely nothing. "Don't cry, don't cry. Don't cry," he quietly said in my ear.

I truly was unsure of how much English Martti did and didn't know, so I kept my response monosyllabic: "I'm sad." I was worried we'd need to resort to his smartphone and I'd have to yell, "Siri, how do you say, 'You've added an unnecessary layer of difficulty to my already complicated relationship and although he and I were going to break up anyway, I've now stained my longest record of being a good girlfriend' in Chinese?"

"Don't cry," he said again. I'm sure Martti is a bright guy, but the language barrier made him sound like a shitty pop song where the lyrics keep repeating themselves until the only way to remove them from your head is to blow your brains out.

"I have a boyfriend."

"It's okay."

"I promise you it is not okay."

Martti shrugged, but only because he didn't know what I was saying. We sat quietly in my room. I couldn't bear to look at him, so I stared at my feet. It was clear he had so much to say, but he didn't know how to say it. It was the most bizarre interaction I've ever had with a one-night stand. *As if they aren't awkward enough.* Our mistake made through physical contact would not be solved through communication, so instead we sat there staring at the ground as if Rosetta Stone was etched into the rug. After a long silence, Martti sighed and looked at me.

"A woman heart is like glass. It breaks." He mimed a heart breaking with his hands and then pointed to my chest. I wondered how long it took him to memorize that phrase. If he said it over and over during his cab ride to the hotel.

"A woman heart is like glass. It breaks," he repeated to the back of the cab driver's head.

"A woman heart is like glass. It breaks," he said with more confidence in the elevator.

"A woman heart is like glass. It breaks," he whispered to my door before ringing the bell.

"Thank you, Martti." I stood up and Martti took the hint. He gave me a second, meaningless hug and dejectedly walked out of the room. I'll never forget how hard he worked to say that sentence and how incorrectly fragile it made me feel. My heart is made of muscle. It is strong and tender, it keeps my body functioning and my mind sharp. It is not made of glass.

A day later, I was on the sixteen-hour flight headed back to the U.S. I spent the whole time crying into my choice of chicken or fish, which isn't that different from any other flight. Something about the plane air makes me weepy.

Usually, landing on solid ground after a long flight is my favorite. The couples kissing, the families hugging, children running around, people drinking alone at 10 a.m.—everything about the airport seems a little better than real life to me. When I landed at JFK, I noticed none of this. I wanted to get out of there and into my bed as quickly as possible. I kept my head down until I got to the baggage claim area.

There was Carl. He was standing in the middle of a large group of Asians, scanning the faces of people walking by, looking for mine. It was the movie moment I'd always wanted. He smiled so big when he saw me, as if the power of our reunion erased the mistakes of my past. I distinctly remember the rough fabric of his jacket, scratching my face when I shoved it into his clothing. He smelled the same as when I'd left him. To the outside world, we were a happy couple reuniting after a long time apart. Our hug was filled with the raw, passionate energy of a paradigm shift. The airport reunion *did* feel like the movies. It was big and dramatic. Carl's face, jutting a foot above the others, will always be seared in my memory. But the scandalous means to my storybook end were not worth it. I didn't deserve that moment.

We walked out of JFK holding hands, knowing that in a month I'd come back to that very same airport with all of my stuff packed in two suitcases and we'd part ways. This time for good. Because relationships, at least the real ones, can't survive off theatrical moments.

LIVE IN A DIFFERENT COUNTRY

Asia was not at all what I imagined when fantasizing about living abroad. My dreams involved a Vespa, a man with a five o'clock shadow, and some sort of vine-covered apartment building with a charmingly chubby landlord who called me "Bella" or "Amor." What I got instead was Taiwan, where the men are hairless, the scooters are clunky, the streets smell like rotting fish, and the apartments are sterile. In a way, not getting my perfect Spantalian life abroad worked out in my favor because I had more to complain about, and I quite enjoy complaining.

My decision to move to Taiwan was made with just about the same amount of forethought as I put into my cocktails. It turned my life upside down. I had to break up with Carl, move out of my new apartment, and give John back to his owner, all in a couple of weeks. It made me miserable, but when I tried to gripe to my father, he wouldn't play my game.

"You did this to yourself, Marina. It's because you're Russian . . ." he told me. "Russians like to create their own problems so that they can heroically overcome them." Which is not only true, but one of my favorite activities.

"Who's going to marry you there?" my mom moaned as we folded my clothes into a huge new suitcase. At the time, I was a twenty-four-year-old who was sleeping with more stuffed animals than men. It was a valid point. Who *was* going to marry me in Taiwan? I'd become good at tricking men into liking me in Brooklyn, but the men of Taiwan would prove to be ill-equipped for my brash personality. The guys I met wanted a peaceful, quiet woman to take care of them and to keep the apartment, and herself, in shape. I was none of those things. Eastern European ladies are like the starter-brand of female—we're too hairy and gain weight too easily to be fetishized. Our tone is masculine and we rarely care who's satisfied with us, least of all our husbands. "No one makes me dinner anymore," my father whined one Monday when he came home from teaching his jewelry-making class. The next Monday, my mom left a frozen pizza on the counter, still in its plastic wrap.

When I landed in Taiwan, I was greeted by an email from Amy, my brand-new pen-pal friend who would become the keeper of all my Taiwan exploits. Amy spent a few years with the Peace Corps in Moldova and had the sage advice of a well-traveled individual:

> You're on your adventure now! Channel that energy into hilarity, projects, blogs, making friends, decorating your new place, and, I don't know, work? Sure.

Amy's guidance combined with my own trial and error produced a small New Country Survival toolbox.

The only thing I couldn't seem to master in Taiwan was dating, which was difficult for me. Aside from criticizing Facebook engagement photos posted by former high school classmates, dating was my second favorite hobby.

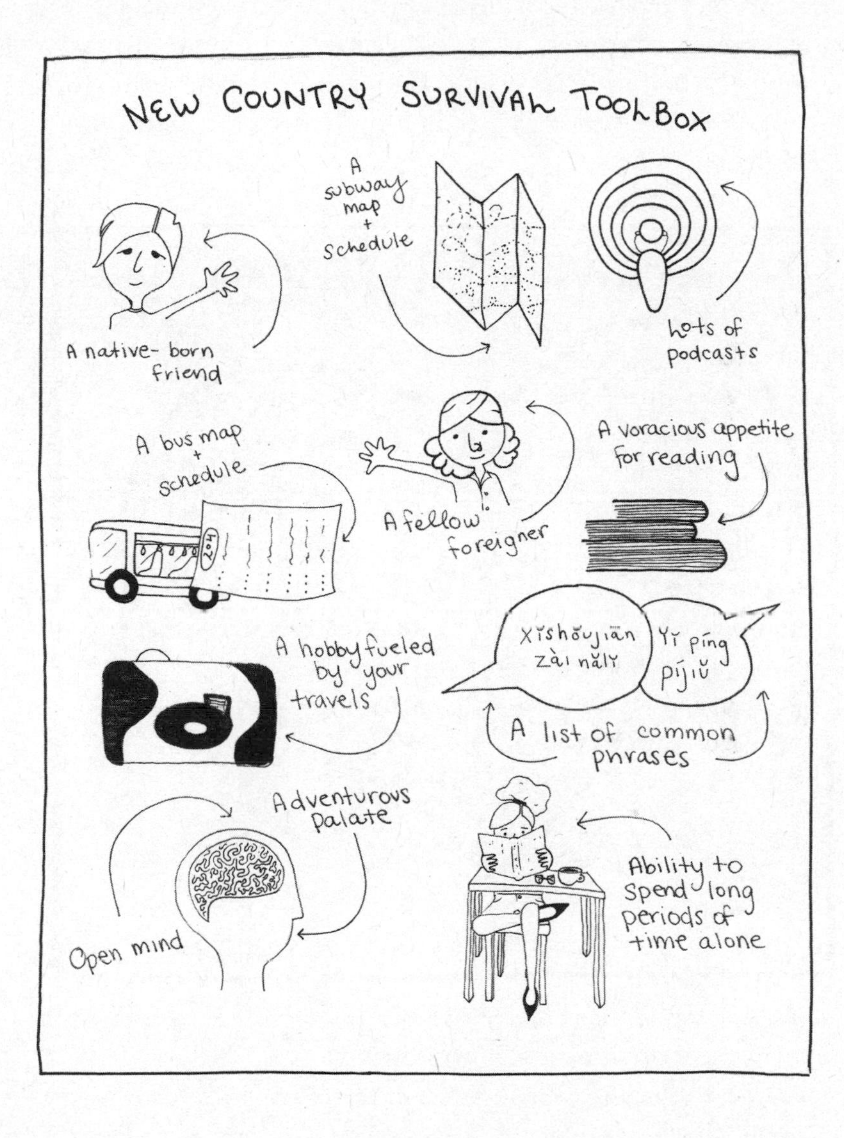
NEW COUNTRY SURVIVAL TOOLBOX
A native-born friend
A subway map + schedule
Lots of podcasts
A bus map + schedule
204
A fellow foreigner
A voracious appetite for reading
Xǐshǒujiān zài nǎlǐ
Yǐ píng píjiǔ
A hobby fueled by your travels
A list of common phrases
Adventurous palate
Open mind
Ability to spend long periods of time alone

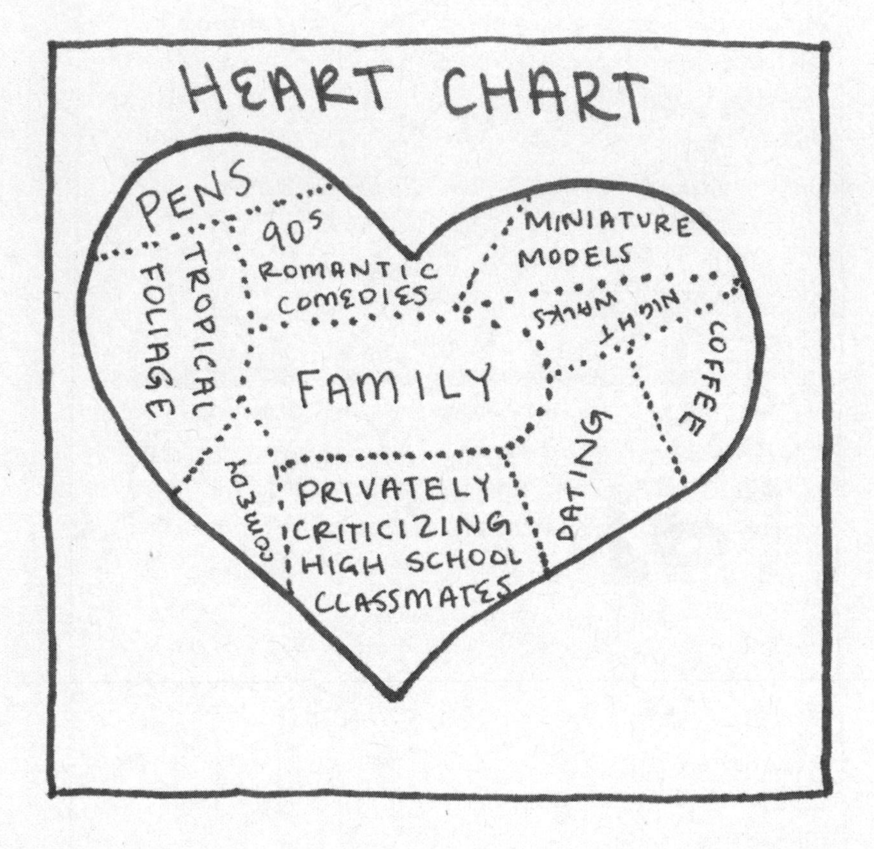
HEART CHART
PENS
90s ROMANTIC COMEDIES
MINIATURE MODELS
TROPICAL FOLIAGE
NIGHT WALKS
FAMILY
COFFEE
COMEDY
PRIVATELY CRITICIZING HIGH SCHOOL CLASSMATES
DATING

The lack of eligible bachelors interested in me was a wake-up call. Going from New York, where I could pick up a guy using little more than a cocktail and a pen, to Taiwan, where men recoiled from my large mouth and affinity for alcohol, was a big adjustment. Subtracting male attention from my day-to-day added a lot of depth to other parts of my life. I began working harder, writing more, running. I actually became pretty trim. Which is a shame, because no one was around to appreciate my healthier body—so for the first time in my life, I began to appreciate it myself. My weekends were spent wandering the city, listening to Savage Love podcasts. Dan Savage, the host, gave advice to people with the filthiest sexual kinks I'd ever heard of as I hiked through national parks, congested subway stations, and buzzing street markets.

Taiwan ignited my love of street photography. In that part of Asia, photography is celebrated beyond anything I've ever seen. One time, in the distance, I saw a large crowd of people gathered around something with cameras in the air. I walked over to see if it was a celebrity or some other marvel worthy of such attention—it was the entrance sign to a mall. My talent for street photography began to emerge, but it was mainly a result of people staring at me, the outsider. I wore my camera at my chest and snapped a photo every time I felt curious stranger-eyes sizing up my furry American body.

Subtracting dating from my life rounded out some rough edges to my personality. But after a while I grew lonely and started to scrounge.

I began hanging out at an expat bar—the expat men in Taiwan are like abductees from a comic book convention. Most were anemic and awkward, possessing an incomprehensible obsession with Asia. It was hard to tell whether they were out of touch because they'd been living in a different country or if they were born out of touch and found a sanctuary within Taiwan. The classic question of which came first, the chicken or the freak?

"Want to see my third nipple?" a guy named Greg asked me on our first date. A real mutant! Greg was in Taiwan studying Chinese, and had the facial features of a toad. I, of course, desperately wanted to see his third nipple, but played it cool.

"Sure, whatever." I edged closer to his body. He lifted his shirt and right there, on his ribcage, was a third nipple. We broke things off shortly after we met. Turns out his third nipple was the most interesting thing about him.

I decided to sign up for Mandarin classes in an attempt to diversify my dating pool. I tried to study the language on my own before moving, but was too cocky about it. "Yeah, I already speak Russian and a little bit of Spanish, so picking up a fourth language should be easy," I said to Karen, the listless bookstore employee who helped me find *Everyday Chinese for Travelers*. I thumbed through the pages and my eyes widened. Each word had a set of lines and dashes hanging over its letters. I'd never seen so many letter-accouterments. Don't even get me started on the netted webs they call "characters." I bought the book, but quickly understood that your tone is the most important part of speaking Chinese. You're required to pitch and dip your voice according to the word. If you mix up the wrong pitch or dip, you completely change the word. My favorite example is *mai*. *Mǎi* means to buy, whereas *mài* means to sell. Mai oh mai, Mandarin is a headache!

I downloaded a Mandarin-language app to focus on my tone. "Cat" I'd say in Mandarin to a puddle of urine. "Apple!" I'd yell at a cab. The only phrase I managed to learn fluently in my two months of self-study was, "I have one son."

My teacher, Dory, was a pint-sized person with an incredible wealth of patience. I came to her apartment twice a week to go over a Mandarin workbook filled with simpleton phrases and large-eyed illustrations. Her apartment was only a couple of train stops away, but I always began the commute extra early to allow for the twenty to thirty minutes I inevitably spent being lost. The street signs were literally in Chinese and impossible for me to navigate. I always arrived on time, half awake and bathed in coffee. I even fell asleep during a lesson and Dory didn't get mad, she just gently rubbed my arm in an attempt to wake me up. Early on in our one-on-one lessons it became apparent that I'd never get beyond the skill level of Sassy Toddler, so Dory let me bring in a self-selected list of sentences to learn. "Where is the bathroom?" "One coffee, please." "I don't usually do this on the first date."

We spent most of the classes saying the same word over and over again until my tone matched hers. "Mandarin is like singing," she told me. You have to pretend to sing, "*Kāfēi.*"

"*Kafei,*" I repeated.

"No, you have to go higher with your voice," she pointed above her head. "*Kā-fēi.*"

"*Kāfèi.*"

More pointing. "*Kāfēi.*"

"*Káfēi.*"

"*Kāfēi.*"

"*Káféi.*"

"*Kāfēi.*"

It was the closest to doing a duet I've ever come. But by the end of that lesson, I was able to order a cup of coffee in Mandarin. I spent a month drinking piping hot coffee in the ninety-degree muggy weather before learning how to order it iced.

My diet changed drastically in Taiwan. I ate what people put in front of me, often going to restaurants and pointing at random numbers, not recognizing any of the Chinese characters. Even though I lived in the Gourmet District of Taiwan, 7-Eleven was my favorite food stop. Unlike their U.S. counterpart, 7-Elevens in Asia carry everything from top-shelf whiskey to raincoats to hotpot soup. I frequented the 7-Eleven two to three times a day, and saw the same attendant during the evenings. I wanted to ask him his name but the phrase was too complicated, and if he responded with anything other than a one-word answer, I'd be stuck in the conversation. Forever.

Jimmy—I'll just call him that—had the night shift, which meant he'd see me at my worst. "The girl with the raccoon eyes came in today," he'd tell his wife when he got home. "She pointed outside, wrapped her arms around herself, then shook her body. She might have something wrong with her head." I hope Jimmy has a wife because I spent far too much time imagining their conversations. Sadly, I never learned anything about him and he didn't learn anything about me, aside from the fact that I have one son.

By moving to Taiwan, I had done an excellent job creating my obstacle, but I didn't have the first clue in how to heroically overcome it. Getting out of the apartment was a challenge; the anxiety of needing to interact with strangers using a combination of pointing and charades was crippling.

On weekend mornings, I'd treat myself to *dan bing*, a traditional Taiwanese breakfast consisting of a thin crepe-like pancake with egg and your choice of stuffing from a local stand. The two ladies who ran the stand, Small One and Tall One, were always hot and frazzled, which is unusual to see in Taiwan—especially considering they were women. Women hold themselves to a high standard of togetherness and poise; Taiwanese people in general do not like to exert themselves. When running in the heat, my complete disregard for getting disheveled always attracted all sorts of stares, but I liked the attention. Let's face it, I am a comic, and a woman—attention is my nourishment. For the first few weeks, I thought there was something on my face because of the volume of people gawking at me, but then I learned it was just

Small One in her element.

curiosity about someone different. In such a homogenous country, my self-imposed isolation turned into individuality—something that was difficult to come by in Brooklyn, where I was a generic-looking Jew in the faceless sea of hipsters.

The women had a method, a flow, to their cooking. Small One would press the scallion pancake dough, and Tall One would ladle egg onto the fryer. You had about 2.5 seconds to place your order. Anything longer than that and you'd be greeted with such a vitriolic stare that it would crawl into your bloodstream and lodge itself in your taste buds, tainting every *dan bing* bite with bitter twinges of embarrassment.

I wasn't that concerned with Tall One; she wore the same glasses—and permanent look of disappointment—as my mother. It was Small One who scared me. Petite things have always scared me; babies, grandmas, unidentified growths—this little lady was no different. For a while, I only had the courage to go to the stand when still tipsy from the night before. I would walk up to the counter and Small One's dark, sweaty eyebrows would say it all, "Oh great, let's watch Ms. America muster up the courage to practice this week's Chinese lesson on us."

We quickly worked out an unsaid agreement: I didn't try to order in Chinese, and they'd give me a plain scallion pancake with eggs. I'd raise my index finger and minutes later there'd be a glorious, steaming egg scallion pancake burning my fingertips. If I had a friend with me, I'd change my index finger into the peace sign and then there'd be two glorious egg scallion pancakes.

One day, I saw a man walk away with spinach sticking out of his pancake. The human condition is an interesting one; our desires always outlast our satisfaction. My pancakes no longer tasted as savory. Something was off. I, too, wanted spinach in my goddamn scallion pancakes.

Dory and I had a new problem to work through together. Spinach. The Mandarin word for spinach is *bōcài*. If you say, "bow tie" with a strange lisp, it kind of sounds like you're saying "spinach." I began my training. "Bow tie. *Bōtài. Bōcài*," I quietly sang it on sidewalks, chanted it in subways, and whispered it on bus stops. "*Bōcài*." People left me alone, "Nothing to see here, just a white girl chanting 'spinach' in Chinese."

The morning I decided it was time for my "*jiānbing jiā bōcài*," I wore high-waisted navy shorts and a white crop top—it was my most prized outfit. It gave me confidence, all of which was needed on my walk to the breakfast stand where the women are brash and the food is banging. When it was my turn to order, I confidently stated what I'd been practicing for a week: "*Qǐng gěi wǒ yīgè jiānbing jiā bōcài*."

The Small One began yelling at me almost immediately. I didn't understand what she was saying, but it sounded something like, "You're a disgusting failure. Hearing you speak makes me wish the meningitis left me deaf in both ears. I hope you choke on a pancake." But I can't be quite sure. The yelling continued.

If I showed my fear it'd only be worse. I loudly repeated *bōcài* in the breaths of her rant. I considered slowly slinking away. "*Bōcài!*" I'd wave before disappearing in the crowd. But I'd still have to pass that same stand every day. The clanging of the spatula would haunt me in my dreams. So, I stood there, repeating *bōcài* to Small One, then Tall One, then The Husband, then The Son. Finally, The Small One reached her tongs into the bin of spinach. My shoulders relaxed and my breathing went back to normal. She drizzled the beautiful leaves on my eggs and they immediately wilted in the heat. Little green smiles curling toward their death.

I overpaid and took my small bag of scallion pancake, egg, AND SPINACH to the park. The amount of pride I felt from five green leaves is indescribable. I'd overcome my fear of communication and busted into a brighter, greener world of achieving small but mighty goals—with a lot of yelling and help from a crew of family members. I fought for this. *Earned* it. I strategically positioned myself directly across from the stand in order to make eye contact with Small One and Tall One as I ate. My teeth triumphantly tore through the flaky crust, my tongue pushed the food up against the roof of my mouth, and a satisfying cascade of flavor swirled between my taste buds. It was in this instant that it became painfully clear my *dan bing* did not contain any spinach, but basil instead.

LEARN HOW TO DRESS MY BODY

My mother's favorite fashion accessory is the cargo pant. "Marina, watch this. Watch!" she excitedly gushed after she first discovered them. She tugged on one of the thirteen zippers and the bottom half of her pant leg dropped to her ankle. "Now they are shorts!" Olga put her sunglasses, loose change, and a water bottle into one of the pockets. "A purse too! Three things in one. I love America." It is the happiest I've ever seen her. I still associate the sound of loose change with my mother.

Olga has a very distinct sense of style: cargo pants, fleece vest, and lots of turtlenecks. My mom does everything she can to cover up her body. She hates her body so much that I once came home to find her completely covered, neck to ankle, in trash bags—going about her housekeeping as if it were normal. It looked like my mom had thrown herself away. She had ankle weights securing a trash bag to each leg, her hair was matted down with sweat, and her face was red from the lack of oxygen. "What are you doing?" I asked.

"Cleaning your mess," she said, crinkling past me in her trash suit.

Like many women, my early style choices were dictated by my mother. Her two closest held beliefs: what you wear should cover up your problem areas, and clothing should only be bought at a discounted price. Once, when Olga picked me up from high school, around the time crop tops and low-rise jeans were the teen uniform, she pointed out the car window, "What is that?"

I followed her finger to see a portly freshman, Julie, running to the bus. Her exposed tummy bounced around as she ran. "Julie?" I asked.

"What, she don't have friends? No one say to her she is too fat to wear this shirt?" My mom has always been a devastatingly blunt person, but the Russian accent makes her sound merciless.

Shopping with Olga meant a yearly trip to Nordstrom Rack, T.J. Maxx, or Marshalls. If I hadn't gained any weight from the previous year, then we'd skip our annual trip. "Oh, Marina, this will look cute for your body," she exclaimed, holding up an XL Billabong sweatshirt during one of those trips. Billabong, a brand created for California surfer culture, was not meant to be worn by a suburban chunkster. The closest I'd ever come to surfing was tripping over my brother's swim goggles. I had no business wearing Billabong, but Olga bought the sweatshirt because "the front pouch hides your stomach." Another sweatshirt perk: I could discreetly flip off skinny classmates from the warmth of that same front pocket.

It wasn't until changing in front of other girls for gym that I realized why my mom encouraged the oversized sweatshirts. "Oh my god, you have HUGE boobs," a classmate exclaimed. And it was true. DDs. I was a fourteen-year-old with the chest of a Renaissance milkmaid. It became clear that my mom wanted me to cover up, just as she had learned to cover herself up. Embracing your body was not something women did in 1970s Russia, at least not in my mom's family.

For decades, women have been expected to navigate a closet filled with acronyms and catchphrases. The LBD. Boyfriend jeans. Must-haves. Athleisure. Classic tee. Investment-piece. Statement-piece. It-piece. Baldgy. Tront. Swisps. Okay, I made the last three up, but I'm sure we're moments away from more made-up words to trick you into overpaying for a shirt or pants. If you're not a fashionista then you're a fashion victim—and no one wants to be a victim.

Like Olga, I never cared about which meaningless fabrics covered my body. I was very proud of my fuck-fashion stance until I realized how many doors being well-dressed can unlock. Writer Caitlin Moran put it best in *How to Be a Woman*: "When a woman walks into a room, her outfit is the first thing she says, before she even opens her mouth." I wanted my outfits to say, "I have arrived."

Just this past month, I had a work party on a Tuesday night. Weeknight work parties suck. In theory, the office is saving more money because people don't drink as much. But also, ha, as if tired and stressed adults are capable of having self-restraint at an open bar.

On the day of the party, all the women were running around the office, trying to get their work done early so that they would have time to change out of their office clothes and into their party clothes. The ones who didn't have time for day-to-night makeovers changed in the supply closet. They fashioned staples and paperclips into safety pins and used hand sanitizer as moisturizer, all the while making sure everyone knew that their bodies didn't usually look like this. "I've gained weight since getting this job! I just can't stay away from the candy dish." "I was skinnier when I bought this dress." "Still working on that baby weight. Do you know where the duct tape is?"

Meanwhile, the men had no sense of urgency, no need to change. They were sitting around, showing each other Gallon Smashing videos on YouTube. (For those unfamiliar, Gallon Smashing is when teenage boys go to grocery stores, pick up two gallons of milk, and violently throw themselves to the ground, causing the milk to spill everywhere. Look it up.) It wasn't fair, but I already knew this. Men have it infuriatingly easy when it comes to clothing.

My brother once came home wearing drop-crotch pants, a zebra-print headband, and a dashiki top.

"Has Mom seen you yet?" I asked when he walked in the door.

"No, why?" he responded. I quickly sprinted to the kitchen, where my mom spent most of her time scrolling through her favorite news blog (eBay), and took a seat at the table.

Olga eyed me suspiciously, knowing that I only showed this amount of enthusiasm when something bad was about to happen. My brother came into the kitchen and she turned her attention to him. I placed my chin in my hands and eagerly waited for the Comedy Central Roast of Sanya Shifrin to begin. My mother slowly looked my brother up and down, soaking his outfit in. "Where did you get that shirt?" she asked.

"A thrift store in Evanston," my brother calmly replied.

"Look at the pants too, Mom. Sanya, spread your legs. Show her the pants," I said. My brother spread his legs to show the crotch, hanging there like those saggy canvas bags placed beneath a horse's butthole to catch all the poop.

After a moment of pensive silence, my mom spoke up, "Can you get me shirt like this?"

"Of course, Ma!"

My mouth dropped open. My brother had already figured out how to dress with confidence, while I floundered in the fashion world. I was quickly nearing the age where one needed to have her "look" figured out (which is twenty-five, by the way) without a clue of how to do so.

My wardrobe was a mixture of high school athletic gear, free T-shirts, and clothing I'd stolen from my former roommates (one male, one accountant, and one raver). On a typical day, I looked like a banker going for a jog at Burning Man. It was not *me*, but the clothes were free and I needed to cover my privates with *something*. Before I knew anything about anything, my simple sartorial rules were as follows:

1. Do not wear more than two colors at any given time.
2. Tight shirts are not flattering on 83 percent of people and should only be reserved for exercise.
3. Blouse buttons are a chesty girl's worst enemy.

It wasn't much, but it got me through the first twenty-three years of my life. Until, that is, I became friends with Noël and Stephen. Two fashionable New Yorkers, one a professional designer, the other a professional gay man. I didn't want to be a fashion victim anymore, I wanted to be fashion survivor, so I asked Noël and Stephen to *What Not to Wear* me.

"You should set this on fire," Stephen said before he'd gotten all the way into my bedroom. He grabbed a sweater I only wore for special occasions—first dates, holiday parties, negative pregnancy tests. It was a large black knit sweater with an extra-baggy collar that hung down to my chest. If I bent down and jerked my body up fast enough, the collar would flip over my face, concealing my head. It looked like an uncircumcised knit-penis. It was my favorite party trick.

"Why? I like that sweater!" I snatched it from his hands.

"It makes you look way bigger than you are," Stephen said. I put the sweater in the bag marked "donations." Noël started grabbing one thing after another, after another, until she was hugging a big ball of clothes.

"What's wrong with all of that?" I asked her.

"It says 'Forever 21' on the label," she curtly replied before throwing the ball into the donation bag.

I'd clearly made a mistake by inviting the disaster duo into my closet but it was too late to do anything about it. We bundled up and headed to Century 21, where Noël and Stephen proceeded to tear apart every single thing I put on my body.

"Thank god I only fuck men!" Stephen cackled when I came out wearing a peasant top with white mid-calf pants. I scampered back into the dressing room and tried on a teal empire-waist dress.

"Oh, my god. Congratulations," Noël exclaimed. She walked up to me and gently placed her hand on my stomach. "Is it a boy or a girl?"

Every time I picked out a shirt or a dress, the jokes came like arrows, slicing through my choices. At the end of the day, I bought two items: a black cardigan and an off-white blouse for $120. The price tag hurt my feelings more than Noël and Stephen ever could.

I got home from that shopping trip, delicately hung the two items in my closet, and didn't touch them again until returning both pieces the next week. The guilt of spending *that* much money on two pieces of clothing got to me. I tenderly pulled my shitty clothes out of the donation bag and hung them back in my closet. I made a mental note of each piece and promised to never wear any of it in front of Noël and Stephen again. Which wasn't too difficult because our friendship ended shortly after that. (Unrelated to my stint at the burn clinic.)

After that experience, I went about my clothing revolution in a gentler way: by parroting. If someone was wearing something I liked, I made sure to ask them where they got it.

My favorite response was from my pen pal Amy. She has

unmatched taste and was the one who taught me about consignment shops, which is a more sophisticated way of saying "thrift store." She's a bloodhound when it comes to lightly used clothing. "See these shoes?" she asked me while holding a pair of white, glossy snake-effect leather loafers which were two sizes too big for her. "These are Tod's and they're selling them for $20." Amy leaned in and whispered, "They're worth over $300." She rolled her eyes and placed them in her shopping bag.

When I wrote Amy to ask about her style secrets, she emailed:

> My aesthetic is "professor chic" and my style icon is Bea Arthur.
>
> My advice is to carry yourself like you're about to go out. I know this isn't always realistic. I have days where I hate every single piece of clothing I own and come to work looking like a crazy. But there have to be some strict rules followed (and only very rarely broken) like:
>
> - leggings are never acceptable
> - find your silhouette and stick with it—only veer away from it if you're 100 percent sure it works from every angle
> - undergarments are never to be seen unintentionally (underwear creeping up/bra straps)
> - AND SO ON. We can discuss fashion further if you don't totally think I'm a snob.

I loved that response so much I wanted to take it as my own. But that's not how style works. You have to grow into it, you have to find what works for you through mistakes and ill-advised "statement pieces." It took me about three years to scrounge together my "look" and I still hit bumps along the way.

Last month, while on the bus in my brand-new, Cyber Monday–sale boots, I noticed the girl sitting next to me trying to sneak a photo of them. She wore ripped, acid-wash jeans and a powder pink sweatshirt that said "No" on it. The bus was so crowded that we were nearly sitting on top of each other and her elbows dug into my ribcage as she centered her phone. I smiled to myself, thinking that she'd taken the photo as a reference for next time she went shopping. I leaned in to tell her that the shoes were on sale at Macy's, only to see she was posting my boots to Snapchat with the copy: "EWWW!! I HATE THESE SO MUCH!" I recoiled in horror. Someone in acid-wash jeans was about to cyberbully me and there was nothing I could do about it.

The truth is I worked really hard on my outfit that day. I was on my way home from a new job on a Comedy Central show hosted by Moshe Kasher, a comedian with a sharp sense of fashion and an even sharper tongue. Everyone around the office was desperate to get a style nod of approval from him. Your day depended on whether or not he noticed your shirt, shoes, hat—and said, "Cool." I started peacocking in a desperate attempt to get his attention, and, slowly, my fashion sense began to change.

One day I showed up in a black romper with a bold pattern, complemented by a fitted black jacket and brand-new white Vans that sported pink flowers. The outfit demanded that everyone notice me, my chest, my style—my existence. I felt great in it. During rehearsal, someone tugged at my elbow. I looked over to see it was April, Moshe's personal stylist. This woman was paid to tell famous people what looked good and what didn't. Prior to this moment, we had never spoken because what would we have talked about? I just stared longingly at her tan skin, tiny body, and effortless style—everyone, except men and celebrity bloggers, knows it takes a lot of effort to look effortless.

"Where did you get that romper?" she whispered.

"Urban Outfitters, online," I whispered back.

That romper became my diploma. I graduated to the other side. The side where *I* was being asked, "Where did you get that?"

I truly believe that style can only be learned through years of mistakes and asking trendy coworkers, "Where did you get that?" You don't have to like fashion or even shopping to leave a lasting impression when you walk in the room. Unfortunately, women have to spend more time and money to look put-together, but luckily women are also prettier and smarter than men so it equals out. Women have more opportunities to send a message without speaking—a powerful tool if you use it correctly.

It took about five years to come up with an affordable, well-manufactured wardrobe that I hate only 20 percent of the time. A pretty good percentage considering the fashion industry survives and thrives on making sure that women are constantly disappointed with how they look.

There is a strong foundation upon which style can be built, and I'd like to share that foundation through some tips I've learned from the wonderful women and men in my life:

1. Don't wear heels you can't run in.
2. Everyone should own one good leather jacket (wonderful at hiding excessive arm hair). You can get a great (recycled) leather jacket for under $150.
3. Flowy shirts look good on everyone, especially women with abnormally large chests.
4. The darker your skin, the better cream looks on you.

5. Own one expensive blazer, they go with everything and can be used for multiple events (from business meetings to convincing your family that you're doing okay).
6. If your top goes past your mid-thigh, it's okay to wear leggings. (Don't tell Amy.)
7. Invest in one nice pair of boots, heels, and shoes. (Wait until Cyber Monday for the sales, and fuck bus bitches.)
8. Vans or Adidas are a fun and comfortable way to make an outfit cooler.
9. Consignment shops in hip neighborhoods are the best place to shop for affordable and durable clothing.
10. Dark multicolored scarves are a good way to cover up the fact that you are a sloppy eater. So are Tide pens.
11. Wear a dress if you want to. I spent many years avoiding dresses because I worried they made me look too feminine and therefore vulnerable. I've since learned it matters more how you carry yourself than what you're actually wearing.
12. Comfort trumps trend.
13. Wash new clothes after you buy them.
14. Hand-wash your bras. (I learned this late in life, and still don't do it. Bad habits and stubborn women are hard to break.)
15. Find a store with good basics and learn how to use them.
16. Don't wear chunky belts.
17. Don't look at the size (my clothing size ranges from 0–10, XS to L).
18. Sew buttons back on within a week.
19. Throw out clothing with holes you can't fix.
20. Don't get mad at resale shops that don't take your clothing; they're just snobs who use their snarky opinions to hide the fact that they're broken people.
21. Sunscreen is your best friend and a literal lifesaver. Nothing's more fashionable than healthy skin.

I am living proof that you can blossom from an awkward caterpillar into an awkward butterfly—a sharply dressed awkward butterfly who commands attention because she is comfortable in her clothing and looks like a consummate, trendy professional.

10

SUBMIT AN ESSAY TO *THE NEW YORK TIMES*

I've always treated the English language with a sort of reverence, mainly because my parents considered me the Goddess of Grammar every time I pieced a sentence together. "Unfortunately, Marina will not be able to make it into class today. She has fallen ill," my father proudly read from a note written by me. "Un-for-tun-ate-ly," he marveled, "Our Manya and her big words!" I fell in love with the practice of putting letters together in new and interesting ways to win over the admiration of Olga and Vladimir.

Learning a second language so late in life was difficult for my parents. I started writing school notes for them when I was seven, work emails shortly after, and years later, Facebook posts to their friends. "Hi, Sue, so nice to hear from you. How are your boys?" To this day, birthday wishes and condolences are still my responsibility. Although they mastered English fluency at an impressive speed, my parents are still coated with embarrassment when their grammar is off.

It is a gift to speak English fluently, and therefore the language should not be abused. I never fell victim to the horrendous massacre that is "internet speak." I don't think I've ever typed *R* or *U* in place of the actual words, and you'd have an easier time convincing me to get a belly button tattoo than to shorten the word *situation* to *sitch*. Speaking eloquently was important to me because it was important to my parents.

Taiwan bolstered my appreciation for the privilege of communicative ease. I became a soft-spoken, shy woman who avoided opening her mouth for fear of sounding stupid. My stomach churned with empathy for my parents: it sucks to not be able to connect with people using your native tongue. I barricaded myself off from the outside world and created a comfortable life within the walls of my English-speaking office. My job meant everything to me, which is a dangerous position to be in, especially overseas.

The first time I got in trouble with my boss, Jerry, I wasn't upset, I was destroyed. The whole situation was especially traumatizing because I knew it wasn't my fault. A coworker had forgotten to upload my story during her evening shift, which was a cardinal sin in my department. The reason I'd missed that the story was never uploaded was because I was on the phone with Jerry, who divulged his feelings of loneliness to me late into the night. My father never allowed us to give excuses when we were blamed for something, and I wasn't about to start throwing coworkers under the bus. Instead, I just stood there, letting Jerry's anger wash over me.

"This is unacceptable. It is your responsibility to check the stories at night. If you notice . . ." He began to dig into me. My nose started to tingle, and the tingling headed toward my eyes. I wanted the conversation to end as soon as possible, but stood there frozen, listening to him yell. At the end of the berating, I squeezed out a "sorry" and headed to the bathroom on a different floor. (Please see: "How to Cry at Work" on page 94.)

By the time I composed myself and came back to my desk, my name had been taken off the schedule. Jerry took away all of my responsibilities for that day—and, as it turns out, for the rest of the week—because my stories were "too much to handle" for me, according to a curtly worded Gchat from him.

My parents raised me with a strict Soviet-era understanding that elders, especially thirty-eight-year-old boss-elders, are never wrong. I was taught to never question an authority figure no matter how wrong they might be. I feared teachers, police, and, most of all, managers, but my biggest fear was getting fired, and that fear only intensified in Taiwan. I'd ditched everything for this job. Getting fired meant I'd fly back to nothing. Jerry's yelling shook me to my core. I took the next day off.

In Taiwanese work culture, women get about three days off a year to *handle* their period so that they don't come into work and drown everyone in their bloody uterine lining—or so it was explained to me. It is my guess that a man wrote this legislation and nobody had the heart to tell him that a period doesn't last three days a year, but, whatever, I was happy to find such a convenient use for my period. Joke's on them anyway, I don't get my period. I mean ultimately joke's on me, because I probably can't have children, but for right now joke's on them.

I didn't want to waste my menstrual leave on moping over the fact that Jerry was probably going to fire me, so I grabbed my laptop and decided to walk around my neighborhood. I weaved through old women doing Tai Chi in the park and grabbed *dan bing* from the corner cart with the angry ladies. I had walked further into the neighborhood than ever before when I stumbled upon a coffee shop. It was everything a young foreigner could want in an establishment: hidden from the street and packed with disillusioned space cadets. Laptops covered in stickers, and arms covered in tattoos, crowded the wooden tables. Bored Taiwanese hipsters worked behind the counter. It even had a name I could pronounce: Yaboo. A mangy orange cat with the same name and a tiny triangle missing from her right ear slept in the doorway. I couldn't have painted up a better place to hide out. A cool-looking Indian chick sat on the plant-filled patio. She had her long, henna-dyed hair secured with a purple scarf atop her head. Her eyeliner was early-2000s thick, but she pulled it off in a Cleopatra kind of way. The patches on her backpack indicated that she was a Westerner, and I desperately wanted to be friends with her. But making new friends as an adult is impossibly complicated, so I walked inside, out of her sight.

I opened my laptop and briefly looked at job postings for Digital Media Producers, Content Creators, Social Media Wizards, YouTube Magicians, Twitter Warlocks, Blog Dads—and all the other made-up titles created in hopes of catching the elusive millennial. I clicked out of all my tabs, overwhelmed with all the application requirements.

I turned my attention to an old essay of mine, written about something familiar. Someone familiar. If nothing else, I still had my words to comfort me. I wanted to revive the essay to upload it onto my small blog, read mainly by my parents. But during the rewrite, the story morphed into something a little too intimate to post.

I was worried someone from high school would get their hands on the piece and spread it across the web-o-sphere, or even scarier, share it with Kevin, the person it was about.

Oh my god, remember that weird girl from 7th grade, I imagined Jenni messaging Lindsey. You know, the one who always wore a leather jacket? Well, she just wrote the most ridiculous thing.

I decided to submit the story to *The New York Times*'s Modern Love column instead. Now, this sounds counterintuitive, yes. Someone who doesn't want the world to read her

MAKING FRIENDS

as a kid...

as an adult...

story wouldn't then go and submit it to one of the largest newspapers in the country. But I truly did not think it would get published. Sure, I had the goal of submitting, but that's as easy as sending an email.

When putting my 30 before 30 list together, I intentionally made the goals as doable as possible. I could've easily written "*get published* in *The New York Times*" instead of "submit an essay," but I'm a realist who knew that my only narrative writing experience was a tiny, self-centered blog read by my parents and a handful of supportive friends. An average blog post would get one to two hundred views, tops—one hundred of which were just my mom refreshing the page. All in all, getting my actual writing published in *The New York Times* seemed impossible and completely out of my hands. Submitting, though, that was something within my control. I attached my too-personal story to the body of an email, constructed a short message, and hit send from a small windowside table at Yaboo.

I felt accomplished and ready to return to work with the added confidence that comes with completing a goal you set out to do.

"Where were you yesterday?" Jerry asked when I came in.

"I took a period day," I told him. And in a way, I kind of did. I put a period on submitting to *The New York Times*, a period on my unrequited relationship with Kevin, and a period on my frustration with work. A big bloody period.

Almost a month to the day later, Daniel Jones, the elusive editor of the Modern Love column, sent me an email. It was short:

> This is a sweet, funny, and well-written essay. I'd like to work with you on it, if it's still available. At the end, you say you're leaving the country. Are you still away, and if so, where? Thanks for sending your writing my way.

I read that email fifteen times before it sunk in. "I'd like to work with you on it." This felt better than when Otto wrote me a song, Erez kissed my face, and Carl greeted me at the airport, combined. A man, a stranger, an editor liked my writing. It was the cracked door needed to believe that maybe I *could* be a real writer.

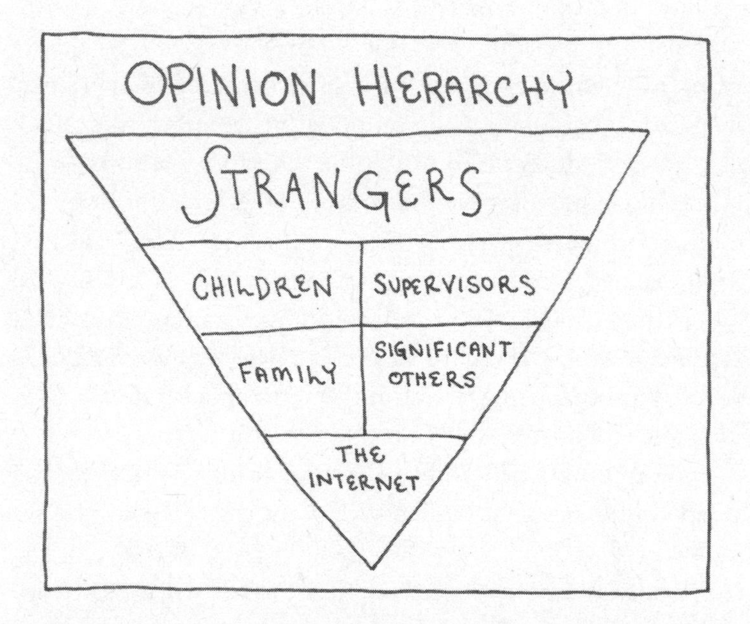

STRANGERS

If someone doesn't know you, but takes the time to give you their heartfelt opinion in person, you should listen. Strangers tend to be the most honest because they don't have anything invested in your relationship.

CHILDREN

Children have not yet been marred by the rigidly cloaked world of adult etiquette, making them brutally honest. If you're working on something, run it by a child first! Unless you're, like, opening your own dildo factory, then maybe wait until they're in middle school—the age kids learn about sex and dildos these days, it seems.

SUPERVISORS

People who are above you in the job food chain tend to give you a good evaluation of things. That is, if they're good at their job. If they're bad at their job, then they're probably going to lie and manipulate you into a little bowl of jelly to delicately place at the foot of their hollow throne.

FAMILY

This is very dependent on the type of family. If your family is like my mom, then their opinion will cut into you with sharpened edges of brutal honesty. You'll always know what your harshest critic is thinking, and that's invaluable. If your family is like my dad, then everything you create exists in a vacuum of magic. You'll have a hard time deciphering whether what you're doing is truly magnificent or not, but your confidence will balloon into an indestructible bubble of light, ideas, and creativity.

SIGNIFICANT OTHERS

Usually, people who are trying to have sex with you are not going to give you a clear picture of their opinion and that's fine, they shouldn't. It's very dangerous to seek the acceptance of your significant other. Just use them for body warmth, intellectual conversation, and procreating—if that's something you're into.

THE INTERNET

The internet is a diseased tumor growing inside of the colon of a murderous hobgoblin. The opinions there might be benign or malignant, but either way, you should cut them out of your life as quickly as possible.

My essay* was published Sunday, April 7, 2013 and it changed my life. It really did. I never actually thought that anyone, besides my parents, wanted to read my writing—let alone pay money for it. I simply sent that essay to a vague address to check a number off my to-do list, not because I thought it'd get published.

As with all life-changing experiences, after the excitement died down I was left with the lessons. Here are the main ones:

- The things you are most scared to share are the ones that are most compelling—I guess that's why gossip mags are so popular.
- It'll take five to six edits (minimum) before a story is ready for eyeballs. Edits are tedious, but they are also the difference between a hobbyist and a writer.
- If you don't have closure on a story in your life, write it for yourself. Force that closure with words and jokes typed onto a page.
- Some stories take years to live and only a couple of pages to tell.
- You may think you've reached the end of a story only to learn it's the foreword to a bigger, better story.

---

* To read my Modern Love piece please flip to page 313.

- Sometimes, taking a "personal" day from a job can change the course of your career better than any eighteen-hour workday could ever hope to.
- Never censor yourself, and fuck anyone who tries to censor you.

Addendum: The day the article came out, Kevin went to Delilah's in Chicago with four of his friends. One friend, Danny, a red-faced triplet with a swimmer's body and a youthful demeanor, did a dramatic reading of the article for the entire table. The other friends leaned in to catch enough lines to use as ammunition against Kevin. Lucas, who is now a lawyer with a chiseled jaw and shaved head, drank a beer next to Danny. I didn't know Lucas at the time, but I'd be at his wedding three years later. Jahd was there too; his real name is John but everyone calls him Jahd. He's a soft-spoken sweetie who gets animated about the state of the world, probably because he ditched normal society for an isolated small-town farm life. Another friend of Kevin's, Sam, sat across from Danny, sipping a bourbon and soda. Sam has brown eyes, a freckle on the bridge of his nose, and a brilliant mind. Remember him.

11

LEARN TO DRINK

I've come to understand that there aren't enough dangerous situations and idiotic mistakes in the world to get me to stop drinking. I may have a problem, but it's not something that really needs to be dealt with until my thirties, I don't think. My complicated relationship with alcohol stems from the fact that there's no such thing as alcoholism in Russia; drinking is just a natural way to keep warm and sane. That being said, my drinking has slowed down in the past few years, and I've finally gotten a handle on how to do it properly.

Before teaching you how to drink, I should level the playing field. (Parents, you can skip to the next chapter now.) In no particular order, here are the most embarrassing things I've done while drunk:

MADE OUT WITH A COWORKER

You know all about this one, so I won't get into it.

TOOK A BATH

My junior year of college, my boyfriend at the time, Jason, a kind engineering student who was built like a tree, and shy like one too, threw a party at his off-campus house, the creatively named Campus View Apartments.

While friends were sipping on Natty Lights and sugary rums, I was doing vodka shots (and immediately throwing them up in the bathroom). This was the year I desperately tried to live up to my ethnic stereotype.

When the party began to pick up speed, I went into Jason's bathroom and ran a bath. As the hot water filled the tub, I added some shampoo—poor girl's bubble bath—and quietly slipped in. I was wearing light blue jeans, a free ResLife tee under a Mizzou hoodie, and ankle-high socks. My eyes shut as the warm water enveloped my fully clothed body. "If Jason doesn't find me within the hour, I'm breaking up with him," I told the fading bubbles. Jason found me twenty minutes later, my eyeliner running down to my collar, my clothes soggy. He leaned in to check if I was still breathing and I pulled him into the bath with me. Later he asked if that was some sort of breakdown. I wonder if he tells his new girlfriends this story.

FELL ASLEEP . . . ON THE STREET

A few months into my new life in Brooklyn, I got invited to a Mucca Pazza show. If you did not come of age in Chicago during the mid-2000s then you might've missed out on Mucca Pazza—a still very-much active thirty-piece punk-circus marching band. One of the thirtyish members in the band used to be a security guard at my high school. Let's call him Kent. He had an odd gait from years of back problems, and told me dirty stories when there were no teachers around. It felt incorrect, but fun too.

One day, I accidentally left my notebook at his security

stand. When I came to pick it up the next day, "YOU ARE A GODDESS" was scribbled on the back page in Kent's distinct handwriting.

A few months after he was hired, a rumor that Kent was inappropriate with the students spread through the hallways, ultimately leading to his dismissal. I was furious. The other girls didn't appreciate his hungry glares like I did. I suspiciously eyed all my thin, blond classmates. Attention came so easy to them that they had the luxury of choosing what kind they wanted—Kent did not make the cut.

Kent texted me months after he'd been fired to invite me to a Mucca Pazza show. Yes, he had my number. "He's harmless," I told my best friend Lauren while looking for the perfect outfit, vagina-deep in her closet. It was the coolest thing to happen to me as a high schooler.

We left our crystal suburban nest and ventured into Chicago to watch Mucca Pazza. They blew our minds. They were big, loud, and unapologetic. It was the most joyous concert I've ever been to.

I saw them twice more in college. And one last time in Brooklyn, shortly after I'd moved. I went to the show alone and spent most of the concert drinking heavily to prove to Kent how adult I'd become. I danced with middle-aged cheerleaders and yelled "Hi" to Kent every time he looked my way. He had more character to his face; it didn't seem like life was too easy for him. At the end of the night, I stayed back and hung out with the entire marching band.

"Can you believe it?" Kent asked them. "I've known this girl since she was fifteen!"

At a certain point, Kent and I left the Knitting Factory, walked around the corner to the Church of the Annunciation, and sat on a stoop to catch up. He pulled out a joint and asked if I wanted some. "Why not," I answered. Grown-up Marina is fuuuuun and not scared of drugs. I took a hit, and my chest caught on fire. Everything slowed down. It became painfully evident how far I was from my apartment and that we were all going to die one day. Death. Death. Death. Kent took another hit and then turned to me, "You want to make out a little?"

I laughed. What a preposterous idea. "You're married," I said, confused. This was at a time when I thought married men were penis-less nymphs who only had love for their wives.*

"My wife and I have an agreement," he told me. I laughed again and hailed a cab. As the car pulled up, Kent remained on the stoop, possibly emasculated. But it's okay, I'm a Goddess and us Goddesses can do whatever the fuck we want.

This was back when you had to give cabs in New York directions to where you were going, a practice made complicated by the fact that I didn't have a smartphone. I was too new, stoned, and drunk to know the first thing about where to go. So I just repeated Fort Greene until something looked familiar enough to barrel roll out of the cab. The last thing I remember is seeing a brownstone stoop that, to my fuzzy mind, looked like my apartment. (I didn't live in a brownstone, nor have a stoop, but the apartment was so quaint and cute that my altered brain tried to convince my messed-up body that this was home.)

A few hours after finding "my" apartment, I woke up to a large man poking my butt with the tip of his sneakers. I'd fallen asleep on a stoop IN BROOKLYN. Not even the nice part of Brooklyn, but the shady nadir where angry immigrants and twitchy drug dealers rule the land. "Ey, yo, girl! Your underwears are showing!" he yelled. He had a friend

---

* Open marriages didn't exist in my limited worldview at the time. I still think they're too tricky of an arrangement *for me* to navigate. I know, I know, it's not "woke," but I don't need my strings getting tangled in another person's strings.

with him who said, "Yo, that's craz-zee" as I pulled down my skirt, proudly dusted off my clothes, and continued the search for my apartment. Two days later, I got a text from Observant Butt Poker asking me out. Apparently, I gave him my number during the exchange? We never went out because it wasn't an ideal How We Met story.

As you progress toward your thirties, an unfortunate thing begins happening: your friends start getting sober. They say things like "Oh, I don't really drink that much anymore," or "My tolerance is so low now," or "You know I can't drink while I'm breastfeeding!" It sucks, but it's going to happen.

No one wants to be the middle-aged, bloated mess of a friend who can't hold her alcohol. It's fine before the age of twenty-eight because no one knows how to drink yet, but drinking properly is truly a skill you should learn by thirty. The earlier the better, if not for the sake of your stomach lining, then for your love and social life.

Every Shifrin family dinner came with a lesson on drinking, but I didn't start practicing these lessons until my hangovers started increasing in frequency and strength. That's the thing people don't know about Russians, their tolerance is high because they work at it, not because they have magical genes (their genes are only semi-magical). You can work at it too with these simple steps:

HOW TO DRINK LIKE A RUSSIAN

Always Have Zakuski (закуски)

I've seen my dad put back four to six shots of vodka at many a family gathering. Not once have I seen him drunk.

"How does *he do it?"* Well, to start, you'll never see a Russian taking shots without zakuski. Zakuski are like appetizers, but we use them as a food-form of chaser. Take a shot, eat a pickle. Take a shot, eat some rye bread with Swiss cheese. Take a shot, eat a spoonful of potato salad. My family likes to have pickles, bread, butter, cheese, potato salad, eggplant salad, herring salad (all three made with an obscene amount of mayonnaise), cold cuts, smoked fish, sauerkraut, eggs, cured pork belly—basically anything fatty—at the shots table. Eating smoked fish or a mini-sandwich with every serving of alcohol consumed can be the difference between a life-shattering hangover and getting up in time for brunch.

One to One

By your late twenties, you should get in the habit of having a glass of water with every glass of alcohol you drink. I hate water because liquids that don't give me a buzz bore me. That being said, water is your best friend on a night of drinking. It doesn't prevent you from getting drunk—my favorite!—but it does help lessen the effects of a hangover. Water also keeps your skin looking taut and youthful, something you won't care about until you do—and then it'll probably be too late to reverse the damage. Have a glass now. Go!

Never Try to Keep Up with Australians

Russians carry the Universal Stereotype Torch when it comes to being heavy drinkers, but it's Australians you have to look out for—those people drink like there's no tomorrow, or today, or yesterday. In general, you should never try to keep up with anyone. Even the phrase "keep up" implies you are not capable of setting the pace and therefore should not attempt to do so.

Don't Drink on an Empty Stomach

If you're drinking on an empty stomach to get drunk faster (I used this logic once upon a time): stop it. Why are you doing that? Save money by pre-gaming or bringing a flask to the bar. Get creative! They have bras that hold alcohol now. One is called the WineRack because I think they were legally required to call it that. It comes in three sizes: Small, Medium, and Drunk. Okay, I'm done. Anyway, this isn't as much a Russian thing as something that I've had to train myself to stop doing.

No Mixing

Russians don't mix their alcohol. It's disrespectful to the alcohol and your stomach. If you're location-hopping, make sure to stay with the same drink. Period. If they run out of what you're drinking then it's a sign to finish up. Beer before liquor will make you a stickler, or whatever the saying, actually is *not* supported by scientific evidence. Mixing alcohols is not inherently bad (Sangria, anyone?), I just prefer not to do it, which has worked out pretty well for me. There is an exception of course: celebratory flutes of champagne. But even those are danger pills waiting to ruin your next morning.

Why Are You Drinking?

I like to check in with myself before I go out for drinks. "Why are you opening that bottle of wine, Marina? Is it because you're celebrating, sad, bored, happy, stressed?" I had a boss who said he only drank when he was happy. He had this theory that "if you drink when you're sad, then you have a problem." I do think there's something to that. If you reach for a bottle every time you've had a bad day, maybe you should be getting your endorphins up through exercise instead.

Drunk People Are Categorically Not Cool

If you've never spent a night sober at a rowdy bar, you should really try it. It'll open your eyes to how incredibly inane and obnoxious drunk people are. All of them. Even you, you beautiful, beautiful Empress. My friend Ryan once gave me some very, very good input: "You turn into the worst version of yourself when you're drunk, Marina." I was twenty-three years old and had no idea. I truly thought I was the ethereal Belle of the Ball during my riotous and frequent nights out. Russian people drink a lot, but they don't like to appear drunk. It's neither glorified nor idolized in Russian culture.

Know Your Drink

I've created an infographic for what and how much to drink depending on the occasion. (Please see next page.)

That's about it. Russians don't like a lot of rules because they won't follow them anyway. Being a smart drinker can suck big time. I get it, it's tedious, and not lit (or whatever the equivalent to that word is when you're reading this). But there's nothing hotter than a person who can hold their alcohol. You can still drink and have fun, but be smart about it, like a Russian.

What I'm Drinking

Girls' Date

RED SANGRIA
4–6 glasses

First Date

WHISKEY
NEAT
1–??? glasses

Gay Date

PINOT GRIGIO
1/2 bottle

Work Date

VODKA MARTINI
DRY
2 glasses

12

GO TO INDIA

I grew up in Skokie, a small suburb in the Chicagoland area filled with a mélange of immigrants. We *were* the melting pot. Growing up in a neighborhood that had every culture splayed out like a deck of cards gave me a chance to peek into all of them.

In elementary school, there was an ethnic hierarchy: The Filipino girls were the first to wear makeup and therefore the most popular. The Chinese girls were focused and athletic. The Japanese girls were the nicest. The Indian girls were graceful and mature, as well as the smartest—this made them accepted by every group. Everyone loved the Indian girls and I so badly wanted to be one of them. They were the largest and most powerful clique. All of the girls wore their dark, black hair in meticulous braids that reached all the way down to their butts. Their skin kept its perfect coloring year-round—unlike my temperamental, pasty nonsense. From October to March, I sported chapped cheeks and cracked, bloody lips, and my hands exploded into red splotches of what turned out to be the beginning stages of eczema. I spent June to August slathered in sunscreen, modeling flaky skin raw from an inevitable burn, and the rest of the year I had scaly rashes crawling across my hands and face. My skin was not made for the outside.

And their mothers! Oh my god, their mothers. The mothers would glide into the school in packs of three or four, wearing the loveliest clothing I'd ever seen. Magentas, lime greens, teals—all of these striking colors filled the parking lot as they marched toward their perfect little children. They accessorized with bare torsos and jeweled foreheads, while Russian women accessorized with cigarettes and sadness. I was jealous.

My adoration of Indian culture, specifically the women, followed me into adulthood. I vowed that once I had money and chutzpah, I'd travel to India—but the opportunity came before I had either. My friend Disha was leaving Taiwan, for good, and invited me to come visit her family in Kolkata. I said yes immediately.

Disha was the same Indian chick I'd seen sitting on the plant-filled patio of Yaboo, the coffee shop I discovered on my *period* day. A week after spotting her at the coffee shop, I recognized her purple scarf and dark eyeliner at a storytelling event in Taipei. We ended up standing in the same circle of expats. Before I could stop the words from tumbling out of my mouth, I'd introduced myself. "Hi, you were at Yaboo two weeks ago. I'm Marina."

"Yeaaahh," she said, stretching out the word in a manner that proved she wasn't in a hurry to do anything. "Yaboo is the shit."

"Yes, definitely the shit."

Like all expat conversations, ours started with "Where are you from?" A complicated question when you're an immigrant who moved six times before landing in Taiwan. I decided to tell her Brooklyn, my last place of residence.

"What?! You're a Brooklyn Babe? Me too." And such was the spark needed to light our friendship on fire.

3 WAYS TO MAKE FRIENDS
(AS AN ADULT)
① ASK A FLATTERING QUESTION
Can you recommend any good books?
Where did you get that incredible shirt?
② FIND COMMONALITIES
"I love whiskey!"
"I live in Brooklyn too."
"Lizzo is one of the most underrated rappers out there."
③ HATE THE SAME THINGS
(AND PEOPLE)

We bonded over female-driven situational comedies, our love of dancing, and the fact that it was nearly impossible for a hairy girl to get a decent wax in Asia. We became each other's heroes, staving off the inevitable loneliness of living in a foreign country.

When planning our trip to India, Disha and I agreed to visit Kolkata in July because we wanted to know what it's like to live *on* the sun. It was so hot that I had to mentally disconnect from my body. *This is just a shell that holds my organs. It's wet and slippery, but that's okay,* I told myself. My previous intolerance for being hot evaporated. I wore the lightest and flimsiest of clothing. My bare skin turned to flypaper, attracting the sticky stares of men around me.

We went to India when Disha's life was in upheaval. She left not only Taiwan, but her boyfriend of a year, which made our trip dramatic and emotional.*

It was my third time traveling with a friend and I was beginning to pick up on what was needed for an Ideal Travel Buddy. I, myself, am not a good travel buddy. I get irritable quickly and usually just want to sit in a café people-watching for hours. Everything I enjoy while traveling can be done at your run-of-the-mill Starbucks. But despite being the third wheel, I was still able to enjoy the trip.

Kolkata is a conundrum. It's simultaneously picturesque and devastating. The decrepit buildings have purposeful hand-crafted architecture that made me want to run my tongue along the details. The faded signs and advertisements added pops of color to the dusty landscape—but they were also depressing reminders that Kolkata used to be brighter

---

* Especially since he decided, last minute, that he wanted to join us. I love drama, so it didn't bother me too much, but it changed the dynamic of the trip from a Girls' Weekend to an "I'm gonna miss you so much, baby. Marina can you give us a minute?" weekend.

ANATOMY of an IDEAL
TRAVEL BUDDY
extrovert
your favorite person on earth*
doesn't mind doing their own thing
laid back
adventurous eater
same energy level
same budget
proficient in foreign languages
good at improvising
quiet sleeper
*ideally someone you're sleeping with.

and cleaner before power shortages and political unrest left it for dead. "We're in the armpit of India," Disha told me as we walked by a man having an intense conversation with a wall. She fanned her arms outward and took a little spin. "It's kind of gross and magical." Disha was completely right. It looked like an ornate silk rug with hand stitching and astounding details hidden under a crusty, untouched layer of grime.

One night, we crammed into a small venue where a family friend was performing with his band, Neel & The Lightbulbs. Everyone had this peaceful air of coolness that I've never been able to harness. My high-strung anxious tendencies compounded with my brute Russian judgment make me a tornado of nerves in public settings. But in Kolkata, it was different. The streets were wild, and the night scene was all about slowing down and being calm. Their nightclubs had hookahs set up at every table, seducing you into taking deep breaths, inhaling poison, if only to watch curly plumes of smoke leave your mouth.

I felt happy for the first time in months, and soon realized it was because I didn't have a phone or internet. Without a connection to work—which had become increasingly hectic—I was able to truly absorb Kolkata. Disconnecting is the proper way to travel.

During our last few days in India, Disha and I aimlessly wandered through the city, gravitating toward street vendors, bright signs, and really anything that piqued our curiosity. During one of our walks, an Indian man at a dilapidated stand caught my attention. He was wearing all white and had his legs folded beneath him in a very meditative pose. His eyes interested me most: they were a cloudy blueish gray color, like a newborn baby's. As we got closer, we realized that he was a fortune teller.

Beside him sat two tiny cages, the size of lunch boxes, each with a bright green cockatiel inside. Above them were three

WEDNESDAY 7 AUGUST 2013

KOLKATA IS TALKING ABOUT

INDIE & LOVIN' IT

The band, Neel & the Lightbulbs, rocked the night as they performed at a city club recently. These young musicians had the crowd swinging and lip-syncing to numbers like *Big mistake, Mister Coolio, House in a car* and more. The boys sang some 18 songs from their repertoire of indie numbers they have written themselves. Pretty talented group, must say! We spotted Bodhi Tree band member **Bodhisattta** and Insomnia's **Tania** cheering the the four boys on the stage. Also spotted was young actor **Sam**, who was lost in conversation with his girlfriend, **Maya**.

Snapshot of me dancing to Neel & The Lightbulbs. The next month I make international headlines for dancing again.

photos of Hindu gods adorned with orange marigolds. "You have to get your fortune told by a bird," Disha demanded.

When we walked up, the man said something. I assumed he was asking my name, because Disha told him, "Marina." He said something else in Hindi and Disha turned to me. "Think of something, a question you have, and he'll answer it."

A rolodex of concerns whirred through my head; millions of questions. Most were vague, like, "How much weight can one lose through sweat?" "Am I barren?" "What's my perfect job?" Before I could settle on one solid thought, the man nodded his head and opened one of the two cages next to him.

The old man waved a little bit of seed in front of the cockatiel, which sprang to life. It bounced over to the envelopes fanned out on the table, confidently plunged its beak into the deck, and picked one out to hand to the man. I wondered how difficult it is to train a bird to pick fortunes for aimless American women. I can't imagine my parents' Yorkie, Tootsie, being responsible for deciding people's futures. I once caught her licking up her own puddle of urine.

The man delicately opened the envelope and dumped out two sheets of paper—one in English and one in Hindi. He handed me the English one. I took a deep breath and read:

Bad period have gone. Good Timing is coming. You will get unexpected money (Wealthy.) For trust you have to work hard, bad and good stars always come side by side to man, but it will be disappeared don't think to be mean or weak yourself. Don't be proud to have wealth. By nature, you are a thoughtful gentleman. Definitely you have a spot on your check. If possible you give milk to dogs.

A thoughtful gentleman indeed. I smiled politely and dug around my bag for some money when he started to speak again. Disha, who was recording the whole exchange on my camera, leaned in my ear, "He's going to tell you the meaning of your fortune now." She pointed the camera at my face, filled with polite, but not genuine, interest.

I stopped digging and began to listen. As the man spoke, I studied the red smudge in the middle of his forehead and noticed that his earlobes had orange powder on them. "Whatever you were thinking, it will be successful," he told me in Hindi. I began to think about my job and how much I wanted to leave. "You will go through a bit of a tough period, but after September, everything will be perfect. You will get unexpected money, but do not feel bad about it." I made a mental note to check my bank account in October. As he spoke, I wondered what he believed more: that his birds predicted people's fortunes, or that American tourists were stupid enough to fall for them. "There are good times and bad times, they come side by side, but they come and they go so don't worry about it, don't stress about it," he continued. A small crowd began gathering around us.

Everyone listened without a flicker of cynicism, as if maybe a little bit of my fortune would sprinkle onto them. "They all want to hear Marina's destiny," Disha said into the camera. I brought my attention back to the man.

"Your thoughts are very pure and good, which will show in your actions. When you have time, go find a black dog and give him some food or milk," he concluded. "Whenever you have time. Don't stress about it." Disha and I raised our eyebrows at each other.

The man then handed me a large coin with an engraving of the Hindu god, Ganesh, the one who looks like a mutant elephant. (According to famed travel site Wikipedia, Ganesh is a sign of new beginnings, amongst other good things.)

Despite how much I tried to avoid it, I became a walking cliché in India. I was yet another thoughtful gentleman, with an enviably peaceful life, looking for some sort of spiritual sign to grant me change. Something to tell me which direction to face. Whether or not the fortune was real didn't matter because I began to believe it.

Disha turned off my camera. "C'mon, let's go find a dog to feed!" she squealed, looping her arm in mine. I handed the man some money and his eyes locked with mine. For a moment, I thought I saw them flicker with something indiscernible. Intrigue? Recognition? Maybe he saw something in my future that amused him? Or maybe it was concern?

We walked off, leaving the man with the gray eyes. I put his coin into my back pocket and didn't think about him again until a few months later when his predictions came true.

13

QUIT SHITTY JOB

Jerry, my boss, and I grew closer as I drifted further into Taiwan. We spent a handful of nights each week sitting in bars, waxing poetic about the declining state of the journalism industry—I could feel myself growing sharper and stronger under his guiding hand. It was game-changing to find a boss who was willing to invest as much time and energy into me as I was investing into my job. Under his direction, my future looked bright and successful. With enough dedication, I could be his protégé.

I first "met" Jerry over the phone. Together we chose news stories to animate during his nights in Taiwan and my mornings in Manhattan. There was a sheen of charming sarcasm coating his every word. For a moment, it felt like I was developing a crush. But in person, it became clear he wasn't my type. He was older and shorter than me; a fair-skinned man who accessorized with nice shoes and beautiful suits. His perfectly pressed shirts vacillated between light blue, light pink, and bright white—I never saw a stain on any of them. He was slow to smile, but when he did, it was flirtatious and sinister. His hair was blond, and I wonder now if he dyed it so. My type is hairy man who looks like he might roll over and accidentally suffocate me in bed. So my maybe-crush on Jerry evolved into a creative-crush and I grew a deep affection for his mind.

Taipei is a small city, everyone kind of knows everyone. One night, about eight months after I moved, an expat comedian (there were about six of us) asked if it was true that I was dating my boss. I lost it. Like a shark to blood, I latched onto the expat. "Who did you hear that from?" "What's their English name?" "What floor?" When you work in a building with three thousand coworkers, it's difficult to pinpoint one single rumor.

There are weird insinuations when a young woman is finding success for the first time (or anytime really). I was devastated to get caught on the wrong side of those insinuations. Later that week, at happy hour, I told Jerry about the rumor, "People think we're dating. People who don't even work with us."

Jerry did this move that I would grow to know very well: he lifted an eyebrow and rotated his whiskey glass. His piercing blue eyes latched on to mine. It was what he did when he was amused. "That's funny," he told me.

"Funny? No. It's sexist. It only boosts your status and makes me into some kind of harlot. It's not funny." I finished my drink and left. Then came this text message from him:

> The thing that bothers me is it's a gross simplification of our friendship. I'd like to think our relationship is more nuanced and textured than that. One day you will write a book and if your time with us is featured in any way, I hope that portrayal is richer and more varied than what this gossip has described.

He knew exactly how to flatter me into submission. I couldn't be mad—he saw me as a writer. He believed in me.

Jerry understood things get complicated, and that's what makes life more interesting. I delicately transcribed his text into my journal and read it back to myself.

There's a moment before someone kisses you for the first time that you can almost pre-feel the kiss on your lips. The exhilarating energy of anticipation creates a phantom feeling of connectivity before it even happens. In the early hours of a random morning, I had this pre-feeling with Jerry.

We spent a lot of time together as it was, but when he and his same-age-as-me girlfriend broke up, our hangouts went into overdrive. Working, happy hours, dinners, grocery shopping, commuting, dancing—we did it all side by side. We could talk until the bar shut down without noticing a moment had gone by. His mind made mine do mental aerobics to catch up, but I loved that about our conversations.

My desperate need to please authority figures combined with his desire to be cherished created a cocktail of codependency; it was like we had a Liz Lemon–Jack Donaghy relationship. Dedicated to the job first, then to each other. It was nice to have Jerry by my side, navigating Taiwan, my weird-ass job, and life in general.

As I got to know him more intimately, I found a man who thrived on the perception that he was stoic and untouchable, despite his desperation for companionship. He was an oxymoron of needs versus wants and a master at manipulating people into fulfilling those needs and wants for him. He was the most dangerous kind of mess: a secret mess. All of his emotions were shoved deep down in his psyche, which meant he was going to blow one day. "I hope it's not in my direction," I told my mom over the phone.

We usually hung out outside of work, but on a slow news day would catch up over Gchat.

Jerry: Hello
Me: Hey.
How was your night?
Jerry: Decent.
Yours?
Me: Good.
What did you do?
Jerry: Went on a date
Me: Oh?
Jerry: Felt artificial tenderness with some flickers of sincere desire
Me: Beautifully depressing
Jerry: I wish we were hanging instead
Me: Haha, so you can roll your eyes at my absurdity and watch me be awkward?
Jerry: Yes, because time spent with you is delightfully unpredictable

Our conversations flattered me in a way that seemed dangerous. But I worked so hard and invested 110 percent of myself into that job, I couldn't imagine a world in which that'd happen. My tongue had yet to taste the unfairness of being a working woman. I hadn't realized how easy it is for a young, smart, diligent person to fall under the spell of an older, powerful man.

One night, after a work party at Jerry's apartment, he walked me to the private elevator on his floor. The elevator sat in a small entryway with a tiny, temperamental light above it. We'd been tangled in an intense conversation all night, but that wasn't different from any other time. What was different about this specific evening was that the temperamental light above the elevator flickered, and then went out. Everything went dark. Pitch black. Have you ever stood in the darkness with someone you're not supposed to kiss? It's electric.

At that moment, I wanted Jerry to kiss me more than anything. Mortified by my desires and frozen in the darkness, I searched for something funny to say.

Suddenly, his hands wrapped around my waist and he gently pulled me in. It was like he was listening to my mind. He leaned in, his chest lightly touching mine, and I could smell the fresh pear finish of the Glenfiddich twelve-year on his breath. I inhaled, parted my lips, praying that we aligned our faces correctly.

And then the elevator came. The doors opened and the hallway was flooded with light. We simultaneously took a step back. His face had the same surprised look that was on mine, and we began to laugh.

Our relationship moved away from a quirky *30 Rock* dynamic into something cloaked in complexity.

After the elevator experience, I promised myself not to get that drunk around Jerry ever again. This job, our friendship, meant too much to me to sully it with drunken kisses. I needed him and had a striking suspicion that he needed me too.

My new agreement with myself was tested on Jerry's forty-fifth birthday when he invited the entire staff out to a shots bar. Shots and coworkers are like fireworks and dogs in that they should never mix. I decided to refrain from drinking that night. Before you applaud my incredible self-restraint, also know that I was devastatingly hungover from hanging out with Disha the night before.

The bar was called AQ, which stands for Alcohol Quotient. The shots cost a little over a dollar and were brought to you on a clear tray, nine at a time, like pigs in a blanket meant to be mindlessly popped into your mouth. It was insane.

I arrived late because of the slight heel on my new boots, which made them difficult for me to walk in. I'd packed a pair of Chucks for just-in-case (it's good to always have just-in-case shoes during a night of drinking) but was too proud to change into them. Minutes after I got to the bar, it became clear I'd wobbled into the *wrong* one. It turns out AQ is a franchise with multiple locations.

By the time I got to the correct AQ, an hour late, I was greeted by a sad sight. Jerry, my friend, my boss, the man who had invited the whole staff to his birthday party, was sitting at the corner of a long, white table with only two coworkers, a couple, Peter and Charlotte. I was mad at my other colleagues for not coming to his birthday party, but understood why they hadn't.

Things at the office were prickly and growing worse by the week. The company objective was pivoting every few months, and we were all scrambling to keep up. We were instructed to illegally rip news videos from reputable sites and repackage them with animation for our own channels. It felt wrong to steal other reporters' content, but I wasn't comfortable questioning authority, especially when I was *best friends* with that authority. Jerry was caught between demanding CEOs and disgruntled employees. It was making him stressed, tired, and angry. The disorganization of the company, on top of Jerry's mood swings, was giving me motion sickness.

It became difficult to defend his decisions to my resentful coworkers. We rarely knew what our job responsibilities were, and it was making everyone frustrated. A handful of people quit almost immediately after getting hired. Peter and Charlotte were actually in that handful.

"Marina, you're here!" Jerry slurred when he saw me. He got up a little too fast and stumbled over his chair. The most composed man in Taiwan was tanked. I didn't want anyone to see him this way, especially our other coworkers. My instincts were to get him home, tuck him into bed, kiss his forehead, and tell him he was a special boy.

"Take a shot!" Jerry yelled, sloshing his tray of drinks toward me. I noticed that Charlotte and Peter had their very own trays sitting in front of them. "There are two left, one for you and one for me," Jerry said.

"What are these?" I asked.

Jerry stared at his tray for a good long moment. "Well, there's . . . Let's see . . . There was tequila here"—he pointed at a row of empty spaces—"vodka here, and now we have whiskey. You love whiskey." He shoved the tray under my nose. The scent made me want to gag.

"You should go home," I told him. Jerry's wheels began turning as he pieced together how drunk he was. He put the tray down. Right at that moment, when it seemed that Jerry was about to realize it was his time to go home, another coworker named Michael came in.

Michael was newer to the team and had a passion for the job that I was quickly losing. His exuberance annoyed me in a petty way.

Michael didn't even sit down. "Are those whiskey shots?" he asked, eyeing Jerry's tray.

"Yes. Yes! Do you want to do one with me?" Jerry responded.

"Of course, birthday man."

Before I could intervene, the two did a shot. *Was Jerry going to throw up in front of us? We'd obviously have to shut down the company if he did. I mean, no boss can come back from vomiting in front of his subordinates. Right?*

"Karaoke?" Michael said.

"Karaoke!" everyone simultaneously yelled. Jerry's crushing desire to be adored was taking over his instinct to be a polished and refined enigma. His status as a demigod was quickly diminishing in my eyes. Demigods don't get this trashed.

Jerry pulled me aside and slurred into my ear, "Whatever

you do, don't let me have any more." My new assignment emboldened me. Jerry entrusted himself to *my* care and damnit I was going to excel. "I'll get you some water from the 7-Eleven," I told him. When I leaned in to make sure he heard me I noticed his face looked wearier than usual.

"Okay, thank you," Jerry said before immediately hailing a cab to the other bar. *Or not*, I thought, and crawled into the cab behind him.

The karaoke bar, MayBE, was not like the traditional private-party rooms that are popular throughout Taiwan. Instead, they did karaoke in a sing-a-long manner, with stray microphones floating throughout the lounge. They played a lot of Western indie-rock, so I was at least able to bob my head along to the wailing. It was one of my favorite places in Taipei, but that might've been because it was close to my apartment. My enjoyment of a bar is inextricably linked to how close it is to my bed.

Jerry and I walked in to find Peter and Charlotte already seated with drinks. "Here you go, birthday boy!" Peter handed Jerry a cocktail, which I intercepted.

Michael came in shortly after us and headed straight to the back of the bar, where a man, who looked like the owner, sat watching over the sweaty drunken mess of his kingdom. Michael said something in the owner's ear, who then looked over at our crew and pointed to Jerry. They both nodded, then Michael came back to join us.

"What was that?" I asked.

"Nothing." Michael smiled.

"Nothing" turned out to be a drink made specially for the Birthday Boy. It was called "Baby Sleeps Three Days" and from what I remember there were five different types of liquor in it. The drink had a sort of blue glow that stressed me out. The owner came out from behind the bar, gingerly balancing the umbrella-capped glass of poison on top of a tray, and started singing Happy Birthday. The whole bar joined in. My gaze moved from the drink to Jerry, who was the happiest I'd seen him in months. A whole bar, singing to him. Happy birthday from all of his new friends.

The owner made it to Jerry and everyone raised their glasses. I surreptitiously grabbed the drink out of his hand as he toasted the bar. "I'm getting you water," I told him.

"No, it's my drink. Give to me!" he howled, lurching toward me. I pulled the drink back.

"Wet blanket!" Charlotte yelled.

"BOOOOO," Peter chimed in.

"Oh, this is straight-up bullshit," I sneered.

Jerry grabbed the drink out of my hand and chugged it. Everyone cheered and I took a mental snapshot of the moment. Does that ever happen to you? You have a sobering second where you're like, *Wait, what the fuck am I doing?* Everything became so clear. The drinking, the late nights, the running errands, the weekend breakfasts—my boss and I were inappropriately using each other in a pseudo-relationship and neither of us was going to get out alive. I no longer felt the need to take care of him. The spell was broken and all I saw was a lonely forty-five-year-old man with lots of money, and little else.

"Smells Like Teen Spirit" exploded over the speakers and the whole bar devolved into head banging. I'm a sucker for a rowdy crowd and a good song so I got up and began to dance. Jerry stood up to dance with me, but he couldn't even stand straight. "I'm going to leave," I yelled over the music.

"Stay for a little longer," he pleaded.

"No, I mean, leave Taiwan," I told him.

"No, you're not. You'd be making a big mistake. You haven't even worked on good projects yet. I promise they're coming," he told me. "Besides, you're not allowed."

"This is an absurd conversation to have right now. You're drunk," I told him.

"You brought it up."

"I shouldn't have, just forget it."

"You have so much potential, you have to stay. Until you at least get to two years."

These kinds of business promises are a common tactic to get employees to stay in a job longer than they want. Sadly they rarely, if ever, pan out. I sat back, sipped some water, and kept an eye on Jerry's alcohol consumption. By the end of the night, he'd had a total of thirteen drinks. I made a tally in my notebook.

Around one a.m. Charlotte yelled, "I'm bombed!" and the night was brought to an abrupt end. As usual, Jerry and I shared a cab, but unlike usual, we headed to his apartment first. He couldn't even sit up straight; I was genuinely worried he'd choke on his own vomit and die in that cab. Shadows from the city lights danced across his face while he made a series of unfortunate sounds.

"You're not going to leave," he said.

"Yes, I am," I responded. We sat in silence for a moment. I chose my next words carefully. "I know it's hard, because we're friends, but you have to let your employees move on when it's their time to go." We pulled up to his apartment and Jerry got a strange look on his face. His red eyes blurred behind a layer of . . . tears? "Are you—" before I could finish the sentence, he bolted out of the cab. I'd never seen a middle-aged drunk person run so fast.

I paid the driver and scrambled out of the car only to sit down on the sidewalk and wriggle out of my new heels. *Thank god* I had those Chucks. I jammed my feet into the shoes, tied my laces, and took off after Jerry.

He wasn't hard to find. He'd made it about halfway down an alley before leaning up against a wall to catch his breath. Perfectly silhouetted by a streetlight, his whole body convulsed in these big heaving dips. *Oh no, he's puking*, I thought.

But upon closer inspection, I saw it was much, much worse: he was crying. Hard. Harder than I'd seen anyone cry. There is no bigger turn-off than seeing someone you idealize in their feeble human form. I turned around and began running in the opposite direction. "I'm going to get you some water and food," I yelled over my shoulder. "Don't move."

I ran to a 7-Eleven—seriously, they are everywhere in Asia—and grabbed two bananas, two bags of nuts, and two water bottles. When I got back to Jerry, he'd calmed to a silent cry. He was sitting on the ground, scrolling through his email and whimpering. I handed him the water and put my arm around his shoulders. We sat there for a long time. A young, directionless girl, and a broken birthday man—huddled on a curb.

I used to take these month-long sabbaticals from drinking to make sure I didn't have a problem—and to lower my tolerance when a couple glasses of wine were no longer getting me buzzed. The last time I did one of these idiotic sabbaticals was on September 1, 2013. I was on the graveyard shift, which meant taking a break was going to be easy, considering the workday started at prime drink time.

Our graveyard shift was a living nightmare. My coworkers and I showed up to work one day and there was suddenly a night shift. Everyone grumbled, and one person quit on the spot. I was kind of intrigued. "Maybe I'll eat less and get thinner," I whispered to Cathy as she sat with her mouth agape.

As a person with shaky mental stability, flipping my schedule from day to night equaled destruction. I'd survived the first night shift, a few months earlier, but this one was different, more venomous. The apartment above mine was being remodeled and construction would start early. It sounded like two jackhammers having sex. I'd arrive home around 5:30

a.m. and the renovations would start promptly at 8:00 a.m., giving me two and a half hours of uninterrupted sleep a day. One morning I was woken up by one of my framed photos flying off the wall and landing on my chest.

After Jerry's birthday, I had begun to pull away. I stopped responding to his nonwork texts and stopped seeing him outside of the office. The dinners, the rides home, the drinks—I put an abrupt end to all of them. Frantically looking for a new job, and worried that Jerry would be personally offended when he found out, I began to phase out our fake relationship with a real breakup.

One morning, in a private act of pettiness, I defriended Jerry. Not a day after the defriending, Jerry sent me a curt email. The subject line read "Your phone" and the body, in one sentence, instructed me to return it to his desk immediately. Something inside me cracked, though not because of the phone. I couldn't care less about that thing, I barely used it (aside from navigation). It was his intentional attempt to make my life more difficult that upset me the most. Jerry wasn't a mysterious leader with a hard shell and a soft heart; he was a trifling bitch. He was flexing his power and constricting my ability to work. His fangs were out, and they had more reach than mine.

Even though I was checked out at that point, it was important to me that my previous nineteen months of dedication did not go to waste. I made sure to work harder and smarter than ever before, if for nothing else than a letter of recommendation.

One day, shortly after he took my phone, I came into work a few hours early. I couldn't sleep with the construction and wanted to utilize the company gym. Whenever my mind feels a little sick, I like to focus on making my body stronger; remind myself that it's all just muscle matter that needs to be stretched and strengthened. I dropped my stuff off at my desk, and ended up getting roped into helping coworkers who were behind on their deadlines.

While waiting to be sent articles to edit, I hopped onto Facebook to respond to a cousin who was trying to reach me. (No smartphone, remember?) My Gchat went off and I clicked open the tab, expecting a frantic coworker, but instead I got a message from Jerry:

Jerry: This is ridiculous.
I'm balancing two production slots while you're not even working.
You know what? You can do two slots tomorrow.

My shift hadn't even started and Jerry was already reprimanding me. I've never felt comfortable having serious work conversations over Gchat,* so I did everything possible to keep things professional.

Me: Okay.
Jerry: I'm too busy for this. I'm working double time and you're on Facebook or Gchat or Tumblr.
Me: Just waiting on VO from Chris and Michael before we worked on the stuff we had outlined earlier . . .
Jerry: I don't need your excuses, Marina. I'm sick of it. Sick of everyone saying they can't keep up. People think I push too hard, yet I'm not seeing any results otherwise. You've wasted everything I've handed to you . . . ruined every opportunity. You meet every task with a lackluster attitude . . . You have the possibility to accomplish great

---

* You better believe I saved every character Jerry typed. Gchats live forever. I cannot emphasize this enough. Always conduct yourself like your computer will be hacked and everything you've typed into that metal box will be emailed to the *last* person you'd ever want to see it.

things, in my opinion, but you haven't fully dedicated yourself to this job and that's why you are where you are.

The irony of him using Gchat to criticize me for being on Gchat was not lost on me.

Gone were the days of flirtatious messages, they were now malicious snubs constructed to hurt me. We were in the shit now. The problem wasn't his double-sided personality, it was the lack of consistency between the sides. I could not adapt to someone who unexpectedly wavered from kitten to snake.

I watched Jerry decimate my work schedule. He stripped me off my favorite project and took away all of the responsibilities I'd worked for over the past nineteen months. It wasn't his first time lashing out at me for something unrelated to work, but it was going to be his last.

The next day I walked in on Michael and Jerry, nose to nose, arguing . . . about me. Michael was attempting to defend me because he'd noticed that I was being unfairly treated, while Jerry staunchly stood by his decisions. Jerry *hated* having his authority questioned. It was a surreal experience to hear my name yelled in a quiet office, with neither party knowing the subject of their argument was standing right there. They didn't see me until I had to walk in between them to get to my desk; the embarrassed silence that followed was revolting. It was time to give notice. I emailed Jerry asking if we could set a meeting as soon as possible.

Jerry knew every intimate detail about me and he was using his knowledge against me. When you're the child of immigrants, your parents insist that you do two things in life: 1) Marry someone within your culture, and 2) Work harder than everyone around you. I had about as much enthusiasm for marrying a Russian man as I do for getting a back-alley vagina wax, so I focused all my energy into work. That's why, when Jerry messed with my work schedule, my responsibilities, and finally my coworkers, I knew he was specifically targeting my emotional vulnerabilities.

After I sent my email, I received a Gchat from Jerry saying that he would only meet with me under the condition that a manager was there. *You almost kissed me on the mouth, why does our meeting need a chaperone?* I obliged and immediately emailed the managers on our floor asking them to meet with us the next morning. "I'll come in at eight a.m. if it helps," I wrote in the email, planning on sleeping at the office.

"I'm not getting involved in your lovers' quarrel," one of the managers responded. I was heartbroken. My attempt at being a work-appropriate professional woman had backfired. I told Jerry we needed to meet as soon as possible, but he never responded. This spiral of negativity is eternally seared into my consciousness; *never let your boss become emotionally close to you.*

Without my best friend, alcohol, to ease me through the last week of my shift, I had to get creative with my stress relief. I began to take refuge in the small oasis of tranquility that was our voiceover rooms; they were these awesome, closet-sized, soundproof rooms with padded walls. When the tension was unbearable, I headed downstairs, turned on Kanye West's *The College Dropout* album (basically the song "Gone" on repeat), and slammed my body from side to side, bouncing off the padding, desperately wanting to be gone. I danced hard, kicking my knees up high. Some people had cigarette breaks, I had the voiceover room.

The security guards in the lobby must've thought I was insane. I'd go to record a voiceover, be in there for five minutes, and come out drenched in sweat, panting as if I'd just finished a marathon. *What if a camera caught me doing this?* I thought shortly after discovering my new favorite form of stress relief. The CCTV footage would've been bonkers.

Then it hit me: *This should be on camera.* I loved sending my friends and parents lo-fi videos with little updates—kind of the single gal's version of home videos. The next day, I brought my Canon G12 and waited after my shift to hit record. I put on "Gone" and danced on desks, in empty offices, and in the voiceover booth. I propped my camera on books and cubicle walls. I hung it from mic stands, waiting for it to stop swaying to hit record. I awkwardly kicked open a bathroom door and hopped from side to side as it closed. The whole thing took about fifteen minutes to get on tape.

Since the construction was keeping me up during the day, it was easy to get the video finished quickly. I spent a few days editing, and a few more figuring out what to say in the scroll on the bottom. I wanted to announce that I was quitting, but also wanted to protect Jerry, just in case he ended up seeing it:

> It's 4:30 a.m. and I'm at work. I work for an awesome company that produces news videos. For almost two years I've sacrificed my relationships, time, and energy for this job. And my boss only cares . . . about quantity and how many views each video gets. So I figured, I'd make ONE video of my own. To focus on the content instead of worry about the views. Oh, and to let my boss know . . . (dance break). I quit! I QUIT. I'm gone.

If my life were like a movie, I would've posted my video to the company website, flipped everyone the bird, and boarded the first flight back to the U.S. But I couldn't do that, not to Jerry. Even though our lovely friendship had turned into something vile, I didn't want to hurt him or cause him to lose *his* job—which he probably should've considering I wasn't the last woman he manipulated with his power.

I titled the video "An Interpretive Dance for My Boss Set to Kanye West's 'Gone,'" and uploaded it to my YouTube channel under the unlisted setting. I sent a private link to my parents, a couple of friends, and two equally discouraged coworkers. Fewer than ten people. Within a day it had almost one hundred views.

Back at work, Jerry still wouldn't meet with me. Short of not showing up anymore, I was running out of options for quitting. I began to wonder if he was planning to fire me. . . .

My last graveyard shift marked exactly one month without alcohol for me. (It also happened to be the last day I'd ever work for Jerry, but I didn't know that at the time.) I decided to break my drinking fast in order to celebrate surviving the shift. I brought a bottle of Jack Daniels to work, waited until my last stories were uploading, and poured it into three red cups. One I left on my desk. One I gave to Michael.

"Shit," he said, shaking his head.

"I know."

One I took over to Jerry. It didn't feel right, drinking whiskey without him. I couldn't separate the smell from the way his one eyebrow would raise when he was about to say something mischievous. Or how he made me feel smart and interesting. Or how crowded bars melted into the background when he and I were talking. I missed our friendship regardless of how twisted it was.

"Whiskey?"

"Yeah, thanks," he said. And he smiled at me. A slow, warm, genuine smile. The way he'd smile at me when I told him all my kooky ideas or made fun of his cynical worldview. He probably thought it was a peace offering. We clicked plastic cups and each took a sip without breaking eye contact.

Michael and I got off our shift a little early and decided to see off Peter and Charlotte, who were leaving Taiwan for good. Their cab was coming in the early hours of the morning and we were all going to stay up until it did. Charlotte ran from room to room, packing last minute items while Peter, Michael, and I drank and smoked—complaining about work the entire time.

At about four or five a.m., the cab came, and we helped them drag their suitcases to the curb. Michael and I gave them big hugs and watched as they pulled away. A small pit formed in my stomach. "*Go with them*," it whispered. It felt as if Peter and Charlotte were driving out of the hurricane, while I was facing toward it.

"Food?" Michael asked.

"Food," I answered.

We got in a cab, or maybe we walked, the night begins to get hazy at this point. I remember we ate at one of those places where you order at the window and sit on the street. You get a plastic bag of noodles that you dump into a container of soup, and then you mix the two together to create the most satisfying drunk breakfast you'll ever eat. All for a dollar. At some point during drunk breakfast, Michael and I decided it'd be good to watch the sunrise from his roof. He was one of those "one more" people when it came to drinking, and unfortunately, so am I. When you get two "one more" people together, the drinking only ends when one of you blacks out, makes out, or passes out.

Maybe it's because my endorphins spiked, or the overwhelming beauty of the quiet city, but this next part of the night is vividly scorched into my brain. We sat in two plastic chairs on his roof and watched the sun sneak over the horizon. Michael began to talk about how abhorrent the graveyard shift was, and then, unexpectedly, he burst into tears. Loud, heaving sobs.

"It's not fair. It's not fair. It's not fair," he repeated, crying into his chest. All these men and their tears! I grabbed the bottle of whiskey and took a giant swig. The kind of swig you see in the movies, when you think, *They must've replaced the alcohol with juice because no one can drink that much without puking.* It did taste like juice. Apple. I rubbed Michael's back, trying to get him to calm down.

Then I remember walking down his stairs, giving him a hug goodbye. "We made it out alive," I whispered in his ear. There was a cab and that's it. That's all I remember.

I woke up at six p.m. the next day—not in my apartment. Without a clue of where I was or how I got there. There were Band-Aids on the insides of my arms, and my first thought was that I'd tried to kill myself. Then I realized they were covering up IV holes. There were tattered men lying around me, also hooked up to IVs. There were nurses checking stats, a desk, and not much else. I slowly got up and floated to the small front desk. I had no idea how to say, "I fucked up, huh?" in Mandarin, so I just swayed wordlessly. It was clear that they didn't speak English because they silently handed me a plastic bag with all of my belongings and a bill. The bill, by the way, was $20. I still don't know what that place was. Hospital, maybe?

I went outside and grabbed a cab home. The sun was setting and the air felt unchanged. An entire day had disappeared from under me, and everything felt the same. Instead of feeling shame, as is customary when I've put myself in a potentially life-threatening situation, I felt nothing. Death had sniffed around my body and all I could think was: nothing.

I got home, plugged my dead burner phone into the wall, and noticed there were about eight missed texts, most from my landlord, Sue, and a couple from some coworkers I was supposed to meet for dinner. *Guess they didn't think to call the local hospitals.* I promptly threw up, showered, and then headed out to meet up with my coworkers, who, by the way, would make awful detectives in a missing persons case.

"This job is killing me," I told them in between sips of ice water. Michael was there to corroborate.

We gossiped about work and what we wanted to do with our lives. I made fun of myself for drinking too much and told them we should all leave to start our own company—a conversation every single downtrodden employee has with her coworkers at one point or another.

At about 4:30 a.m. we all went our separate ways. I decided to kill some time by walking home because my body hadn't adjusted from the nightshift yet. I put on "Gone" and popped my ear buds in.

I walked down Ren'ai Road, arguably the prettiest road in Taipei, and marveled at its stillness. There's something tender about an enormous and busy road lying dormant. It's similar to seeing a dog shaved like a lion; ironically poetic and slightly sad. As I walked through the empty lanes, I felt like the only living girl in Taiwan. A twenty-five-year-old *girl*: negligent with my body, thoughtless with my mind, careless with my career.

I turned onto Xinsheng South Road, nearing my apartment. The neon lights of the long-closed stores danced off the palm trees. The security guard on the corner slept, like he did every single morning. The peaceful night brought everything into focus. I had to destroy our relationship in order to preserve myself. I pulled out my phone and texted Michael:

Marina: I'm going to post it.
Michael: Burn that motherfucking bridge down.

I posted "An Interpretive Dance for My Boss Set to Kanye West's 'Gone'" that day. It hit 19,783,020 views before it was pulled off YouTube.

14

BECOME FAMOUS

Before posting the video, I washed my hair, made my bed, and invited fame into my life. Just like that, like an honored guest I was eagerly anticipating.

Quitting on YouTube started out as a joke idea, created out of ludicrous fantasies, but it became a reality the night I woke up in the hospital. Something inside of me broke. It was clear that I wouldn't be able to work in the same, blindly trusting way ever again. I had to be smarter, tougher, and more calculated with my career. I vowed to never again allow a poisonous work environment to seep into my bloodstream. A career rebirth was on the horizon. Cue: fame.

My craving for fame began after I saw what it could do for small-time writers. My life in digital media was entangled with the need for views, clicks, and likes. The more views my animations received, the more it meant I was doing a good job. The more visitors my blog attracted, the more it meant I was succeeding as a writer. The internet was building a vapid infrastructure of faves and likes; my salary and emotional stability became dependent on it. I went from a generic attention whore to a full-blown attention addict.

"You need to add more boobs to the thumbnail," Jerry once said while looking over my shoulder. "It will get people to click." I was working on a story about a Ukrainian woman who had demolished her body with plastic surgery in the hopes of looking more like Barbie. I added four more sets of breasts to the thumbnail, and our view count jumped to over 700,000, making me an official member of the Capitalizing Off Women's Insecurities club. It made me feel powerful and masculine, like Jerry.

The benefit of writing for a big company is that there is an established voice that's going to make money. All you need to do is show up on time and write in the voice of the company. When you write for yourself, you have the opportunity to choose your own words, your own voice, but the getting paid thing gets a lot trickier. In short: you have to be known to get paid.

The day my Modern Love story was published in *The New York Times,* I was certain I'd made it. It was something written on my own, for myself, and *The New York Times* published it. There's a current of excitement that runs through your body when you stumble on something you know you can do for the rest of your life. Especially when that something requires little more than a laptop and a room.

You begin to envision an existence where you work from your small apartment, occasionally stepping out for coffee at a charming café. The only schedule you watch closely is your menstrual one, and when people ask what you do, you can giggle and say, "Oh, I work for myself." I wanted to giggle and say that.

After *The New York Times* article agents and publishers reached out to ask about me. "What are you working on?" "Do you have a novel?" "Any samples?" I didn't have any of those things so I utilized the fake it 'til you make it mentality. Maybe if they gave me a week, I could come up with some sort of writing to prove my worthiness. "Yes, it's true," I'd smugly tell future panel moderators, "I wrote my first film in a week. You have to rise up to the opportunities handed to you." But that's not how anything works. Good writing takes effort, time, dedication. It took me fifteen years to go from writing about Kevin in my diary to writing about him in *The New York Times*. The agents and publishers eventually grew disinterested due to my lack of samples and quickly moved on.

Only one agent, Tamara, seemed serious about working with me. "What kind of books would you like to write?" she asked over the phone.

"Essays," I told her. It was the only writing I knew how to do. Well, that and credit card deals, or topical animations, but essays were my favorite.

"You can't do essays," she told me, almost too quickly. As if she had known I was going to say "essays" and was prepared to intimidate the idea out of me. I was confused. I'd just published an essay in *The New York Times*. Ever heard of it, Tamara? What more could you want?

"How many Twitter followers do you have?" she asked.

I quickly pulled up my Twitter account and looked at the number. It was fairly high. "Almost two thousand," I confidently told her.

"Oh, so basically nothing," she said. I winced.

"It's nearly impossible to sell a book of essays from an unknown writer. No one knows who you are so they're not going to want to read about you," she told me. Ah, she had me there.

It makes sense, of course. Publishers want to buy a book that they can easily sell. One *New York Times* article does not a writer make.

Tamara, like the other agents who were initially interested in me, disappeared shortly after she appeared. I was left with this deep pit in my stomach, like I'd missed a chance to succeed.

According to comedy lore, Donald Glover got his first writing job (on *30 Rock*) because he had two scripts and multiple sketches ready to go when someone important asked if he had any writing samples. I felt like this was my Donald Glover moment and I blew it.

But there's no such thing as a big break—just little pushes forward in the endless pursuit of success. If being published in Modern Love didn't generate enough attention for me to leave my job and become a full-time comedy writer, then I was going to fight for more. Shortly after my conversation with Tamara, I invited fame to come into my life using a method handed down to me from my mother.

Olga spent most of my childhood hopping from one addiction to the next. There was the year that she was obsessed with the Atkins diet; our dinners were just slabs of steak with cheese for dessert. Then she was addicted to Olympic swimming; I came home to pictures of Lenny Krayzelburg posted all over the walls. After that, of course, was the self-help book compulsion; the whole family developed an unusually sunny outlook on life. It felt like we were normal for a moment. That addiction only lasted a summer, but it was my favorite. I still fondly remember reading *The Secret* which teaches you to manifest things by making physical and mental room for them—I was desperate enough for fame to give The Secret a try.

During the overnight shift, I spent my sleepless days cleaning up my internet footprint. Deleting old photos, college videos, and anything that didn't make me look like the fun, laid-back professional that I'm not. I ripped my stand-up videos from YouTube and edited them down to forty-five-second digestible clips—my best jokes from my best shows. I created and designed my own website (the one I still use today) with links to everything I was proud of: marinavshifrin.com. (That's marinavshifrin.com.)

I began sharing more photography on Instagram. I tweeted one to two jokes a day, so that if anyone scrolled through my feed, they'd know that I was a good joke-writer. I wrote flowery Yelp reviews and even won Yelp's "Review of the Day" right before my video went viral. (There is a very entertaining comment thread in which Yelpers try to figure out if I was a bot created by Big Advertising.)

Every inch of my social media was meticulously curated with things I am most proud of. I was constructing a hologram of my life and damn did it have a nice sheen to it.

Editing the video of my dancing around the office was an exercise in observation. I watched countless viral videos, trying to figure out what they had in common.

Pooling all knowledge together, I put my mediocre-to-poor editing skills to work. I made sure my video was under two minutes long, knowing that most people wouldn't watch anything longer. I began with a close up of my face, staring right into the camera and through the screen. It was the familiar locked eye-contact that most YouTubers use, but this was a little a different. Instead of the cheerful "Hi, guys," I wordlessly stared, adjusting the camera as if something important was about to happen. I added scrolling text so that those who couldn't watch with sound would still know what was happening. Exactly one third of the way through the video, when viewers' attention would naturally wane, I added a little cliffhanger: "Oh, and to let my boss know . . . (dance break)." This kept people watching until the end, which ensured their views were counted. I don't want to brag, but it's *nearly* a perfectly constructed viral video.

Want to hear a secret? I never told anyone this because I thought it made me sound maniacal, like a malicious media manipulator. But now I'm older, a little more confident, and

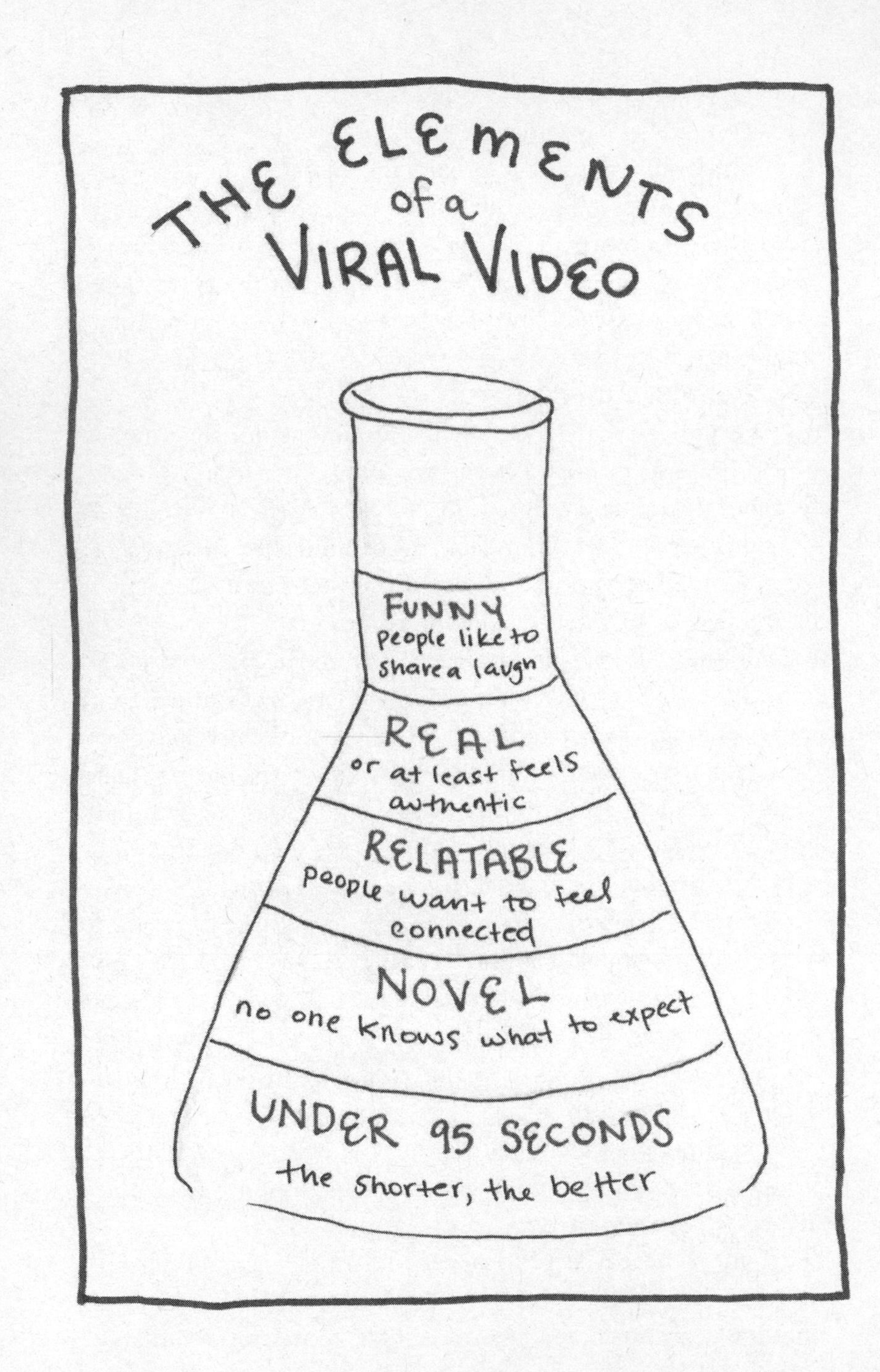
THE ELEMENTS of a VIRAL VIDEO
FUNNY
people like to share a laugh
REAL
or at least feels authentic
RELATABLE
people want to feel connected
NOVEL
no one knows what to expect
UNDER 95 SECONDS
the shorter, the better

I care less about what Jerry and other lecherous men in power think of me: the video I posted, the one that got over nineteen million views, was the second video I'd created. My previous attempt had been made a week earlier. The two videos are nearly indistinguishable. I dance in the same way, in the same places, to the same music—the only difference is, in the first video I'm wearing a gray baby-doll dress cinched at the waist with a thin red belt. My hair is down and bouncing around my shoulders, and if you play the video slowly enough, you occasionally catch a glimpse of my Ninja Turtle underwear. "You look like a slutty nineteen-year-old intern," Rebecca said after I sent her the video.

"I do?"

"I can see your underwear! People are going to put screenshots of your butt on Reddit."

"Who? My parents? No one is going to see this," I told her.

"Yeah, but what if they do?" She had a point.

Before you release anything into the world—your résumé, a photo from a night out, a long Facebook post chronicling the demise of modern-day democracy—make sure that your underwear isn't showing, literally and metaphorically. It is perfectly okay to recruit a Rebecca for these purposes.

So I went home and looked through my closet. Everything I owned either had holes or stains, or it was too short. Everything except for a beautiful, forest-green corduroy blazer that my stylish pen pal Amy had gifted me a month earlier. Because Amy is a New York public defender with wild amounts of confidence, I trusted that the blazer would project a similar image of maturity and grace. It was the nicest piece of clothing in my closet, and when I wore it, I too felt like a badass NYC lawyer.

I put on the blazer, reshot the video, re-edited it, and then . . . made a viral video pros and cons list, probably the first and only one of its kind.

9·20·2013

CAREER SUICIDE

PROs	CONs
· a way out	· unprofessional
· clever	· no more $
· forces me to start over in a career I want	· no more health insurance
· opportunity to take comedy seriously	· will never get hired in the corporate world
· can take down if it doesn't get enough views	
· no longer under Jerry's* control	

*Jerry's real name redacted

Ultimately, my decision to make the video public came down to this: Jerry stripped me of my voice, work responsibilities, and my trust in authority figures. The morning I woke up in a hospital with the crushing disappointment of being alive, it became clear to me that there was truly nothing to lose.

I posted the link to my Facebook page at 7:15 p.m. and went to bed. My heart fluttered and blood rushed through my body. It felt like the night before the ACTs. The anticipation of what was to come was too much to take.

Ten minutes later, I got out of bed and checked my computer. Seven likes on Facebook. I considered deleting the post. "Whoa, this is gonna go so viral," an old resident from my RA days, wrote. Instead of deleting the video, I sent it to Gawker's tips email with the subject line, "This is how I quit my job yesterday." While I was typing, a message popped up on my screen. It was from Jerry: "Resignation accepted." That's all he wrote. It was over. I got back in bed and waited for the construction in the apartment above me to start.

At 4:42 a.m. Taiwan time, 4:32 p.m. New York time, Gawker posted the video on their page. Soon after, the *Huffington Post* posted it too. Which meant my video made the digital news cycle, the same one I checked every morning for my stories. I wasn't able to go back to bed, so I sat at my computer and watched the internet devour my video. My YouTube page showed the view count at 301-plus. It was the magic number we were always trying to hit at work: 301-plus meant there were so many people watching that the analytics system couldn't keep up.

I got up and started pacing. "Don't mess with me, Jerry. I SAID, DON'T MESS WITH ME." My pace turned into a hop and I began chanting, "Don't mess with me. Don't mess with me. Don't mess with me." I am not someone who talks to herself, but on this morning, I needed to share my news with someone, even if that someone was a wall. My chanting was so loud that my neighbor filed a noise complaint. The apartment above me was getting demolished with jack hammers, and I'd earned a noise violation for my first expression of elation in a year. Whatever. I was done being quiet. I'd finally gotten the attention I wanted, and all it took was emotional manipulation, a hospital stay, and a little bit of dancing.

Jerry messaged me again at nine a.m. asking if we could get together. "We should meet to discuss a few things, away from the office."

A chill ran through my body. In the years that have since passed, I've thought about those four words a lot. "Away from the office." Where did he want to meet? A restaurant? His apartment? An abandoned parking lot so that he could slit my throat and hide my body? I still don't know, although I'm deeply curious. Jerry, if you're reading this, were you going to kill me?

We agreed to meet in the cafeteria of our office building. Before I left, I grabbed the coin from India, with Ganesh on it, and slipped it into my pocket. *You will go through a bit of a tough period, but after September, everything will be perfect.* It was September 30.

This time, a manager was there to moderate the meeting, the same one who didn't want to get involved in our "lovers' quarrel." We stood at the elevator in the lobby and waited for Jerry to come down. When Jerry arrived, we got in the elevator with him and I simply said, "Hi." It was probably too cheery, but whatever.

"Give me your ID," he responded. I pulled my lanyard out from under my shirt, over my neck, and handed it to him. Snipped the umbilical cord. Tears of exultation welled up in my eyes. But I did not cry.

"Please don't fight," the manager pleaded to what felt like

nobody. The three of us silently rode the elevator to the bottom floor and picked a table in the corner of the cafeteria.

As soon as my butt touched the seat, Jerry launched into all the reasons I'd failed the company. He told me that I had squandered all the opportunities he'd given me. I thought about the time we'd almost kissed at his elevator. He told me I'd ruined my future. I thought about the time he cried in my arms. He told me that I probably wouldn't get hired anywhere ever again. I thought about the time we slow-danced to techno. I let his words wash over me, tumble off my skin and onto the table.

That moment launched the development of an impenetrable wall that I'd keep between myself and my bosses, managers, superiors—all of them—for the rest of my life. Jerry handed me a stack of resignation papers (all in Chinese) and leaned in. "I don't ever want you setting foot on my floor again," he seethed. I nodded, signed the paperwork, and handed it back. He stood up and walked out of my life, and back into his own.

Moments later, a manager came down with a cardboard box (just like in the movies!) of my things—a bag of tampons delicately balanced on top. The image of this married, polite British man gingerly collecting my stuff, making sure to grab my loose tampons, entertained my buzzing mind for months to come. Back in the daylight, a sense of ease washed over me. I put "Gone" on my iPod and walked to the bus stop with my cardboard box in tow.

Meanwhile, my video had taken on a life of its own. Everyone was watching me, but no one was looking at me. I faded into the background of Taipei. Without a job keeping me there, I was just another traveler, passing through. The video metastasized into a huge story. Reporters I'd never spoken to wrote long speculative articles about who I was and why I made that video. Some places reported that Taiwan had abusive work environments. Not true. Other places reported that

I was an entitled twenty-two-year-old who came from money. Not true, but thank you. People hailed me as a hero and as a cunt. My weight, face, nationality, hopes, and dreams were all dissected in comments sections and think-pieces.

This experience is pretty standard for anyone who goes viral, but the odd thing about my case was, as you know, I didn't have a smartphone. It added this game-changing layer of mystery to who I was. I couldn't run my mouth, or tweet about my experiences, or do anything that would ultimately make me look like an idiot. I watched from the outside—a spectator to the madness of my own virality.

As a spectator, I began to see things about fame that I deeply disliked. It turns out, if you want fame, you have to hand over control. Control of your image, tastes, desires, because it's simply impossible to control how everyone consumes you, millions of people's opinions, and their perceptions. That control is handed to producers, managers, journalists, bloggers, whose job it is to shape you into a digestible snack.

The reason I always loved stand-up comedy so much is that you get to control how the audience perceives you. "Look here," you tell them as you raise your right hand in the air. Their gaze goes to your right, and you steal their money with your left. But once you reach a certain level of notoriety, you become an object to consume—which is a dream for any creator, but when you're a twenty-five-year-old who still hasn't quite figured out who she is, it's scary to hand those powers off to the internet.

Going viral ultimately made me feel alone. The internet kept using my name without my permission, which drove me crazy. Marina Shifrin was used on the Yahoo! landing page and placed into an article about why millennials are the worst generation. It was added to the dark web where trolls bragged about knowing my address. Little bits of me were strewn through the internet at an impossible pace. I felt helpless, a little cockroach scuttling around exclaiming, "I'm not a kike-bitch!"

I needed attention to "sell myself" but didn't like the labels I was being handed. What can I say? I'm a broad who's hard to please. It became clear that fame and control have a contentious relationship and I could only choose one.

Things started going downhill after a girl from my past, who had once told a handful of our fellow eighth graders that I smelled like farts, friended me on Facebook. "Wanted to see how you were doing!" she wrote. The immature part of me felt satisfied that she wanted to hear from me, and the logical part felt infuriated. All these unwanted people coming into my life. I deleted my Facebook (a process which took an unnecessarily long time) and felt even more disconnected.

I retreated into a shell of self-doubt and worry. I didn't want to say or do the wrong things and risk disappointing everyone around me. I didn't want to leap into another job, because I was still shaken from my last one. I was in decision-purgatory, passing up opportunities left and right—all the while getting daily emails from reporters asking for exclusive interviews. "What's next for you?" or "We just want to understand millennial culture." As if I had the keys to unlocking questions facing our generation. Fame sucks. It sucks big, unwelcome dick pics.

"I hate people who want to be famous," my comedian friend Daniel once told me. I was indignant. A comedian who doesn't like fame? It didn't seem possible, but then again, Daniel is a weirdo whose diet consists mainly of sugary cereals and fried chicken, *also* he doesn't drink. He is an enigma.

"How do you mean? Don't you need fame to be a successful comedian?"

"I don't begrudge anyone who wants to keep working and

wants to be successful at their job. It's people who indiscriminately crave fame/attention/notoriety/whatever, and don't really care how they get it that drive me nuts," he told me. His words stuck to my brain. Is there a difference between wanting fame and stumbling into it?

After experiencing a taste of fame for myself, I can say this: No one should desire fame; they should desire the pursuit of success. Sure, the two can exist on the same planet of aspirations, but focusing more on your integrity than on fame is what will ultimately lead to your happiness. Striving to be famous is like striving for a body made out of candy—it's a nebulous goal that shouldn't be on your list of things to want.

I began to cringe every time someone called me famous. "I told my parents a famous person is coming to my wedding," a friend told me after my video went viral. I wanted to shake her and yell, "I'm not famous! That's not fame!" But her eyes were so earnest and her spirit so supportive. I smiled through clenched teeth. "It'll be great."

I'm sure some of you are reading this in a crappy apartment, eating a can of Sriracha-soaked beans, and praying for fame. If that's your situation, I bet hearing someone (who used to be in your position) complain about going viral is straight up annoying. I'd be annoyed. But I'm not completely writing off the concept of fame. Fame can be very beneficial and life-changing, but also, it should not be anyone's aspiration. My heart breaks when I see infantile YouTubers baring their souls to the hollow abyss that is the internet, hoping, praying that someone notices. The magic is in your voice, not how many people hear it.

If I haven't deterred you from craving fame, then at least make sure you're ready for all that attention. Heavy is the head that wears the crown, so you need a neck strong enough to support it. Make sure you've spent the last few years focusing on your art and why it makes you excited. Make sure your posture is right and you can answer any question asked. Make sure your samples and confidence are ready to be shoved through that cracked door. And also make sure that you know what you want to do once the fame has subsided. If it's doing what got you all that attention in the first place, then you're in pretty good shape, my friend. At the end of the day, you will only have what you put out into the world, regardless of who recognizes it.

I've learned that fifteen minutes is the exact amount of fame that's useful for most level-headed creative people. That's the exact amount of time needed to make strong connections without ruining your personality or private life. Fifteen minutes lets you hold on to your voice and your ideas, while still navigating who you are.

My only mistake when inviting fame into my life is I didn't specify the type I wanted. (NPR-level fame where people know my voice more intimately than my face.) I got more attention in those fifteen minutes than I could ever need in a lifetime. It cured me of my addiction, like a child forced to smoke an entire pack of cigarettes.

Moving my concentration away from fame opened up space for me to figure out exactly what my next steps were. About a year after the buzz from the video died down, a year after it was posted, I washed my hair, made my bed, and invited good work into my life.

15

MEET ROE CONN

Middle school was the first time I had a locker. Well, that's not quite true; there were lockers at East Prairie, an enormous K-8 school I attended until the fifth grade. But the hallways were anarchic territories, rife with opportunities to get your face shoved into one of those metallic deathtraps. Lockers weren't your friend; they were cold and unrelenting surfaces into which you'd get body-checked. I stand corrected—middle school was the first time I had a locker *in the suburbs*. The hallways of Sherwood Elementary were overflowing with spindly, weak-wristed Jewish kids who didn't physically bully you, but preferred the emotional kind.

In my new middle school, lockers were a safe-space of creativity. How you decorated the inside dictated who you were as a person. Did you choose Backstreet Boys or N*Sync? Britney or Christina? B*Witched or Spice Girls? My locker was papered with photos of Roe Conn and Garry Meier.

Roe and Garry, a WLS 890 AM radio duo, were my tween obsession. Garry was a radio personality behemoth, on the air for twenty-two years before he and Roe got together. Roe was the rising star of talk radio, debuting on WLS a short six years earlier. Unlike their cheesy counterparts on FM radio, Roe and Garry were quickly cementing legend status with their charming chemistry and sharp perspectives.

My favorite photo depicts them standing together, Roe a little bit in front of Garry. Roe is wearing a leather jacket and a black undershirt. His arms are crossed, and he's scowling into the camera like he's disappointed with you. I love the look of disappointment. It pushes you to try again, harder this time. Garry is behind him in a white shirt and black blazer. He wears a supportive smile; he seems a little gentler, brotherly even.

Roe and Garry's voices provided the soundtrack to my childhood. From two to six p.m., Monday through Friday, their words echoed through the house, bouncing off the walls and into the furniture.

We crowded around my parents' white Hamilton Beach kitchen radio (which doubled as a can opener) every day to hear Roe and Garry deliver the news. Olga and Vladimir listened to practice their English, and I listened because these two men knew how to capture the attention of my parents. As I got older, I genuinely felt connected to them: Garry with his logical and witty worldview; Roe with his sardonic, self-deprecating jibes. Their individual perspectives fit together like the cogs of a sophisticated pocket watch.

Radio lends itself to fantasy. It ties up your ears and leaves your mind to wander. I imagined their office as this cool smoke-filled room filled with leather-bound books and Emeralite lamps. My favorite segments involved the clink of a glass or rustling of papers, which added a few more items to my mental picture. I yearned to be a part of their lives and devised a plan to make it happen.

Like most teenagers in the early 2000s, I eagerly awaited my sixteenth birthday because with it came the promise of a driver's license. But unlike most teens, I wanted my license for the strict purpose of meeting Roe and Garry. I had come up with a poorly envisioned scheme where I'd wait outside the WLS building after their shift and "bump into" them. (They traveled as a pair in my mind.) I'd tell them about my years-long dedication as a fan—and they'd be amused because most of their listeners were middle-aged. Naturally, I'd ask for a tour of their studio and they'd oblige. At the end of the day, Roe and Garry would call their wives—they lived next door to each other—to explain that their Greatest Fan was in the studio so they'd be late for dinner. They might even interview me! It was going to be the best day of my life.

My suspicions that the world was a cruelly constructed mechanism created to torture and disappoint me were confirmed on the day of my sixteenth birthday when *The Roe and Garry Show* went off air. My idols, my friends, had thrown in the towel after nine years together on the very same day I was allowed to stalk them without the help of my mother. A few months later, Roe came back and started *The Roe Conn Show*. It was weird hearing him alone on the airwaves; nevertheless I took my obsession for the two of them and focused all of it solely on Roe.

My unbridled affection for Roe followed me through high school and into college, where I studied journalism. My new plan was to study radio broadcasting and do everything I could to get a job at WLS-AM. "I'll clean the toilets!" I wrote in my journal.

On the first day of my freshman year, I got an application for KBIA, the University of Missouri's radio station. I neatly filled it out and never turned it in—my fear of failure impeded my opportunity for success. *If achieving life goals were easy, everyone would be firefighting astronaut millionaires.*

When you're constantly scavenging for opportunities, the right ones eventually begin to present themselves. The second my resignation video went viral, I got emails from every news organization large and small for an interview. It was only a matter of time before WLS reached out. I was, after all, a Chicago native. There was a hometown angle to the story—it was too good of a hook to pass up, the producer in me knew that. I sat by my computer and patiently waited for Roe to come to me. And eventually he did, in the form of a producer writing to see if I could come on *Windy City LIVE*, a local morning talk show on WLS-TV.

I was in the middle of my I'm-not-a-psycho-just-a-normal-girl-who-happened-to-quit-on-the-internet-and-wants-to-be-taken-seriously-as-a-comedian-I-know-that-doesn't-make-any-sense-more-hyphens press tour and rapidly getting bored with talking about myself. I limited my interviews to a few places: *The Queen Latifah Show* because I love her and the *Today Show* because it's the fucking *Today Show*. I turned down *20/20*, VH1, the *Wall Street Journal*, and a handful of other places. If I was getting sick of talking about myself then other people were *definitely* getting sick of hearing about me.

But this, this was different. This was an opportunity to finally meet Roe. I immediately wrote the producer back, agreeing to come on the show. Any chance to meet Roe Conn? I'm obsessed, I added.

That's wonderful!!! Thank you!! You won't regret it. We can have you on the show on Monday the 14th. Will that work? she wrote back. I told her it would work and privately wondered if she was ignoring my inquiry about Roe Conn.

The night before the show, I sent her another email: Where's your studio? Does it share the same building as WLS-AM radio?

190 N. State Street . . . yes in the same building. =) she responded.

I came a few hours early, and hung out in the greenroom with a flamboyant makeup artist and a young talent scout. Greenrooms are secret clubhouses filled with free snacks and drinks. The nice ones look like modest-budget miniature hotel lobbies; the shitty ones look like abandoned living room porn shoots. None of them have windows.

The makeup artist complimented my hair thickness and then asked for a photo together. I said yes, uncomfortable but touched by his warmth. At this point, my video had slowed to around 14 million views, but the excitement was re-ignited because "Gone" had re-entered the Billboard Top 100 charts. My fifteen minutes of fame subsequently stretched to sixteen.

The tranquility of the *Windy City LIVE* greenroom was interrupted when an entourage of people stormed in. They were swarming around a tiny blond girl wearing a short satin skirt, gunpowder top, and leather jacket. Her clothing reeked of expensive panache. I quickly recognized her brushed-out eyebrows, ski-slope nose, and pouty lips. Chloë Grace Moretz looked just like she does in her movies; youthful, sly, perfected. She had the air of someone who was going to meet about thirty to fifty people that day.

She came with her own makeup artists (plural) who twirled around her in a synchronized dance of compliments and grooming. The *Windy City LIVE* makeup artist tried to sneak his hands in there, but was elbowed away by a member of her entourage. She didn't say much, just stared at her own reflection as her flock of employees made undetectable changes to her perfect face. At one point, she asked them to "fix her knees." A makeup artist pulled out a palette of different skin tones, dropped to his knees, and began smearing concealer onto hers.

I went to the bathroom, pulled down my pants, and examined my own knees. The left one had stubbly patches of hair and the right one had a permanent black mark due to bits of gravel shoved so deep beneath my skin that they became a part of my body. A pair of nicely heeled feet entered the stall next to me and I grew self-conscious. I flushed the unused toilet bowl and stepped out of the bathroom only to end up face to face with Chloë Grace Moretz. I scrambled for something to say.

"Nice shoes," I told her.

"Miu Miu," she said.

I'd never heard of the brand Miu Miu before and just assumed it was a quirky famous-girl "farewell." Something yelled out before getting on a private jet: "Ciao, Miu Miu!"

Chloë Grace (or is it just Chloë?) went up first; she was eloquent and kind as she covered all the talking points needed to advertise *Carrie*. Her knees looked incredible. I went second and babbled through my now infamous job exit. I sat with Val and Ji Su Yuk, the two hosts for the day, as they asked me questions about my video. I tried my hardest to convey my personality in the seven-minute interview. I was so focused on not saying anything incorrectly that my mind went into autopilot. The lights, mugs, smiles, audience, hosts, it all circled around my face.

". . . And you have a list of thirty things to get done before you turn thirty, and how old are you now?" Val asked me.

"I'm twenty-five."

"Twenty-five, okay, so what did you have on this list?"

"Well, one was 'quit my job' which I accomplished"—the audience chuckled—"and another one is to meet Roe Conn, who I know works closely with you guys."

"Meet Roe?" Val baited me, "Why would you want to do that?"

"Because he's so dreamy and I love him," I said.

"Dreamy?!" came Roe's voice from behind me.

As you move further into your life, a thin layer of cynicism begins to form around everything. It's easier to shirk experiences with an eye roll instead of risking the possibility of your true unfiltered vulnerabilities rising up to the surface. When Roe's voice came from behind me, I nearly fainted from elation. My desire to be cool and in control melted out my butt. I was seven years old, running to the can-opener radio at 1:59 p.m. to be the first to bring Roe and Garry's voices into my home. Roe wasn't a radio celebrity, he was the narrator inside my head.

In an act of instinct, I lunged at his body. "Can I touch you?" I squealed, wanting to make sure he was real.

I'd mapped out a million ways to impress him, but when it came to actually meeting Roe, I turned into a Chihuahua trembling at the sight of her idol.

"I'm touching Roe Conn," I yelled to the surely uncomfortable audience.

"Oh my god, she's shaking," Val said, placing her arm on mine. "So why is Roe so dreamy to you?" she asked, trying to regain control of the segment.

"Yeah, I'd like to hear this." Roe pretended to straighten his tie, much to the delight of the audience.

"Oh my god, I called you dreamy and you were right behind me. I'm sorry, I know you're a taken man," I realized out loud.

"But you don't mean it in *that* way, you mean like you want to work with him," Val continued, salvaging what was left of the interview.

"Yeah, whatever," I said, not breaking eye contact with Roe. This elicited a bigger response from the audience. Not all people get to meet their idols, but when they do, especially if they're women, they probably shouldn't say they'd do "whatever" when offered a career opportunity.

I decided to reel myself back in and explain to Roe how much he meant to my family and the Russian Chicagoland community. I told him that he inspired me to go into journalism and how I left the industry because it was not operating to the standards taught in school. "But I'm twenty-five years old, I don't know anything," I concluded.

Here I am with both hands clasped onto Roe's arm and my back turned to the two nice women who were interviewing me.

Which is true, you don't know anything when you're twenty-five. You only know what's happened to you, and while that's valuable *to you*, it's probably not valuable to anyone else.

"Well, listen . . . we might have a job for you here," Roe told me.

"Ha, okay." I responded, thinking it was a joke. The audience erupted into applause, and Val began to throw to commercial. I turned to Roe and gave him a "Wait, really?" look. He smiled and gave me a warm nod. I've rewatched this interaction thousands of times. We have an entire conversation with our eyes and it's caught on camera. For the better part of sixteen years my adoration for Roe was limited to a little plastic box in the kitchen. It was a one-sided relationship where Roe spoke to me and I listened, picking up on his humor, guessing his jokes before he said them, laughing into my homework. In that split second, in front of a studio audience, our wordless conversation was two-sided. I could've died in that moment. I really could have.

After the taping, we stood at the corner of the stage and chatted—like the old friends I always knew we would be. I told Roe the truth about what went on in Taiwan, ripping other reporters' videos, the complicated relationship with my boss, the pressure to get views over truthful and honest reporting. Roe lowered his voice and told me he was in the same boat, that things in the radio industry were changing and not for the better.

It's heartbreaking to hear your idol tell you he's struggling with his career. It's a pattern that happened a lot after that video went viral; people I respected from different facets of life began reaching out to admit they were disillusioned with their jobs too. Former teachers, other journalists, friends' parents—I began to worry that adulthood was just a series of jobs, each making you more miserable than the last.

Roe and I only talked for about fifteen minutes before he got pulled away to start his workday. "We can't offer you much," he told me as he was leaving, "but we would truly love to have you here."

The next morning, I was in Target buying ice cream for my dad when Roe texted to ask if I wanted to join him on his radio show that day. I've never wanted to time travel more than in that moment. What I'd give to go back to my sixteenth birthday and find teen-me sitting in bed and crying about Roe and Garry going off the air. I'd gently brush the hair out of her fat, bumpy little face and scream, "You don't even know, homeslice!" Then I'd slap her-me, so that she-I would know it was real, and dive out the window.

I was on a train into the city a few hours later. This time I only touched Roe at a high-school-gym-teacher level of inappropriateness. I brought him gifts from Walgreens, many of which were inside jokes from the show, and we had an on-air conversation that lasted thirteen minutes and fifty-six seconds. (Our interview is still in my iTunes. It came on in the middle of a make-out session once; I made the dude stop kissing me and listen to the whole segment.) Roe sent me this magnificent text later that evening:

> Just wanted to say what a pleasure it has been to meet you. If you want to pick up something part time while you're plotting the next moves you have a standing offer. In the meantime, stay in touch. Feel free to bounce anything off me. You have all the characteristics of a HUGE STAR: smart, driven, fearless and talented. You'll be surprised how rare that is.

After that video went viral, I had a lot of people asking me many kinds of questions. "Where do you work now?" "Are you crazy?" "Will you marry me?" One I got most often was, "Do you regret it?" This, in my opinion, is a frivolous question. Why ask someone if they regret something? It's done, we are in the present, the now. That being said, I don't regret it. Of course not. That video flung open all the doors I'd been dancing around. I was granted a chance at a new life, wrestled back control of my voice, and got to use that voice on my favorite radio show with my childhood hero.

My one unchanging fantasy, since I was seven years old, had been to work alongside Roe Conn. But when the opportunity actually presented itself, it didn't feel right. My passion for journalism had evaporated.

Sometimes, when you get to a place you've been fighting to get to your entire, short life, you realize you don't want it anymore. For a while, I carried a lot of guilt about this. Not pursuing journalism after all the money and time I put into getting my degree felt like a waste. But all that stuff doesn't mean anything. Strangely enough, it was Roe's text that gave me the confidence to turn down his job offer and pursue comedy full-time.

When chasing the dreams you set up for yourself at eighteen or twenty (or seven), it's important to sit down and reevaluate those dreams every now and then. You can do it when you're twenty-five, or you can do it when you're twenty-nine, but it's best to enter your thirties with a strong understanding of your evolving desires, limitations, and successes.

There is a pattern with creatively successful people: they usually start out in a job that's near what they want to be doing—across the street even—but it's not *exactly* what they want. Sometimes they figure this out after a year; it took me almost ten. Eventually they switch into what they've always wanted to do and work harder than everyone around them to stabilize again. This is what's great about being twenty-five. We get to change our minds, jobs, partners, opinions—it's an age of options. Having too many options can be debilitating, but it can also be the difference between mediocrity and superiority.

I leaned into my decision to pursue a career in comedy with such exuberance that I fell into the middle of Hollywood. And no, I don't regret that either.

TAKE A CITY BUS TOUR

I went on a sightseeing bus tour in Chicago. That's it. Holy cow, not everything has a lesson.

17

DO A LATE-NIGHT SET

On September 15, 2009, I performed for the first time on a small stage in a tiny bar called Eastside Tavern. Eastside was a sanctuary for the freaks of college-town Columbia, Missouri. The owner, a guy named Sal Nuccio, was so New Jersey that his middle name was "You got a problem?" Sal maintained a bar with the kind of boundaryless grit that I'd later learn to love on the East Coast. The brick interior was always dimly lit, dimmer at night, of course, and plastered with vintage Creature Feature posters: Godzilla, King Kong, Dracula, The Mummy—they all silently watched as we made poor decisions. Eastside became my world.

Here is the first joke I ever told:

I met a girl who had a lily tattoo on her foot. I told her I thought it was beautiful and she said, "Thanks, it's a lily, because that's my name." That's so cool. I can't do that. My name is Marina. I can't get a harbor tattoo on my foot. "Thanks, it's a marina, because that's my name."

It took me four years to scrounge together the courage to

Strange Stand-up Ranked

5. OPENED FOR AN INDIAN ACAPELLA GROUP

4. GOT PEED ON DURING A BASEMENT SHOW
(it was a dog, but still)

3. PERFORMED AT TWO FUNERALS
(one willingly, one accidentally)

2. PERFORMED FOR AN AUDIENCE OF THREE MEN IN AN EMPTY APARTMENT

1. WATCHED TWO MEN JERK EACH OTHER OFF DURING MY SET AT A TIKI BAR
(coincidentally, this is the title of my second book.)

perform in front of a minuscule crowd on a Tuesday night. The joke landed. I got my first laugh and knew I'd be back the next week, trying to get the crowd to laugh harder. My set only lasted for five minutes and two seconds, but it forever changed me.

Stand-up comedy was the first thing I did solely for myself, by myself. F.M.B.M. If you haven't figured out an activity you can do F.M.B.M., I highly suggest you get to it. Painting, running, sewing, writing, masturbating—everyone needs something to stave off the occasional bouts of sadness that come with adulthood.

I was twenty-one years old when I found stand-up. I've performed in so many odd places and have had so many bizarre experiences that it forced me into becoming an evolved and cultured human. Finding a F.M.B.M so early in my twenties shaped me into the sturdy woman I am today: a sardonic, mischievous woman who likes a stiff drink and a good laugh.

The most frustrating and simultaneously liberating thing about stand-up is that there is no formula. You just keep creating and trying and hustling until you die. Really, that's how everything is—there's no correct way to become successful.

Too many wide-eyed bushy-tailed youths are told there is a "secret" to success (college, networking, connections, corporate ladders). That's why there are so many overeducated, underemployed people. Too many people follow a "formula," rendering the initial formula stale—or "hack" as we say in the comedy community—and therefore useless. The only people who should be using formulas are scientists and babies.

I told jokes on stage for the better part of six years and learned a lot—things that bleed into the real world. Things that I'll share with you now because I think they're important, and not just for stand-up.

STAND-UP BASICS FOR THE REAL WORLD

Start Small, End Big

A lot of people start doing stand-up in their hometowns before making the move to New York, Chicago, or Los Angeles. It's a lot easier to start in a softer, safer space like a small community before flexing your muscles in front of a big-city crowd. There are merits to throwing yourself into a big pond when pursuing your dream career, but you're not going to get the kind of support and failure-forgiveness that you'd find in a smaller scene.

Find the Funny

This is somewhat of a buzz phrase that's used by many writers and comedians. It requires one to assess a situation and identify what could be considered funny. It's particularly useful when something devastating happens. Maybe not that day or the next, but eventually laughter will sweeten any sadness. What can use more sugar than sorrow? Next time you have a particularly rough day or unpleasant experience, make like a comedian and find the funny.

Respect the Light

Comedians get "the light" when it's time to wrap up and get off stage. It's usually a small light (I've seen red lightbulbs, flashlights, and iPhones used) in the background, and it's a cardinal sin to ignore it. (Unless you're Dave Chappelle. There is no light for Dave Chappelle.) You get the light in real life too; a tiny indicator in the background—maybe even in the recesses of your mind—to let you know it's time to wrap up the conversation and get "off stage." Refine your ability to know when it's time to leave a situation. Don't run the light. Respect the light.

Know Your Audience

Comedians have an intimate connection to the people they are talking to, their audience. A sometimes unhealthy but nevertheless symbiotic relationship. Sure, we don't know details, but we get a sense of who they are by the way they exist in a space. When you're talking to a person, or a group, make sure to pick up on social cues. Who are they? What are they wearing? Where are they from? Where do they want to be? Spend some time listening to their body language and words before inserting your personality. This is particularly beneficial with friends; like, for example, if your friend just lost her grandma, maybe wait a minute before complaining about your messy roommates.

Always Punch Up

This is one of my favorites. It's the idea that if you are going to make fun of someone—which I love to do—make sure they are a level or ten above you. For example, making fun of homeless people is mean-spirited but, making fun of celebrities is cathartic. Whether you're a comedian or not, make sure the people you're being catty about have some privilege over you. You can still be derisive without being cruel.

Support Your Peers

The comedy community is filled with the most delightfully wonderful and supportive assholes I've ever met. It's an industry run on friendship (Abbi and Ilana, Jessica and Phoebe, Amy and Tina, Richard and Gene). I'm inspired by the level of camaraderie. Yes, we have big enough baggage for you to live inside, but we all still manage to celebrate our own people. Everyone is constantly trying to get their friends booked on shows, and we are the loudest and cheeriest when one of us catches a break. Now, it's okay to be jealous—it's normal to look at your own shit when a friend gets something you want, but it's also important to channel that jealousy into self-improvement. If you compete with anyone but yourself, you're always going to lose. Plus, being supportive of those around you will make its way back to you, I promise.

Remember Names

When called on stage by the emcee, it's polite to give a nod to comics who came before you, as well as to the emcee. It can be difficult to remember names in high-pressure situations, so I like to write them down with a little note. My friends think I'm absurdly good with names, but the truth is I write down *everyone*. (Phil—wears a pinky ring; Sandra—told joke about fart-grandma; Toni—blond dreads.) People who giggle and say "Oh, I'm horrible with names" are liars. They simply don't care enough to pay attention, which is good for those who write down names (like you and me) because the courtesy of memorizing someone's name will give you a leg up in any situation.

Two-Drink Max

This is a personal rule, but if I have a big show, I only allow myself two drinks. If you're going to an important event and want to leave a good impression, you should limit yourself to two drinks. You're going to break this rule, as I have, but it's still good to have it in your head.

Everybody Bombs

Stand-up is imperfect. That's why I love it. I've seen the funniest people on earth have horrible sets—it's sadly comforting to me. What do comics do after they bomb? Get mad and then try again the next day (or, sometimes, that same day). It's easy to feel like your idols are perfect all-stars who are constantly shitting out gold, but we all know that everyone misses now and then; the successful ones get back up and try again.

End on the Funny

A simple rule to joke writing is saving the funniest part for the end of your story, or even for the last sentence. The punchline, if you will. For example: "Pregnancy is my least favorite test. I was horrible at test-taking in college" is not as funny as, "I was horrible at test taking in college. My least favorite test was pregnancy." I always try to finish everything on the joke: stories, meetings, emails, fights. The last impression you give should be a good one. What better way to end things than with a laugh? Ha.

After every show or mic, my dad would ask the same question: "How'd you do?"

"No idea." I'd always black out with stress and have trouble remembering anything that happened after my feet touched the stage. Often, I couldn't hear the audience because my inner voice was ringing in my ears. I started taping my sets to watch them later. But have you ever tried watching yourself on tape? It's a horrendous exercise in unwavering confidence.

The performance anxiety never got better. I spent the beginning of all my shows in the bathroom, stress-pooping. I wish my stress manifested itself in a more endearing form. Hot girls throw up when they're stressed, weird girls fart into a toilet bowl. Shitting yourself before going up onstage isn't as cute as throwing up. Believe me.

Here's the thing: I want to be a comedian with every fiber of my being—but I just don't have what it takes. I hate repeating jokes, inviting acquaintances to my shows, and asking for stage time. I grew tired of the unending harassment, sometimes physical, from a surplus of creepy comics* and the late-night open-mics spent telling jokes to other jaded stand-ups. As I got further into the world of stand-up comedy, I began to realize that my favorite part was *writing* the jokes. I loved pulling out my little black notebook and scribbling something funny, something that *might* make people laugh. I loved playing with the words, rearranging them, rewriting them, adding them together, until there was a whole set with segues, punchlines, tags, and more.

Stand-up is the most useful tool for a comedy writer; it's the fastest way to workshop your jokes to find out if they're truly funny. But I also have to be realistic. There's this glamorized idea, enabled by Olympic sports packages and memoirs, that if you put your entire soul and body into a dream, it will happen. Most people who are successful have a highly stylized story of how they got to their cushy throne—in the face of nothing, they clung to something, and that something was hope. It's very sexy, but sadly not realistic. Sometimes people aren't cut out for certain things.

The thing about reevaluating the goals you set for yourself when finishing college is that you sometimes have to come to terms with the fact that those goals are no longer feasible. You've experienced such dramatic shifts that those goals

---

* However I'd never give creepy comics the type of power that comes with taking credit for ruining my baby career as a stand-up.

become alien to your new life. That's okay. It's smarter to let go of old goals so that you can focus on more attainable ones.

My thirtieth birthday is drawing near and I am no closer to a set on *The Tonight Show*, which means disappointment is rolling in. Do I feel like a failure? Yes. Many people know me as their stand-up friend, a label I'd been pushing for the better part of six years. I don't want to let people down, or let go of what I thought was one of the more interesting parts of my identity. But part of growing up is readjusting your expectations to fit your new life.

Unfortunately, goals change shape, and sometimes you bomb. I failed at this goal, but what I gained was an undying passion for comedy writing. I figured out a way to make my interests work with my severe performance anxiety and unwavering need for job stability. And *that*, I'd take over any five-minute set.

18

TELL A STORY AT THE MOTH

Storytelling is a lot like stand-up, except gentler. It's the milkshake to stand-up's cocaine-infused vodka. You could go up on stage and do Lamaze exercises for five minutes and storytelling audiences would all but give you a standing ovation. Stand-up audiences are different, especially the open mic ones. In order to get a reaction at an open mic you have to tear your heart out and hold it, still beating, above your head—even then, the reaction is fleeting, a glance up at best. Most of the "audience" at open mics are just comedians impatiently waiting for *their* chance to get to tell *their* jokes. I got so used to telling my jokes to the tops of heads and faces illuminated by the blue glow of a screen that it became difficult to know what was funny. Besides, my jokes were always these long-form monologues; I'd spend three minutes setting up the premise before even getting to a punchline—not exactly a crowd pleaser.

After a couple of years of consistently doing so-so at comedy shows, I began to consider the fact that my voice might lend itself better to storytelling. As with anything, the best way to figure out whether you'll like it or not is to simply do it. (Unless it's suicide; you should research that first.) And the best way to figure out if you like storytelling is by getting involved with The Moth.

The Moth has real audiences, real recording equipment, and real stages. I was first introduced to the event through The Moth Radio Hour—an NPR show/podcast that kept me company in the large swaths of silence that followed my move to New York. I'd walk around, listening to strangers' stories about their family, loves, losses, and so on. Sometimes a comedian would be featured on the podcast, and they'd always be charming, touching, and most importantly, hilarious. I started going to The Moth's events at Southpaw, a cool music space two minutes away from my apartment. (The venue has since been replaced by something called NY Kids Club.)

In case you're interested in telling a story at The Moth too, but have no idea where to begin, here are the first steps I took:

The Moth in 5 Easy Steps

1. Find an event near you at TheMoth.org/events. Make sure it's an event marked "StorySLAM."
2. Prepare and memorize (no notes) a five-minute-long story relating to the theme of the night, with a compelling beginning, middle, and end.
3. Go to the event. They're usually well attended. If you want to tell a story, you'll have a soft and supportive audience. If you simply want to observe, you'll be treated to ten stories.
4. Fill out your name and contact information on a release form, usually located on the stage near a frazzled staff member. When you're done, fold it up and put it into a tote bag with the other storytellers' forms.
5. Wait.

The problem with going to raffle-decided storytelling events in coastal places (i.e., New York or Los Angeles) is that everyone is either looking for their big break or practicing for their big break. The raffle-tote often balloons to the size of a pillow with its storyteller stuffing crinkling inside. A lot of writers, actors, and comedians, all trying to wow the overtly supportive NPR crowd, attend the events, which—if you're a spectator—makes for a very entertaining show. But if you want to tell your own story, the odds of being picked decrease in bigger cities. Although I went a handful of times, I never got up in New York. It was too popular and too many people wanted to share stories.

It took me two years of attempts before I finally got up on the Moth stage. At the time, I was living with my parents, unemployed, and knee-deep in an international controversy. In the month since my video went viral, journalists from all over the world had been calling, emailing, or just writing up stories about what they *thought* happened in Taiwan. I deleted my Facebook account, logged out of all my other social media, and began life as a digital hermit.

Being back home for the first time in seven years was an impossible adjustment. My parents waded into this stage of life where they constantly annoyed each other and began pulling me into the center of all their fights. My teenaged brother was *in love* with his girlfriend and wouldn't stop bragging about it. I once walked in on him Skyping with her . . . while butt-naked. His chair was strategically positioned in front of him, Austin Powers style, but I could still see his girlfriend's horrified full-screen face. "Get out of here, I have diarrhea!" he screamed. Which is a very odd reaction given the situation. Needless to say, I made sure to spend as much time as possible away from home, performing in the city.

After a stand-up show one night, I asked a group of friends if any of them wanted to come see The Moth with me the following Tuesday. Everyone started making excuses except Sam, a newly single friend of Kevin's. Sam had high cheekbones, a sharp wit, and an intimidating intelligence. It turned out he was a fan of The Moth as well. Sam scrawled his email into my planner and we agreed to meet the following Tuesday. (Told you Sam would come up again.)

On the day of the show, my parents asked me to stay home; the weather was horrible and they didn't want me driving to the city alone. After several rounds of negotiations, they agreed to let me drive to the nearest Metro station and take the train the rest of the way. Being in the city of Chicago during the middle of a snowstorm is kind of magical. It's even more beautiful when you haven't seen the snowy city in nearly a decade. It almost feels like you're being gifted aesthetic perfection just for getting your ass out the door.

I slipped and slid my way toward Haymarket Brewing, where Sam was waiting with a beer. We'd come to the event nearly two hours early because the shows fill up quickly and we wanted to get good seats.

"Wanna grab some food?" Sam asked as we scanned around the nearly empty venue.

"Good idea."

He ordered a pizza and I ordered salmon and a glass of whiskey. Sam was delightfully easy to talk to and seemed to be completely oblivious to how attractive he was—I love hot, slightly insecure men.

At one point during the meal, we got into a weird debate over who has a smaller dad. "My dad is pretty tiny," I told him. "He's, like, under five-five."

"Oh, that's nothing," Sam said, "My dad is five-three."

"Wow, that is pretty small."

"Yeah. They should wrestle," he exclaimed, before immediately hanging his head in shame. "*They should wrestle?*" he whispered to himself.

"Is the pizza not good?" I asked, noticing that he'd only eaten half a slice.

"Oh no, I'm just full," he sheepishly told me. "Would you judge me if I took it to go?"

"I'd judge you if you didn't," I told him. By the time we finished dinner, and got a to-go box for his *entire* pizza, the venue was standing room only.

"This is weird, I'm being weird," Sam said as the clunky pizza box knocked into people's backs. His nerves were tangible, which oddly calmed mine.

We found a little table near the stage and piled our coats on top of the to-go box to keep it warm. I walked up to the front, dutifully filled out my name and contact information, and prayed that they didn't pick me. Truth be told, I had nothing prepared, but I didn't want Sam to think I was a coward, so I entered anyway. Thankfully (as per usual) I was spared by the raffle.

After the show, the two of us stayed for a third drink. We talked about our regrets (which was the theme for that night), high school, Chicago—he was the exact opposite of me, but we somehow managed to find things to talk about. I told him about my upcoming move to Los Angeles, and he told me of his childhood on the West Coast. At the end of the night, he offered to walk me to the Metro station.

"It's on the way home," he told me. This was a lie.

The sidewalks had turned into large sheets of ice with newspaper and gum frozen beneath. I accepted his offer because I wanted to make sure someone was there to witness how many times I fell on my butt.

When we got to the station, Sam hopped onto the train to continue our conversation. It cost him twice as much as the L train to take the Metro, but I didn't know that. We climbed to the top level of our cabin and watched tired Chicagoans shuffle in. A woman with a red nose scrolled through her phone, her lips occasionally curling into a smile. Two teenagers tried to distance themselves from the exhausted, yet watchful eye of their parents. A large man fell asleep with a bucket of fried chicken precariously balanced atop his exposed belly. We quietly giggled while the train rocked us back and forth. On the stop before his, Sam rested his arm on the back of my chair and I gently leaned my neck back so that our bodies were touching. It was exciting and innocent at the same time.

When the train slowed for Sam's stop he stood up and I followed his cue. We turned to each other, and he leaned in to give me a matter-of-fact kiss. As if our mouths were not supposed to be anywhere else besides touching each other. It was a very practical kiss. I did *not* expect the night to end with a kiss or I would've—I don't know—had gum or something. Before I could gauge whether or not there was chemistry, Sam pulled away. It was so classy. He was so classy. He gave me a little goodbye smile, turned around, and immediately tripped over a seat. He laughed, waved the pizza box in the air, and got off the train as quickly as possible. I was left wondering when we'd see each other again.

I didn't have to wonder for long, because we made plans to attend the next Moth show a week later. The theme was "Home," which was fitting because not only was I living at home for the first time since I was eighteen, but it wasn't going well; my parents were fighting about strange things like egg sandwiches and stains on ceilings. My brother's girlfriend reminded me of every teenage girl who had ruined my high school years. And I was still getting rape threats from strangers on the internet. Needless to say, I was miserable. But misery lends itself beautifully to art and what better way to ease all that misery than writing it into a story that strangers could laugh at.

This venue was larger and yet, again, Sam and I weren't

For Russians the only thing worse than being dead is being alive. Later that night my dad tried defend my mom, "Don't get mad at mom, ~~[illegible]~~ She is just nervous about college costs."

~~Although~~ That's ~~basically~~ the dynamic of a Russian family humor + tough love. We might've left Russia, but my parents kept up with many traditions including ridiculing your children and using alco[hol] as a problem solving mechanism. I hated it. Things remained tense ~~[illegible]~~ until a few years after the "roof incident" → Then everything changed. I became best friends with my parents, mainly because I moved away.

A couple of pages from my "Home" story,

irst to Missouri, then to New
York, and eventually
to Taiwan.
It seemed like the further
way I moved, the closer I
became with my parents.
~~It's funny how your percept~~
~~on of your parents changes~~
~~as they move into your~~
~~social periphery.~~ I started
talking to them everyday.
I started talking *about* them
everyday. They became
legends among my friends
they even got a celebrity
couple name: VOLGA
Volga became a part of
everything I did and do.
They are my loves, they
are my life.
A few months ago, I
left Taiwan and decided to

written on the train ride into the city.

able to snag seats. We did, however, find ourselves very close to the bar. First dates and bars go together like sugar and spice and everything nice. I was on my second drink when they picked my name. I froze. My stomach climbed up into my throat. There wasn't even enough time for me to go the bathroom. (I told you I'm a nervous pooper.) My legs turned to jelly like in one of those stress nightmares. Sam squeezed my arm and gave me a little shove toward the stage.

My previously prepared stories covered everything from animals to second chances, everything The Moth had ever thrown my way, but something about the story I had written for this night felt scarier. It was about my parents, two people I had consistently and ardently kept protected from being negative subjects in my writing, people I'd only spoken about in the most flattering ways. This story was not complimentary. It exposed the cracks in my family, and discussing those cracks made them feel deeper and more real.

The audience that night was kind and attentive. They laughed, gasped, and fell silent when I wanted. The lights were so bright that I couldn't see anyone in the room. I stood at the mic and just barreled into what I had to say. My family's fights, my embarrassment about living at home, an ill-executed attempt at running away (as a twenty-five-year-old), the difficulties of adjusting to the realization that your parents are flawed—all of it was in there. At the end of my story, someone in the audience yelled "awesome," and I wanted to hug the stage. Instead, I plunged my hand into the tote bag and pulled out the name of the next storyteller.

Telling a story to an audience as big, patient, and kind as The Moth's was an exhilarating feeling. It made all the lonely nights of nervously standing in dark corners of different bars, waiting to hear my name but leaving unsuccessful, worth it. The biggest rewards go to those who are patiently persistent and The Moth gave me the biggest reward of all.

I got back to Sam as the applause died down. He placed his hand on my back and whispered, "That was amazing." His affection enveloped my whole body. I bathed in the warmth of his touch and the applause of the audience. Returning to The Moth despite not being called onstage so many times had yielded a night I'd never forget and, it turns out, returning to dating after so many failed attempts yielded the man I'd eventually fall in love with. The real kind of love. The kind of love that takes over your life and soul, only to leave you floating on a symbiotic cloud of mush.

Of course, at that moment, none of that entered my mind. It wasn't even on the horizon of conscious thought. All I could do was bask in the small moment of happiness, found in the chaos that was my life.

19

FALL IN LOVE (FOR REAL)

I used to love fighting. There's a thin line between anger and passion, and I was constantly dancing around it. Dramatically yelling, dramatically making up, and then repeating it all over again. With Sam, fighting is no fun. My favorite hobby, ruined by the man who loves me. Now we just walk around pouting, each one trying to look sadder than the other, until one of us breaks and we make up.

The way couples fight can predict relationship longevity. Sam's anger manifests itself like a stove—he heats up fairly evenly and it takes a while for him to cool down. But once he's cooled, he's completely over it. My anger manifests itself like a suicide jumper—it bubbles in my head for days, maybe even years, until I'm standing on a high surface threatening to end it all. I'm never fully cured of my anger, I just file it away for another time and place. Through practice and patience, Sam and I have each learned a variety of methods for handling the other's anger. I just need to step away and let him cool, and he knows how to gently talk me off the many different ledges I've found myself standing on.

I guess that's what happens when you fall in love—you learn how to fight properly. Which is a good thing, because on the particular night I'm about to talk about, we got in big, fat, stupid fight. Most of our fights are usually pretty dumb and, well, this one started because of our dinner with a newlywed couple, Lucas and Soo.

We were visiting Lucas, Sam's lawyer friend from college, and his beautiful new lawyer wife, Soo, in their beautiful new apartment, filled with beautiful new appliances that had been gifted to them at their beautiful wedding. They had invited us over to use their laundry machine, because our apartment doesn't have one. Although they are our age, Soo and Lucas have their lives together in a way that Sam and I don't. They both hold high-paying jobs. They have a patio, and more than one bottle of wine. Not to mention an in-unit laundry machine—truly the greatest sign of economic status in a city.

Sam packed all of our filthy clothes into a suitcase (bought for potential backpacking trips) and we burst out of our apartment just in time to see the bus pulling away from its stop. I was already in a bad mood because social events make me surly, and missing the bus didn't help.

Sam ordered a car while we bickered over who, in the relationship, had a dilly-dallying problem. It's very hard to have a decent fight when yelling the word "dilly-dally" at your loved one over and over. When the car pulled up, we both struggled to get the suitcase into the trunk. Then we proceeded to sit silently the whole way there. (If you're fighting in public you should break up immediately.) *What a sad vacation for these two,* the driver must've thought.

When we got to Lucas and Soo's we turned to each other and kissed. We knew better than to bring our bad energy into the apartment of newlyweds; bickering, like pet names, is best left at home. "Let's keep it together," I told Sam as he dragged forty pounds of our literal dirty laundry to a dinner party.

As at most adult dinner parties, the conversation went from "Would you taste your own breast milk and which method of ingestion would you use?" (yes, and eye-dropper) to "Farts." I was regaling the table with a story about how all the married couples at my new job claimed to *not* fart around their partners. I couldn't believe it. Might I remind you that I work with comedians, and farting is taught in Level 101 of Hilarious Comedy School. I've been endlessly fascinated by how relationships work, especially shiny new marriages—and luckily Soo and Lucas were game for my inappropriate questions.

"They're lying," Lucas said.

"There is something wrong with them," Soo yelled from the kitchen. She was putting the finishing touches on a cumin-roasted veggie plate, a recipe she had gotten out of a book gifted to them at their wedding. Did I mention the wedding was beautiful?

"It's not healthy to hold in that many farts," Sam told the table. "This herb salad is delicious, by the way, Soo," he yelled.

"We started farting around each other like two weeks in," Lucas told us.

"We do everything in front of each other," Soo responded, coming in to enjoy her work.

"Everything?" I asked her.

"*Everything.*"

I turned to Lucas, "That doesn't bother you?"

"Nah, we're pretty open. I mean, it only bothers me when I'm trying to brush my teeth and she goes to take a shit, I guess," he told me. My eyes momentarily bulged before I remembered to bring my face back to a neutral position. I looked over at Sam, who dropped his jaw and then promptly closed it. Sam and I had been happily dating for over three years at this point, but the bathroom was still a mysterious territory. It was the only room in our minuscule apartment with a door, so it always remained shut during private bathroom time.

When we got back from Soo and Lucas's, Sam went in the bathroom to brush his teeth. I came in, pulled down my underwear, and sat on the toilet. As a joke, obviously. I wasn't going to do anything. But then Sam screamed "NO!" at such an incredibly high pitch that I burst into laughter and accidentally unleashed a torrent of urine so loud it sounded like I'd dumped a fish bowl into the toilet. Sam immediately stormed out and I knew I was in trouble for breaking the sanctity of the only private room in the apartment. I finished peeing and walked into our kitchen where he was pouring a glass of water.

"I'm going to bed," he said, before stomping up to our loft.

I co-opted his anger into mine, as I am wont to do. "How come you get to fart in the bed and I can't pee in front of you," I yelled up to the loft. "It's sexist." He didn't respond, which annoyed me even more.

I'm not sure where urine and flatulence fall on the sexism scale of feminist concerns, but I was ready to make it my cause. In an act of defiance, I avoided the bed and curled up on the couch with my other boyfriend, Laptop.

Before Sam and I got to this stage—the "fighting in a tiny apartment with no doors in LA" stage—as you'll remember, we accidentally ended up at The Moth show together. At the end of that evening he gave me a quick kiss. That's it. I always thought that if I had the perfect first kiss, the kind where everything slows down, lines up and falls into place, then *that's* when I'd *know*. Most of my "first kisses" up until Sam were completely fueled by alcohol and therefore blurry in my mind. But with Sam nothing stopped. There were no violins, just a drunk guy with a tub of chicken resting on his stomach. Sam tripped, I laughed, and we said bye.

The kiss was so sweet and polite that I didn't even know what it meant. Did he like me? Was he just being nice? Was it on purpose? I didn't know that he'd be the one to turn my life on its head. To tie up the loose ends, answer the questions, and fill in the blanks.

"You'll *know* when he's the one," my mother once told me between breakups. "When I met Papa, I just *know*."

I have a theory that a lot of young women are told these kinds of lies by their well-meaning mothers. I also got a lot of, "You'll meet the one when you least expect it!" which just makes it sound like I'll meet The One on my wedding day.

I always think everyone is The One when I start dating them. Those first few months are as exciting as any relationship is going to get. Then it just gets kinda mundane, and I grow uninterested.

Sam was a little different. We actually met for the first time when we were nineteen years old. I was in Chicago, visiting Kevin's frat because I'd just lost my virginity and a fraternity is the perfect place to peruse as a newly initiated sexual woman. Sam happened to be one of the slew of men I met that night. I don't even remember specifics from our first encounter. In fact, I don't really even remember meeting him, which is a big bummer. Over the years that Sam orbited Kevin's friend group, I ignored him as a potential hook-up because, quite frankly, he was too attractive for me. Who would've guessed that eight years later Sam and I would be sharing a bed, legs intertwined and hands searching for warm pockets of body.

Living in Chicago after Taiwan, I wanted someone to keep me distracted from the fact that I had blown up my career and was living with my parents. Sam had an apartment in the city, and was still so devastatingly fetching. I had gained some confidence and lost some inhibition in the years since we'd met and decided he was a great distraction. Here is an email I wrote Amy about Sam:

> I like him, Amy. But my guard is SO HIGH. Especially after New York and Taiwan. I just have not had great

> experiences with men and I am a little worried I am jaded or overdoing it. I don't expect it to go anywhere with Sam, but I want to continue seeing him while I am here.

That's exactly what we did: continued to see each other. We saw each other the next week and the week after. We continued seeing each other weekly until two months later when I moved to Los Angeles. Sam stayed with me the night before I moved. In the morning, I drove him to the Metro Station in Highland Park. As the train pulled up to the stop, he gave me a kiss. This time, it had more depth, more meaning. Our mouths knew each other now, and our souls were getting there too. We said our goodbyes, but when Sam got out of the car, he leaned back in as if he had forgotten something.

"Hey, I love you," he told me. Then he turned around and got on the train.

It turns out "real love" is as simple as talking to the person you love every day. Even when you're mad, or tired, or distracted, or happy, or sad. I wrote this email to Amy about six months after Sam told me he loved me:

> Sam and I are great. I love every follicle, freckle, and part of that man's body. I love his mind. I want to smash my face into his, until our teeth tangle up and we have to breathe each other's air. He's my favorite person and I'm his. That's all I've ever wanted, to be someone's favorite. He's calm and balanced. He brings some peace to my life and I add spice to his.

And that's about it. I always thought the indicator of a good relationship was how little you have to say about it. That's really when you know you've found The One; when your relationship becomes boring, uncomplicated. In fact, there was no revelatory moment when I *knew* he was The One, just little pushes toward each other until there was nowhere else to go. I used to send Amy emails filled with thousands of words, trying to dissect the men I was dating. "What does he mean, 'I have strep throat'? Is he lying?" Or "Why did he kiss me on the forehead instead of my mouth?!" Or "Dating a man twenty years my senior isn't weird, but I feel like it should be! Is it actually weird?" With Sam, there is never much to share other than, "We're great!"

Don't get me wrong—I miss the indulgent nights when my organs were soaked in wine and I divulged the filthy details of a new love interest to a close friend. But after a while even close friends get bored with your love-drama, especially once those close friends have settled into their own secure relationships. You don't want to be that thirtysomething showing her texts to a friend saying, "But what does it *mean*?" Being loved opens up space in your conversational real estate for more interesting discussions, like identity politics, misogyny in classic literature, and when Paul Rudd is finally going to age.

It turns out the greatest love stories are often reserved for the characters who live in them. They are omitted from the page, and composed instead with knowing looks, stolen touches, and wordless exchanges. These love stories take place over decades, and follow a steady path without the conflict needed for a truly captivating tale. They're simple and private.

At about three a.m. on the night I decided to sleep on the couch, Sam realized I wasn't in bed. He peeked his head over the top of the stairs. "Honey?" he said, waking me up from my fitful slumber. "What are you doing?"

"Nothing."

He had cooled and I had stepped back. I gathered my blanket and slowly marched upstairs to the loft. Sam was already back in the beginning stages of sleep. I got into bed, tangling my legs into his, hands searching for warm pockets of body.

20

MOVE BACK TO NEW YORK

My first apartment in New York was on Ryerson Avenue in Clinton Hill. There was no internet, no air conditioning, no kitchen (except for a mini-fridge next to the bed), and a community bathroom, which I shared with my hot Brazilian neighbor, Cahue, who had loud Brazilian sex with his hot Brazilian girlfriend. I took the apartment because it was only $600 a month. I gave my landlord $1,200 (half a year's rent in Missouri) and moved in on the same day. My first week was spent sleeping on the two towels I had stolen from my parents' house.

The apartment had a lot of quirks. My landlord, who was polite enough to light a horchata-scented candle before smoking weed, lived on the ground floor; my room always smelled of cinnamon, vanilla, and marijuana. Our building sat next to an abandoned lot filled with feral felines. I spent many sleepless nights listening to the unmistakable yowl of a cat in heat. It was hard to sleep in that apartment. I once woke up to the feeling of someone moving my hair out of my face in a gentle and intimate manner. I brought my hand to my cheek only to realize it was a cockroach scampering toward my mouth. Maybe for a kiss? Either way, I slept sitting up for the rest of that week.

Another time I accidentally dropped my Chapstick on the floor and saw it roll to the other side of the room. The building's entire foundation was distorted, making everything feel a little off; it was a funhouse reflection of an apartment—but my calves were getting so strong.

My mind often wandered toward the people who had lived in that room before me. Did they move on to greater things? Apartments with bathrooms, maybe? Or did they get swallowed up by the city, falling through one of those cracks I kept hearing about?

A month after I moved into that apartment, the New York summer heat found me—it rose up from the fiery pits of the subway and entered my second-floor room with such vigor that it felt as if I might melt through the carpet. It was the kind of heat that sits on your chest until you cry uncle and seek the cool refuge of air conditioning. But the thing is, my room did not have air conditioning, so I spent my summer wandering grocery store aisles instead.

At the pinnacle of the heat I got my very first yeast infection. Everything in New York City was on fire, including my crotch. Mazel to me. I finally understood the obscenity that is being a woman.

I spent half of my meager weekly budget to buy an oscillating fan from a furniture store on Myrtle Avenue. The man who sold me the fan asked if my husband was going to help me carry it. Instead of simply ignoring the comment, I yelled, "I'm alone!" and stormed out of the store. I carried the fan the eight blocks to my apartment. Zero help from my husband needed.

At home, I moved the mini-fridge in front of my bed, opened the door, and stuck the fan in front, creating a makeshift air conditioner. I took off my pants, pointed the fan at my exposed crotch, and lay there. The cool air hit me at the same time as the smell of baked bread. This was no way to live.

The next day I went back to the furniture store and bought a real air conditioner, proving to the same salesperson that I could do this, too, without a husband. My feminist anger gave me superhuman strength as I carried the fifty-pound unit out of the store. But after about four blocks my arms gave out.

When I get frustrated, really frustrated, like "carrying a fifty-pound air conditioner home on the hottest day of the year, but you have no upper body strength and a yeast infection" frustrated, I tend to shut off. My mind goes blank and my body does what is needed to get the job done. I lugged that infuriating box of steel and plastic to the nearest bus stop, clumsily rolled it up each step of the bus—much to the chagrin of the driver—and didn't even have time to pull out my MetroCard before we got to the Ryerson Street stop.

It had taken me forty-five minutes to get home from what should've been a ten-minute walk. I briefly considered asking Cahue to come help me carry the thing up, but didn't want a man to rub his man-strength in my face. I had been taught to be so fiercely self-reliant that, at a certain point, I got *too* "I-N-D-E-P-E-N-D-E-N-T do you know what that mean?" to ask for help.

The worst part about carrying an air conditioner up two flights of your scalding building's stairs is that once you make it to the top, you want nothing more than to be rewarded with the sweet, sweet relief of manufactured cold air. But instead, you have to set it up, getting increasingly hot and bothered—might I also remind you that, at the time, my nether regions felt like I'd had a one-night stand with poison ivy.

I kicked the box into my bedroom and tore it apart, using my last remaining ounces of energy to hoist the thing onto the ledge, keeping it in place by shutting the window. I'd later learn that you're supposed to secure air conditioning units to prevent them from murdering the person who lives below you. (My landlord is still alive.)

The unit was crooked, but it didn't matter—there was a new, colder machine at which I could point my itchy vagina. I have never, ever, felt as accomplished or as proud of myself as on that sweaty evening sitting in front of my newly installed masterpiece.

That's what I love about New York. You have to *earn* everything. Instead of bragging about the good things in life, people like to out-difficult each other. "Oh, your apartment is 300 square feet? How spacious! I live in a plastic container under someone's bed."

What would be known as tragedies anywhere else in the country are viewed as triumphs in New York. It's like a big expensive obstacle course. Your calves get stronger as you scale the subway steps, your tongue gets sharper after getting groped one too many times, your skin gets thicker as flakey person after flakey person disappears from your life, your brain gets smarter as you pinpoint how you're about to be taken advantage of. You learn the physical weight of things you buy because you have to carry them home and up the stairs. I'll never look at watermelon the same again.

New York is a city that keeps you on your toes. "You're not living if you're not struggling," the subway hisses as it blows hot air in your face. This ideology is even baked into clichéd idioms—"If you can make it here, you can make it anywhere." I so desperately wanted to make it in New York because then, then, I'd get my free pass to anywhere.

When you work so hard to earn the affection of a city, you get fooled into thinking you love it. And I really loved New York. I loved New York so much that I hated Los Angeles. I don't know why, it just seemed like the right thing to do.

Los Angeles
Brooklyn

"Ugh, I could never live in LA," I said on countless dates. "I need a real city, you know?" Yeah, Marina, a real city for a real deep gal.

That's why I surprised everyone, including myself, when I moved to Los Angeles. It was never part of my grand, master future plan, but people with big offices and a lot of money offered me the opportunity to develop my own show, and I took it. I packed up two suitcases, kissed Sam goodbye, and flew to Los Angeles—a city I knew nothing about.

One of the first things I learned in Los Angeles is that if someone says they want to "develop a show" with you, that means absolutely nothing. It's like giving someone a promise ring, except there's no ring, and the promise is kind of shaky too. Now, when Los Angelinos hear that I turned my life upside down because of a development deal, they laugh. It's a fun inside joke.

LA presented new, unexpected obstacles. In New York, the obstacles are visually splayed out in front of you. It's an upfront city. In Los Angeles, the obstacles are hidden in disappointing phone calls, offhand remarks, and the constant competition of living in a city where everyone around you wants the same thing. Los Angeles is tricky because she's pretty, and everyone knows pretty girls are very good at hiding the scary. I spent my first year buried in a cloud of aimless depression that would be too boring and unfunny to even write about. My relationship with Los Angeles began to improve only after Sam decided to join me.

"I think I'm going to move out there in December," Sam told me over the phone one day.

"Well, don't do it on my account. Do it because you want to," I responded, not wanting to bear the weight of his life change.

"I am doing it on your account, and you'll just have to be okay with that," he told me. And I was.

OTHER THINGS I NEVER HEARD BEFORE MOVING TO LOS ANGELES
"It's an open secret."
"Hurry up and wait."
STOP
"How the sausage gets made."
"The meeting is in a bungalow."
"I'm Armenian."

Sam said goodbye to eight years of memories, friends, and experiences and moved to Los Angeles eleven months after I did. We spent the first two weeks of 2015 together in bed. Not the sexy kind of in bed, but the flu kind. As soon as we could each sit up, though, I dragged him to the closest bar to celebrate.

On the walk over, we held hands and peeked into apartment windows. We kissed on crosswalks and basked in the warm January air. At the bar, we raised our glasses, and I began a toast, "To being one step closer to moving to New York!"

Sam put his drink down. "What?"

"Well, since you're here now, we can start making our three-to-five-year plan to end up in New York," I told him. I've since learned that if a person moves across the country to be with you, the first point of business shouldn't be discussing your next life-shattering move. Apparently, it upsets said person who just moved.

The thing I love about being single—and I *loved* being single—is that you're in charge of your own life. I always worried that I'd have to give up my hobbies in order to make space for someone else's. What if I fell in love with someone who wanted to live in the suburbs? Or someone who was allergic to dogs? Or someone who didn't want kids, or worse, did? My mind always raced with all the reasons my nonexistent relationship was doomed. This was my biggest fear about settling down.* I didn't want to be held back from achieving my goals and dreams, like returning to New York City.

"I am not moving to New York," Sam sternly told me.

"How do you know?" I asked. I've always let opportunities govern my zip code, so I didn't understand his way of

---

* Why is it bad to settle, and good to settle down? I could never tell the difference between the two.

thinking. What if he got his dream job in New York? What if I did?

"Because I just moved here. I'm not moving again," he told me.

I used to think that New York was the only city for me, but that's ridiculous. A city is not made for an individual, it just gives you a place to sleep and eat while you figure out what's *for you* on your own.

People view different parts of the country with their preconceived notions: New York is too dirty, Los Angeles is too fake, Chicago is too cold, Austin is too weird. But the truth is, any city you live in is what you make it. Sure, I hate the heat, the beach, healthy eating, and just about everything else that makes Los Angeles unique, but I like palm trees, twisty streets, creative people, and the fact that Sam lives here too.

When putting together my 30 before 30 list, I didn't think about how one goal (fall in love, the real kind) could interfere with another (move back to New York). Being in love sucks balls because it means adding someone else into all the decisions in your life, making things like spontaneously moving more difficult. But it also means that you have someone to help you carry an air conditioner up a flight of stairs.

That night at the bar, I let go of moving back to New York. It wasn't easy. But it opened up space in my heart for Los Angeles, and for the first time in my life, I don't feel like moving anywhere else.

21

BUY REAL FURNITURE

For most of my twenties, all of my earthly possessions could neatly fit into two suitcases. My motto was "You shouldn't own more stuff than you can pack in a couple of hours." All my moves were handled by myself with my own bare hands. I preferred it this way; it made me feel tougher, like I was physically *earning* my new life.

I am very anti–owning things, mainly because I never had the money to buy anything, but also because I moved eleven times in six years. Eleven. Two of those moves were international. If an engagement ring is a sign of commitment to a person, furniture is a sign of commitment to a place—and I was never ready to commit.

Pieces of furniture are like little anchors to adulthood. They give the people who enter your home something to talk about, a way to figure out your style, values, tastes, if you have money, etc. Furniture comforts you when you want to rest and weighs you down when you're restless.

When I moved to Los Angeles, my life was disastrously unstable—no job, no prospects, and nowhere to keep my underwear. It also became clear that I'd need furniture. Unlike New York, Los Angeles had space. Lots of it. Rooms were bigger, yards were wider, and the rent stayed the same—I could no longer get away with my two-suitcase life.

Tired of particleboard pieces designed to disintegrate at even the slightest mention of the word *move*, I turned to my old friend Craigslist. You can learn a lot about your new city from Craigslist; popular things to steal and resell, which neighborhoods have nice stuff (and therefore overpriced apartments), the trendiest adjectives. For example, an armoire can be "organic," and if you add the term *midcentury* to your noun, that noun grows exponentially in price but not necessarily in sophistication.

My first piece of furniture would be a writing desk, obviously. A desk was an accurate reflection of who I was, or at least who I wanted to be. The nice thing about Craigslist in a city like Los Angeles is it's filled with people who have good taste and are in desperate need of money. Flailing actors getting rid of clothing. Struggling set designers hawking curtains. Stressed stylists selling jewelry. People in LA are constantly giving up on their dreams and moving away, meaning the deals are plentiful. I quickly found a desk.

It was forest green and labeled as distressed—a descriptor I'd never heard used for a table before. I thought only unmarried Jews and trapped animals could be distressed. The desk was wide, with two thin drawers, listed at $300. I offered $150. It was more than I'd spent on anything in my apartment, but it was time to invest in my new city.

The seller responded saying that she couldn't go lower than $300. Soon after, I received a second email from her saying she couldn't go lower than $300. And then a third email with the same thing. I shrugged, figuring it was a bug in the system, and put it out of my mind. That night, Miss Table sent me a fourth email apologizing for accidentally spamming my inbox and offering to knock the desk down to $190 due to the inconvenience. Ah, the art of negotiation!

The desk was just as beautiful in real life as it was in the photos. I borrowed my friend's car to pick it up and was treated to a glimpse into Miss Table's home. I love looking into the homes of strangers. My favorite activity is walking around at night, when apartments are illuminated, and peeking into people's lives. *Oh, they decided to put the TV there? How curious*, I think while strolling to the next apartment.

I gave her an envelope with $190 inside it, and moments later, I had a desk. A desk without an apartment, but still, I owned something. Something with years of notes imprinted into the wood. Something that anchored me to Los Angeles. Something that ended up fitting perfectly into the bedroom of an East Hollywood apartment I moved into a week later.

My whole room was designed around that desk. I wanted to hang it on my wall like a work of art, but instead etched "I AM ADULT, HEAR ME ROAR!" into the wood. As I collected more things to complement my forest green desk, my room filled up with my *own* stuff. Previously, I'd been sleeping on borrowed bed frames, keeping my clothes in borrowed drawers, and cooking with borrowed kitchenware. None of my apartments had felt like home, just spaces I shared with people. That desk was the beginning of my carving out a *home* in my new city.

It was the centerpiece of my room, and then . . . I moved. Again. But this time, for the first time, it was in with someone—Sam. We rented a U-Haul on a warm Saturday morning, combined my stuff with his stuff, and moved to a small but bright loft with high ceilings and a tiny kitchen*—a loft we still live in today. It has eighteen plants, fifteen of which are alive. Photos of our families are nailed into the walls and books are organized by color. We have big bulky couches which will be a pain to move. On warm days, the three little boys next door shriek with elation as they beat each other with empty water bottles.

When it gets too hot, Sam and I have to sleep on an air mattress on the ground floor. We can't shower when the neighbors are showering, and a condo is loudly being built next door. It is our *home* and I absolutely love it.

The desk, however, does not fit into my new life. Now it sits in our garage, adorned with empty shoe boxes, reminding me of a time when things were stable for a moment.

Maybe one day when we have enough room for our own spaces, I'll bring the desk back inside and put it in front of some large windows with a view of palm trees. I love palm trees, especially how they look like large swaying lollipops at night. I'll sit at my green desk and swell with pride thinking about a young twentysomething Marina who moved to Los Angeles with the hope of becoming a writer. She was unemployed and had zero sense of where her life was going, but she had a desk. A desk that supported her elbows as she wrote

---

* The same kitchen where Sam asked me to marry him two years after we moved in together.

all the ideas that led to her first job, which led to her second job, which eventually helped her afford an apartment with large windows and a view of palm trees.

Or I'll just resell it on Craigslist for three hundred dollars. The important thing to remember here is you shouldn't get attached to things. Especially when you live a life in motion.

22

SELL A PAINTING

I'm not really a *painter,* just a person who scrolls through Etsy and thinks, "Well shoot, I can do that." To actually have the focus to sit still, pull something out of your head, draw it on a piece of paper, redraw it until it looks better, and then paint it is not easy. Selling something you've made is even harder.

That's why the earth isn't overflowing with modern artists. Although I've never fully understood the weird, weird world of modern art, I've always appreciated the work needed to get your paintings into a gallery. That's all being a modern artist really is—defending your work. All museum labels should simply read: "It *is* a painting! Yes, it is! YES! Yuh-huh."

I always thought that if I sold a painting—and not to my parents—it'd mean I was a true artist. A person who could live off of what her freakishly small but powerful hands create. It's a fantasy that plagues anyone who has even a modicum of artistic skill.

The nice thing about going from fifteen-hour workdays in an office to freelancing full-time—or, as my parents like to call

PROCESS ICEBERG
ART
RISKS
DRAFTS
FAILURE
PROCRASTINATION
DOUBTS
PANIC
EMOTIONS
REJECTION
NAPS
MESSINESS
MISTAKES
EXHAUSTION
EDITS
NOTES
SKETCH
RESEARCH
INSPIRATION
DEDICATION
SACRIFICES

it, "unemployment"—is that I finally had a chance to put my grand theories to the test. Instead of sitting at my desk thinking about how I *could* be a painter if I had the time, my new wide-open schedule gave me the chance to actually do it. I bought brushes, pencils, watercolor paper, an assortment of paints, and sketch books. That's the only thing I splurge on: art supplies. As I write, I'm wearing a fifteen-year-old shirt with large holes under each armpit and what look to be bite marks in the back. I don't have a car or food in my fridge, but there are twenty different types of paint brushes in a jar on my desk. My whole life is lived on the budget of, well, a struggling artist, but not when it comes to tools. Short of a kiln, I have just about everything needed to make any kind of art. It's important to be ready with the materials when inspiration strikes.

But my dreams of becoming a painter were quickly dashed. Turns out, when you make the leap from a corporate job to working for yourself, it's difficult to paint when most of your free time goes toward being curled up in a ball, on the floor, rocking back and forth, repeatedly mumbling, "What have I done?" Even if you don't have the debilitating anxiety of most creative people, it's very difficult to get motivated when you have an entire day to fill. There are just too many distractions. In the time it took me to write that last paragraph, I moved from my desk to the couch, but then needed to use the bathroom. While in there, I began to part my hair down the middle—just to see what it looked like—but then noticed that the soap dish was overrun with scum. I went into the kitchen to get a scrubber brush from under the sink and found this beautiful vase I forgot I had. There are these huge leafy palms on the property across the street that would look breathtaking in that vase. The property is going to get demolished anyway, so it really wasn't trespassing when I went over there to get them. Honestly, I saved the palms from getting destroyed. The thing

I didn't account for when *saving* them was how thorny the stems were. Those suckers slashed right through the skin of my knuckles. It's hard to bandage knuckles. Did you know that? Anyway, my injuries made it too difficult to type, so now it's the next day and I haven't even gotten through the intro of this story.

All this is to say I was only able to paint three things in the eighteen months I was "freelancing"—a robot, some ham, and a Nutella jar. I painted them to fill my bare walls because I hate blank spaces. My aesthetic is kitschy cluttered, but with purpose and sentiment. I like to keep every square inch of my walls covered with photos, paintings, posters—anything that brings warmth to my soul. Sam is the exact opposite. He likes "the beauty of clean lines and white space." If you split our apartment down the middle, one side looks like a Japanese lawyer decorated it, and the other, an Eastern European hoarder. It's as if our apartment has multiple personality disorder.

Every day I was unemployed, I'd sit at my desk waiting for inspiration to strike. Nothing. I put a blank piece of watercolor paper in front of me and wait longer. Nothing. Willing ideas to come into my head didn't work either. The secret about creation is that sometimes inspiration never strikes—you have to go in and yank it out of your big dumb body.

I forced myself to draw something. Anything. I drew what was sitting in front of me: a Nutella jar—very indicative of the kind of depressing work-from-home-unemployment life I led.

I drew the bright and hopeful imagery on the container. Flowers, hazelnuts, a butter knife, jar of milk, and toast. What a sweetly serene snack. The label makes it look as if their clientele uses a small butter knife to delicately smear melty chocolate onto a piece of toast—as opposed to a sad spoon, mindlessly shoved into one's gaping maw at two in the morning. I drew the quiet hope of that label and then painted it while listening to Rihanna. This is what I ended up with:

ella ella eh eh eh

When I finished, I posted it to my wall (like the kind that separates rooms, not the kind that creates a falsified digital projection of who you are) and took a photo. *Then* posted it to my falsified digital projection wall.

A few hours later, Brenda, a stand-up comic I met at a mall comedy show (it is exactly what it sounds like), asked me if she could buy the painting. There's nothing like the feeling of someone offering to pay for something you genuinely enjoyed doing. It makes you think that you *can* open that greeting card company, onesie design business, or personalized magnet shop. Some people spend their whole life—and savings—chasing this feeling.

When I told my roommate-at-the-time, Ted, that I'd sold my painting, he laughed and said, "No offense, but someone *paid* you for that? I could've painted it in my sleep." His comments bristled against my sensitive skin. Maybe he could've painted it in his sleep, but he didn't. He didn't take the time to sit at his desk and stare at a blank sheet of paper and then fill that sheet with pen and watercolor. He didn't expose his painting to the bitter internet, or offer it to Brenda for $20. He didn't bring it to her apartment or make small talk as she wrote the check. He didn't come home and delicately hang the check next to his jar of paintbrushes, to remind himself that he *can* paint. So, you can go ahead and suck it, Ted.

Selling a painting was fun. I can see why so many people are attracted to the idea of leaving it all behind to become an artist. Writing is a continuous grind of balancing budgets, personalities, and expectations. To sit around all day and paint, now that feels like *real* art. I was completely seduced by the idea of living a solitary life as a painter. But if I ever were to leave the writing world and enter the painting world, I'd eventually find cracks and flaws in that one too. I'd get bored, lonely, broke, and turn to friends who were still pursuing careers in comedy writing—growing jealous as they moved forward and away from me.

At the end of the day, writing and painting aren't that different anyway; they're both about someone trying to expose themselves while eliciting an emotion from the audience, the viewer. I got my small taste of what it'd be like to be a painter, and while it was fun, I was already embarking on a new life, doggedly dedicating myself to comedy writing. It was time to stop distracting myself with tangential interests. I guess that's what most people call "commitment," a term beginning to seep into my life with a terrifying frequency. When it came down to choosing between making more paintings or focusing on writing, I chose to focus on writing because "*I took an oath that I'ma stick it out till the end.*"*

---

* As Queen Rihanna put it in her 2007 hit, "Umbrella."

WATCH ALL THREE GODFATHER MOVIES

I can't remember a time when my parents' toilet didn't have a Mario Puzo book resting on the tank. My father has read every one of them—*The Fourth K*, *The Sicilian*, *The Last Don*, *Fools Die*, and of course, *The Godfather*. "*The Godfather*," my dad says, "is the only movie that's better than the book."

I never understood Russian men's infatuation with mob movies. According to Vladimir, *The Godfather* is the greatest story ever told. A story filled with "love, heartache, romance, action, and everything you could ever want to feel, Marina." Maybe it's the romanticized corruption, or the unapologetic display of masculinity that's quickly falling out of vogue in progressive circles, but whatever it is, *The Godfather* strikes a chord with my dad.

He used to splice footage from *The Godfather* into our own family movies. When I say, "family movies," I mean feature-length films created by my dad and his friends (whom I call my uncles—it's a Russian thing). They've shot a total of five movies and one music video under the umbrella of their "production company," FimFilm. At FimFilm, my father is the writer/director, my Uncle Fima is the cinematographer, my Uncle Mark is the producer, and the rest of us are extras in their slow descent into madness.

In one of their later movies, FimFilm rented a horse-drawn carriage for a scene. The families all clambered into our minivans and drove into the city early one winter morning. My aunts, scantily clad in flapper gear (wardrobe was not era-accurate; everyone wore what they felt prettiest in), piled into the carriage and popped bottles of champagne at ten a.m. on a Sunday. The scene required my uncle Mark, who was cast in the role of famed Russian poet Aleksandr Pushkin, to kiss on the women in the carriage. He smooched their necks and cheeks as they poured champagne everywhere. It was the most scandalous thing I'd ever witnessed.

In another movie my dad and the family dentist, who I call Uncle Sasha, play two Olympic divers preparing for a match. The scene required them to sit in a "hot" tub while drinking wine. I love this scene because in one of the outtakes my dad yells, "Осторожно! Яйца!" which translates to "Be careful! Eggs!" It's how I learned the Russian slang for *balls*.

Sometimes if the shot was too ambitious for FimFilm, they just borrowed scenes from famous movies, one of which was *The Godfather*. When I finally watched the Godfather movies, I had the peculiar feeling of recognizing scenes that my father had snuck into our own family videos; Vito Corleone seeing Ellis Island for the first time; the expressionless stares of the Italian immigrants on the *Moshulu*; Sonny being treated like target practice. When I was younger, I had no clue these clips came from *The Godfather*. I just assumed it was some weird Russian reference I was not getting.

I began watching *The Godfather* because of my own strained relationship with my dad at the time. It wasn't a dramatic strain; I didn't punch him in the face, beat his sister senseless, or put a hit out on his dad (all of which happens to Michael

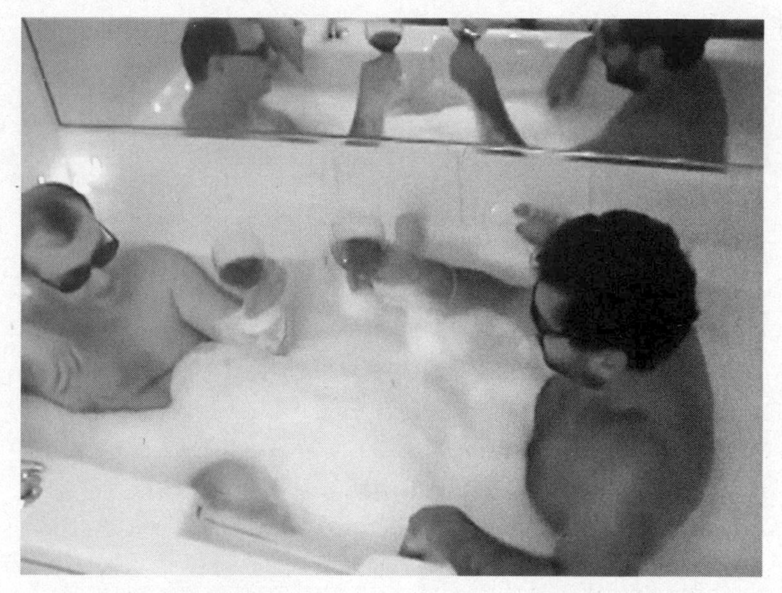

Uncle Sasha (left) *and Dad* (right) *as Olympic swimmers.*

Corleone in the first movie), but it was a strain nonetheless. We were having political arguments, and for the first time in my twenty-nine years I felt completely disconnected from Vladimir. Our conversations were wrought with mean snipes coming from both sides. We used to teetertotter between our different viewpoints on the same seesaw; fiscal conservatism on one side, social liberalism on the other. Then Trump got elected and my father moved to the swings, as I sank into the mud.

I began calling home less and less in an attempt to avoid our strenuous discussions, but soon began to miss my dad. I missed his affinity for circumlocution. His stories have these wordy leadups that rival Tolstoy and often take you down four different paths before you even get to the beginning. I missed his wry humor and how quick he was to point out the discrepancies in my dilemmas, or how he asked for my opinion when it came to dealing with my riotous little brother. I missed our rambling conversations about writers, painters, poets, and art in general. When I miss someone, truly miss them, I envelop myself in their interests, so I sat down to watch *The Godfather.*

It took me three weeks to watch all eight hours and fifty-seven minutes of *The Godfather (I, II, III).* Three emotionally taxing weeks, complemented with a lot of killing, rules, delightfully Italian names, and "The Family." They were long-ass movies created in a time when attention spans were different, more forgiving. It took a lot of self-restraint not to reach for my phone to look up actors, reviews, and quotes during the slower scenes, but at the end I reigned queen over this goal.

THE GODFATHER I

Immediately before watching the first movie, I got into a sixty-eight-minute-long political debate with my dad because he was teasing me for going to a Women's March. "I have problems,

Marina, no one's marching for me," he told me. "I don't know why you waste your time with such things." At one point during the conversation, Sam, sensing the rising tension, scribbled "You're beautiful and I love you" on a piece of paper. It made me cry.

I got off the phone, ate my dinner—my jaw tensing with each bite—and watched *The Godfather*. This is a movie about the importance of respect and fulfilling your roles as required by your gender. "A man who doesn't spend time with his family can never be a real man," as Vito Corleone puts it. In part one, Vito Corleone, the founder and Don of the Corleone mob family, begins to grow older, his son Michael has to decide whether or not to take over the business of money, murder, and power. At the conclusion of the first movie, Don Vito Corleone ages out of his position as head of the mafia empire and Michael is called upon to fill his role as the Godfather. It is a position Michael promised himself he'd never be in, but at the end of the day, family comes first, regardless of your personal desires.

Becoming the Don means Michael is now the patriarch, a lion, protecting everyone in the family *and* the (mob) Family. That's very much the position my father played in my own life. Except instead of the mafia business, he was in the jewelry business—and it stripped him of his time, sanity, and health. My dad was always exhausted when he came home. He'd walk inside, head straight to the bathroom, and rub bright blue astringent all over his face. His day was so deeply ingrained in his pores that the cotton pad would turn black with layer upon layer of glittery jewelry dust. "See this, Marina?" he'd say, showing off the sparkly pad. "This is all the work I did for you today."

My dad hated running his own business. In his fantasy world, he was a painter in some villa near the ocean. During the evenings, he would sit at a table overflowing with alcohol as men came to kiss his pinky-ringed hand and women brought over course after course of carbs. His family and friends would all live in the same neighborhood, and he'd continue using his status as the head of the household to solve problems, protect his children, and eliminate anyone who threatened his kingdom. But at the end of the day, your "in real life" family comes first, so he saved his imagination for the movies and spent most of his time inside of a small office in the Jewelers Row District of Chicago.

I've always been unabashedly thankful for everything my dad did for me. That's why it was difficult when our conversations turned into these long, laborious debates where no one won and we barely pulled ourselves back together in time to say "I love you" at the end.

The next week, multiple news stories of horrendous politics broke. Trump fired so-and-so, appointed so-and-so, tweeted this-and-that, none of it good. All that came to my mind as I read each story was, "What does my dad think?" "How could he possibly be okay with this?" "But really, what does my dad think?" After our previously charged conversation, I could sense a fight brewing, so I took a little break to let my emotions cool before calling my dad again. I ordered Thai and watched *The Godfather II* instead, feeling simultaneously close to and so far away from my own father.

THE GODFATHER II

The Godfather II awakened a sort of dormant teenage lust I didn't even know was in me. If you have never been treated to the absolute fucking pleasure that is a young Robert De Niro, please take a moment to Google him, then maybe google yourself. He is one hot slice of lasagna.

This movie is an exciting representation of the American Dream, where you can lie, cheat, and kill your way to the top. Where everyone around you will bow down to your power.

It's unapologetic about its masculinity and reflects a time where the fantasy of America wasn't as convoluted as it is today. We jump back in time to see the newly orphaned Vito Corleone's immigration to America and learn that his birth name is Vito Andolini. Corleone was a last name assigned to him by an immigrations officer, poached from the Italian city from which he came. This scene is a reminder that your roots are so deeply imbedded in your person. For Vito, his native city ended up becoming a part of him legally. It's so poetic that I can't stop thinking about it. It's the American Dream with the simultaneous realization that you cannot escape your motherland. If my immigration had gone anything like Vito's, I would've been Marina Moscow—I could've gone into pro-wrestling (or amateur porn) with a name like that.

I watched this movie the day Donald Trump issued an executive order temporarily banning citizens of Iraq, Syria, Iran, Libya, Somalia, Sudan, and Yemen from entering the U.S. As an immigrant and a refugee (albeit one whose entrance to the U.S. was fairly undramatic), I was devastated because I understand the power and safety American citizenship represents. I also understand the pain of being bureaucratically separated from immediate family. I so desperately wanted to hear what my dad thought about all of this.

When my father and I argue about politics, both sides come down to what is best for America. To my father, America is a country he fought to live in. He gave up everything to immigrate and molded his entire being to fit into what he thought the country needed. America gave him the space to earn money, buy property, and create home videos that nobody would ever see. He wants to protect this country and his family from the unknown. Tighter restrictions, closing the borders, harsher "vetting" . . . all that stuff. To me, America is a country I fortuitously ended up in. A country that promised "life, liberty, and the pursuit of happiness." Promises of things that I felt everyone should get a chance to have, not just the ones who lucked into it. I want everyone to get a chance at the American Dream, because that's what makes America, in my opinion, a magnificent country. Both my father and I have America's best interest at heart, and that's what makes our disagreements so impossible to navigate.

Vito Corleone shows the promise of America in *The Godfather II*, whereas his son Michael shows what happens when you take advantage of that promise. Michael Corleone's story in this movie is a sad one. As he gains power and strength in his new role as the Don, he begins to grow further and further from his own family, the same family he worked so hard to protect. Unlike his father, Michael is unable to strike a balance between his business and personal life. In the end, Michael's wife moves out, and their lives become fractured. Everything the first movie showed as impenetrable is gone. We see that families can flex and bend, but that they can also splinter and break. I decided to call my dad.

THE GODFATHER III

"Oh, I do have a middle child," my dad exclaimed when he heard my voice on the other end. He also likes to do this thing where he pretends not to recognize who I am when I've waited too long to call him.

I wanted to talk about the travel ban and to hear my dad's thoughts as an immigrant, but he quickly cut me off. "I don't want to have these talks with you, you're too emotional," he told me. Which is true, but I promised not to be sensitive. My conservative father is the closest thing I have to a window into the opposing party's psyche. All the other Republicans in my life were hiding so far up the elephant's ass that it was impossible to tempt them with civil discourse. Honestly? I wanted to know his thoughts.

We got to talking and it was what you'd expect: a back and

forth of shaky facts, sensational headlines from both sides, confirmation bias, the works. The truth is, my dad is a bigger fan of debate than he is of Donald Trump or the Republican Party.

Oftentimes, our discussions end with him saying, "I don't care that much." But this one was a little different. Toward the end of our call, my dad told me a joke: "What do celebrities hate more than Trump? Finding out that no one cares about their opinion."

I was hurt for three reasons. First, although I don't give a fuck about what celebrities say, a large part of my career is working with them. It is my objective to make a positive statement with my work in the entertainment industry. As is the goal of many in Hollywood. Second, I do all of this to make my father proud. He was the one who taught me about the magic of fantasy. The fact that he was letting his political bias stoke a distaste for the industry I work in sucked. Finally, that is not a joke, it's something written to make people feel bad. The setup was weak and the punchline was weaker. A joke written in malice is no joke at all.

Talking with my dad that night opened a repressed part of my malicious brain, and I let my emotions get the best of me. I quickly Googled some tasteless Holocaust jokes because I wanted to prove that just because someone says something is a joke, doesn't mean you should tell it. I read them off rapid-fire, and the phone went silent. I hurt my dad. Deeply. His hurt was radiating off the receiver. It was buzzing in my ear. I immediately regretted it. Our conversation went from tense but civil to a new level and it was my fault. Then, my dad got on my level.

He told me that he and my mother messed up by letting me leave the house at such a young age. That I didn't get the chance to develop into who I should be. That "Liberal Hollywood" had brainwashed me into an anti-Semitic girl. He told me that he never wanted to have this conversation in the first place (true) and I had pushed him into it (also true). He ended with, "I can't do this anymore, have a nice life." Which felt very final. Like the end of something. The phone went dead and I cried. So hard, in fact, that Sam threw a jacket on me and forced me to take a walk around the block to calm down. I was ashamed at how out of control the conversation had gotten and even more devastated that I had hurt my dad.

The next morning I lay on my couch, wrapped in a blanket, intermittently crying while spooning my computer. I pulled up *The Godfather III*. The final movie in the trilogy is all about seeking forgiveness. Repenting. Michael Corleone is older, and his only daughter, Mary, is helping him run the (now reputable) family business. We follow Michael as he tries to become a legitimate aboveboard leader, to no avail. At the end of the movie, his demons catch up with him, and a hit gone wrong ends up killing Mary, but sparing him. It's tragic. An innocent daughter dies at the feet of her corrupt father. Corrupt not by choice, but by blood, because no man can escape the deeply ingrained actions of his past.

Unlike most people, I loved the third movie. Francis Ford Coppola, much like my father, cast his own daughter in his movie, which caused the familial bonds to seep through fiction and into real life. In contrast to Coppola's movies, my dad's movies were not for anyone, they weren't even in English, but they were self-made opportunities for middle-aged Russian immigrants to provide accessible fantasy worlds to their families. My dad's movies allowed us to tap into the pure ecstasy of working on something we loved with the people we loved. In that regard, The Godfather trilogy, in addition to being a cinematic masterpiece, felt like a reflection of my past.

It's no wonder my dad loves *The Godfather* so much. It shows a world where you can be both the hero and the villain.

Corrupt and moral. A world where the rules require shooting anyone who insults your family. It's much more exciting than clenching your fist and stepping away from someone who tells you to "go back to your own country," or any of the other anti-immigrant sentiments my dad has experienced over the years.

Later that night, I decided to call my dad during a burger walk.* I didn't want to apologize, but I didn't want to fight either. Instead, I told him of my recent accomplishments.

"You know," I sheepishly said, "I finished all three of the Godfather movies."

"Oh yeah? What did you think of each one?"

"Well the first one was obviously amazing . . ." I waded through my thoughts about each movie and then quietly listened as my dad told me his. It was the first conversation, after the election, where we were back to our old selves. Just a dad and his daughter talking art, like two old friends.

---

* It's simple: a walk to get burgers.

24

EAT A MEAL ALONE

There is something uniquely challenging and liberating about eating a meal by yourself. Not the kind of meal you eat over the sink while watching YouTube videos on your phone, but a proper meal, cooked by a stranger, brought to your table by a stranger and taken away by a stranger.

There is an unhealthy stigma attached to being by yourself. In my unprofessional opinion, I'd wager it stems from kindergarten-era punishments, timeouts, and groundings—they all require that the culprit sit alone with her thoughts. Just the mention of eating lunch by yourself elicits universal pity. But why is it so bad? I mean, if you don't spend time with yourself, how will you grow to appreciate who you are?

So much of my early twenties was filled with people, parties, conversation, kisses, screens—every inch of my schedule was packed with something. I couldn't go to bed without a podcast droning or even take a shower without music blaring. I spent many years avoiding my own thoughts.

The constant need for mental stimulation began to cause

5 SIMPLE RULES
FOR DATING YOURSELF
① NO CELL PHONE
not even for photos of your food.
② ORDER A DRINK
or order something you usually wouldn't order for yourself.
③ PICK A NICE SPOT
you've earned it!
★ ★ ★ ★ ★
④ BRING A BOOK
or something you've been meaning to read... feed your brain.
⑤ DRESS UP!
dress yourself to impress yourself

me anxiety. After all, how are you supposed to have any thoughts in your head if you are always filling it with someone else's words? I wanted to get to a point where I was comfortable enough with my own thoughts to be left alone with them.

Living in Taiwan helped; not having a handle on Mandarin or reliable cell phone service forced me to explore a lot of the country by myself, including the culinary world. I eased into the concept of eating alone on park benches and at flimsy tables wedged in alleyways. But in order to truly conquer this goal, I wanted to eat a meal by myself in America, where a meal alone would be chosen and not forced.

On a Thursday evening in June of 2017, I took myself to the Figaro Bistrot in Los Feliz. The restaurant is French themed, so the servers are mean like my family. It sits a few doors down from the Los Feliz 3 Cinemas—a revolving door of weird haircuts, exposed navels, and delicate tattoos. There's a lazy feel to the Figaro; they don't need to try too hard because they have the best real estate in Los Feliz. You have the movie crowd, happy hour crowd, theater crowd, and spiritual, crystal crowd all buzzing around the same intersection.

I sat outside, at a table by the door between two groups engrossed in their phones, though for different reasons. The table to my right sat two women who looked to be in their thirties, having a fight with a third woman, Kate, by text. "See, see?" The woman in the black shirt flipped her phone toward the woman in the white shirt, who didn't look up from her own phone.

"This is the problem. I'm going to say, 'I'm sorry, Kate, but this is what you do, you push people away . . .' God, I'm gonna flip a bitch over this." Black Shirt began typing into her phone, while White Shirt typed in hers. I shifted my focus to the table on my left.

"It's too late to do 'shrooms tonight, let's do it on Sunday," a curly-haired man told the group. Apparently 7:41 p.m. is too late to do 'shrooms, and here I thought it was your forties.

"Can't you just text Carmen?" a redhead with a British accent asked.

"No, Carmen's boyfriend just died," the curly haired man responded.

"I heard it was *ex*-boyfriend," added a very hot woman, who I would come to overhear is an actress, but "not from anything you would've seen."

"I'll just invite her to do 'shrooms with us and then we can go to Wi Spa," British Accent said.

The server, Jennifer, came to my table with my martini and left before I could order any food. It turns out that my favorite part about eating by myself is that I am invisible. Sitting at Figaro reminded me of my high school years, the aimless days spent under the radar. I missed the time before cell phones, when life was rife with opportunities to quietly observe the world and connect to the minutiae of the day.

The girls to my right switched phones and copy-edited each other's texts to Kate while the table on my left was group-drafting a 'shroom request text to Carmen. I was the only one not on my phone.

"Anything to eat?" Jennifer asked. She had eleven pens in her pocket, long auburn hair pinned back with a brown hair clip, coral lips, and drawn-on eyebrows. Would I have noticed the way her nose slightly crinkled when she smiled if I was with a friend, passing phones back and forth? I wonder if I would've noticed anyone: Black Shirt and how she fiddled with her gold engagement ring while trying to compose the perfect text. White Shirt and the way her camo slippers perfectly matched her camo pants. Curly-Haired Man's incessant yammering about his new terrier mix, Birdie. "I started giving her probiotic yogurt because it's good for her little tummy," he told the table as Birdie chewed on a gum wrapper under his feet. The way Hot Woman's pink lace bra peeked out from her beige cut-off tank top. I ordered a beet salad with goat cheese and was rewarded for my choice with a smile from Jennifer.

"I don't want to do 'shrooms," Hot Woman said. "I want ice cream and then I'll go for a run. Get my night high that way." She put a cigarette in her mouth and began to dig in her purse for a lighter. A busboy appeared out of nowhere to tell her she couldn't smoke there. She looked at him dumbfounded, as if he had asked her to eat her cigarette.

The women on my right settled on two separate "we should meet" messages to Kate. It took them an hour and fifteen minutes to compose those texts. I wondered what it felt like to have the kind of privilege to spend an afternoon composing a text to a prickly friend. I mean, ditch the friend and write a movie, ladies. Black Shirt and White Shirt decided to treat themselves to burgers from a restaurant down the street. Jennifer with the auburn hair and eleven pens brought me my salad, then turned to The Shirts.

"Anything else for you ladies?" she asked.

"We're good. Just the check," Black Shirt told Jennifer. She pulled up an order menu on her phone and began listing burger toppings to White Shirt: "You want avo, mayo, tomato . . ."

"Yeah."

". . . and mushrooms?"

". . . and pickles."

"It comes with pickles. Do you want mushrooms?"

"Yeah, mushrooms."

Meanwhile, the table on my right decided that Monday would be the day *they* would do mushrooms, because "there's nothing else to do on Mondays." Which is true in Los Angeles.

For a second there, it felt like we were all at the same table, sharing a meal and casual conversation about mushrooms—in a way, we all were, at least for a moment. But eventually the women on my right went to pick up their burgers. They were replaced by an older couple who wore their glasses on the tips of their noses and loudly read the day's emails to each other. The table on my left disbanded shortly after deciding on Mushroom Monday, hovering at the corner for more cigarettes and conversation. I took comfort in my second stiff martini. At the end of my meal, I waited another twenty minutes for Jennifer to bring the check. The evening dinner crowd gathered at the entrance as the sun was setting. A busboy brought me my bill. I paid, said thank you to no one in particular, and gathered my things. Once safely across the street, I watched as Jennifer bussed the table for two young girls with flawless skin and short skirts.

Eating alone sharpened my wolf fangs and taught me the power of peacefulness. It heightened my sense of focus and connection to the people around me. The fear of loneliness is a strong one that grows each year, fueled by our constant need to be digitally connected, but just like it's important to fan the flames of friendship, I've learned that it's important to do things alone. It gives you a chance to fill your head with your own thoughts and strengthens a sense of security within yourself. I guess that's why 95 percent of people in Los Angeles meditate. Which I would totally try if you were allowed to eat while doing it.

25

COOK A FIVE-COURSE MEAL

My dad used to call my mom Soup Queen. Not the most ideal ranking within the kingdom, but it's true, my mother was a royal goddess when it came to soups. Borscht, solyanka, mushroom, cabbage, various forms of gazpacho—Olga could make all of them from memory.

Soup, I know, is not glamorous, but somehow my mom made it so. Her pearl-painted nails would disappear into a bowl of shredded vegetables, only to reappear moments later clutching a cluster of perfectly cut potatoes. She'd sprinkle the potatoes into her broth and I'd watch as they disappeared into the depths of the pot. The house was constantly filled with the sweet, woody smell of beets boiling in salted water.

Borscht was the specialty of her specialties; the beets drew you in with their unassuming vegginess, the meats gave off the familiar warmth of stew, the spicy mustard kicked you in the face, and the sour cream licked your wounds. Served hot in my house, it always tasted like Russia to me. Before my baby palate could appreciate a soup with such multifaceted flavors, I marveled at the color. God, the color. I used to soak my lips in the broth, hoping that they'd turn ruby red, if only for a moment. (Oftentimes, I ended up with a beet-colored goatee instead.) All of those ingredients join together to make a flavor so perfectly balanced that I could taste my mother's elusive love in every bowl.

"When you grow up, I'll teach you all my recipes," my mom would tell me, stirring her pot as if it were a cauldron, "so that you can make husband happy." It always came down to my nonexistent husband and how to keep him happy. I heard about him every time I walked by the kitchen. "Marina, you have to learn how to cook," Olga would yell after me while peeling potatoes, "or no one is going to marry you!"

In my mother's mind, a woman's purpose is to keep her husband happy and her children alive. That way, her boys can go off to earn enough money to support the family, and her girls can birth bouncy grandchildren to brighten up the tragedy that is life. My mom broke off little pieces of herself and sprinkled them into her children, her husband, and her soups—like a proper Russian woman.

I am the black sheep in my family when it comes to cooking; my sister, brother, and dad are all excellent cooks. My guess is that gene skipped me. It's a goddamned miracle I made it this far into my life, because I have absolutely zero interest in cooking. Up until meeting Sam, I survived on different combinations of canned food with hot sauce, oatmeal, and whole wheat tortillas. Rest in peace, my Single Gal's Diet.

It is insane how quickly a fast 'n' loose woman will get domesticated when she's in love. I started doing novel things, like washing bed sheets, hanging towels, shaving my toes. I even took a slight interest in cooking because Sam likes to cook. I learned that cooking is an easy way to show someone that you love them, and an easier way to fish for compliments. If you put the food you've made in front of someone, they

Single Gal's DIET

+ = BREAKFAST

+ = LUNCH

CHICK PEAS + = DINNER

are obligated to tell you that they like it so that you continue to put food in front of them. It's Pavlovian, or something.

I wanted to use the kind of warmth and love that my mom used in her cooking, but that would require a proper lesson from her. In the years since her children left the house, my mom has been cooking less and less. A while ago, she stopped cooking entirely. Well, that's not completely true. Olga still cooks gourmet meals, but only for her dogs. At first, my brother, dad, or I would inevitably eat the food sitting in the fridge. "What is this? Beef?" I'd ask between big heaping bites. "No!" my mom would shout, snatching the container from my hands, "That's Sherry's chicken liver! Spit it out. She needs it for her poops."

The soundtrack of my parents' house has become my dad wandering from room to room complaining that he's hungry. "You have two hands, you know where the fridge is," my mom yells back. The Soup Queen abdicated her throne and it created a weird shift in my family dynamic. It feels like she lost interest in us, retired from being our mom, and turned all of her attention to her dogs' fecal rhythms. Have you ever been genuinely jealous of a Yorkie?

After my little brother graduated from high school, my mom stopped traveling, and eventually, stopped leaving the house altogether. "What is out there that I can't see in here?" she asked us, pointing to the computer.

"My apartment, for one," I told her.

"Oh, I can see that over the FaceTime."

On the bright side, having an agoraphobic mother is useful in the sense that she'll never pop in on me or judge my blind-to-dust ratio. But I still feel a little abandoned on Adult Island. I swam out here, and instead of gentle guidance, I've been left to fend for myself.

When it came time to attempt to cook a five-course meal

FRI (27) NORMAL POOP (MORNING)
SAT (28) 5 + 5 PRED. NO POOPS
SUN (29) 5 PRED. + ENEMA + MIRALAX 2 SMALL POOPS
MON (30) 5 MG PRED (M) EAT GOOD MORN + AFT. 1p. ANT. 2 SMALL POOPS
TUE (31) ANT. EAT GOOD / SMALL POOP M / DINNER GOOD 1 ANTIB 1 TRAMAD
WED (1) ANT + TRAM, POOP! EAT BR. / DINNER GOOD + 1 ANT. NO POOP.
THUR (2) ANT., EAT GOOD, POOP OK / DINNER OK, POOP, ANT.
FRI (3)
SAT (4)
SUN (5)
MON

A dog-related notecard my brother found in my parents' home.

on my own, it only made sense to try my hand at my mother's borscht. Convinced it'd be really poetic to have the recipe written in my mom's beautiful handwriting, I emailed to see if she could write it down and send me a scan. When she writes, you see a historically perfected form of strokes and ink distribution, each letter more striking than the last. It's art. I used to tell kids in school that she was a calligrapher because I wanted her to be more than just a housewife.

My dad called me back the afternoon I sent the request. His voice was strained from frustration. "Your mother doesn't want to do it."

I could hear Olga in the background, in her signature high-pitched tone, "It'll be faster to send her online link."

"Would it work if I wrote it for you?" my dad asked, trying to make things right. Unlike my mom, who was very present for our upbringing, my dad was always working long hours. Their roles have since reversed, with my dad being eager to please and my mom wanting all of us to leave her alone.

After years of my mom insisting that I let her teach me how to cook, she'd tapped out. My heart sank. When it comes to confronting my mom, I become oddly apathetic. She is this delicate orb I don't want to touch for fear of breaking it. Cracks are already forming in the glass, so instead I hold her lightly, never breathing, always hoping that she will stay intact, fearing what might happen the day she breaks.

"It's not a problem!" I squealed. "I'll work something out, no problem at all!"

An hour later, I received a borscht recipe beautifully written in my mother's handwriting. Clearly, there was a discussion I wasn't privy to. Surely it wasn't pleasant or civil, but something went down in my parents' house to convince my ever-so-stubborn mother to meticulously write out the recipe that she'd promised to teach me years earlier.

Борщ для лентяев

Сварить бульон:

Небольшой кусок мяса с косточкой или 1/4 курицы, 1 луковица, 1 морковка, 2-3 листа лаврушки, 6-8 горошин черного перца. Когда бульон готов, мясо отделить от костей, порезать на мелкие куски и положить в процеженный бульон.

Для заправки:

Нашинковать 3 картошки, 1 морковь, 1/4 среднего кочана капусты, 1 свеклу. Положить овощи в бульон и довести до кипения, убавить огонь, добавить 2-3 столовых ложки - лимонного сока, томатной пасты и сахара. Посолить по вкусу. Варить на маленьком огне 10-15 минут. Дать настояться 20-30 мин. Разлить по тарелкам, добавить сметану, чеснок и траву по вкусу.

Borscht for Lazy People

Boil the broth.
Add a small piece of meat, or ¼ chicken, 1 onion, 1 carrot, 2–3 bay leaves, 6–8 black peppercorns into a pot of water.
When broth is ready, separate meat from the bones, cut into small pieces, and put into the strained broth.
Shred: 3 potatoes, 1 carrot, ¼ head of cabbage, 1 beet.
Put vegetables into the broth and bring to a boil, reduce the heat, add 2–3 tablespoons of lemon juice, tomato paste, and sugar.
Add salt to taste and cook over low heat for 15–20 minutes.
Brew for 20–30 minutes. Pour into bowls, add sour cream, garlic, and herbs to taste.

When the recipe arrived in my inbox, I knew that was the end of my culinary education. There will be no sunlit mornings, my mother and me in matching aprons, delicately rolling out dough for pierogies, discussing ideal husband candidates. My mom will never come to my own kitchen and share a glass of wine as we make her famous cauliflower and broccoli soup, or pass down any more recipes unless I wrench them out of her tired, perfectly manicured hands.

I did cook a five-course meal,* eventually, using recipes that I found on the very same "online" she had originally suggested. It took me four hours, and I only messed up two of the dishes. At the end of the meal, I didn't attract a husband. Instead, Sam washed the dishes, and we curled up on the couch to watch a movie. The next day, he made breakfast for us, like he always does because he likes to cook, and I can now 100 percent confirm that I do not.

---

* If you're interested: Steak, stuffed mushroom caps, salad, spinach balls, and coffee cookies.

Maybe in that sense, I'm not an anomaly in my family. Maybe I am more like my mother than is initially apparent. My mom just pretended for years that she liked to cook because she loved her kids. She gave away little pieces of herself until they were all gone. Then her kids moved out and left her to fend for herself on Adult Island. On my mom's first day alone, she walked to the end of the driveway, cigarette in hand, took a deep breath, and decided she didn't want to fend for herself. So she walked back to her home, once filled with children, and decided to fill it with dogs instead.

Because at least dogs, as my mom always says, "will never leave you."

26

FIND A JOB I LOVE

On March 4, 2015, after almost a year and a half of unemployment, I started my first job after going viral for quitting my last one. A real live "industry" job. That's what people in Hollywood call it when you work in entertainment: "the industry." It sounds shiny, like you should only say it while wearing sunglasses.

I was so excited to work in an office with real people again that I left my apartment extra early, getting to Hollywood Center Studios at five a.m.—two hours before the work day started. The salmon-colored slabs of building caught the rising sun, making me feel like anything was possible—in a way that no other workspace ever had. I got to Stage 2, where I'd be working for the next two years, and rubbed my hands across a small bronze plaque that read: THE LUCY STAGE: ORIGINAL HOME OF "I LOVE LUCY" 1951–1953.

During my sixteen months of unemployment, I had begun to understand why housewives sleep with their gardeners and/or drown their children. When you spend too much time cooped up at home, your idea of reality starts to shift; your head begins to imagine alternate lives, and your body wonders if you should pursue them—like becoming a Nutella-jar artist.

I was constantly dizzy from all the contradictory feelings churning through my unemployed soul. Similar to Elisabeth Kübler-Ross's Five Stages of Grief, I experienced five stages of emotion while looking for my dream job.

Unlike the Kübler-Ross model, which at least boasts the concreteness of death, this model can't promise you anything except the unwavering pressure of pursuing a job you love.

A few months ago, a guy I used to work with in Taiwan messaged me. He wrote of his struggles committing to a full-time creative career and how he was hoping to have a conversation that was "less airy-fairy 'follow your dreams' stuff and more about, you know, how to ensure you stick stubbornly to the path you've marked out for yourself." My job, at the time, was taking notes and getting coffee for writers, yet he thought I'd cracked some secret code to career happiness.

It wasn't until I started receiving messages like this one* that it became clear to me that maybe, simply by pursuing my passions, I'd figured something out. Yes, my first job in the industry was thankless, poorly paid, and didn't include any writing, but I was working beneath real comedy writers (my office was literally *under* theirs), with real comedians, and others who knew how to get paid for making people laugh.

---

* After my video went viral I received many emails from strangers asking for advice on how to pursue their dream career. If you are one of those strangers reading this right now, thank you for reading, I love you. As for advice on how to pursue your dream career, the first step is to leave the job that's making you sad. But do it in a tactful way—unless you need to blow up that life, in which case may I suggest a not-negligible number of sparklers that spell out, "I QUIT."

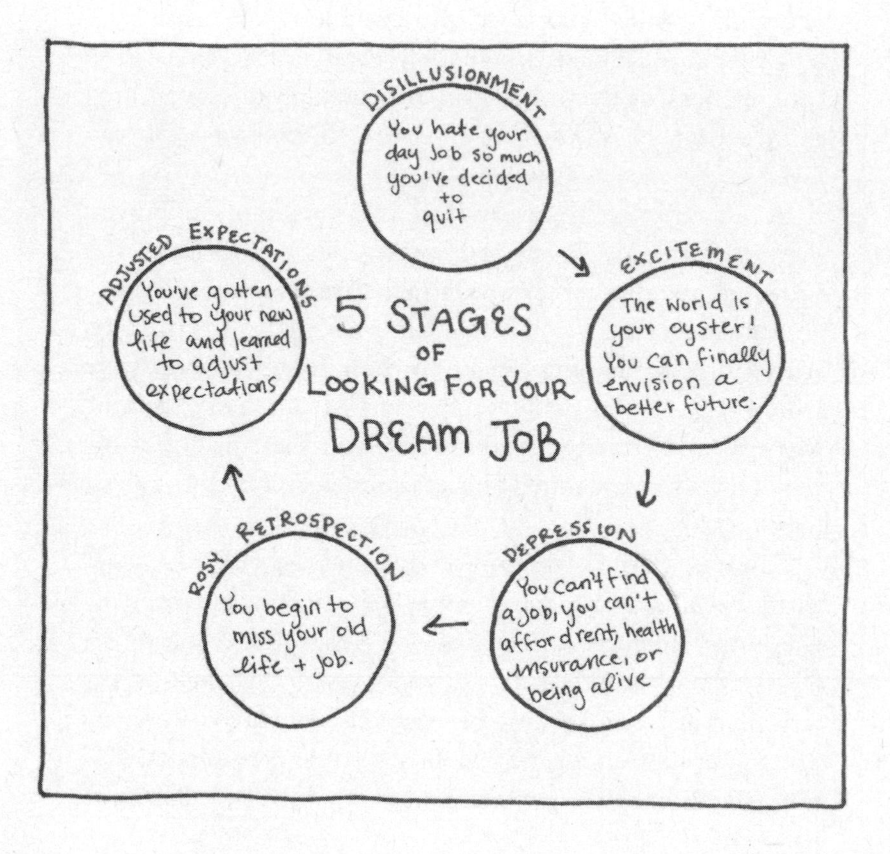
5 STAGES
OF
LOOKING FOR YOUR
DREAM JOB
DISILLUSIONMENT
You hate your day job so much you've decided to quit
EXCITEMENT
The world is your oyster! You can finally envision a better future.
DEPRESSION
You can't find a job, you can't afford rent, health insurance, or being alive
ROSY RETROSPECTION
You begin to miss your old life + job.
ADJUSTED EXPECTATIONS
You've gotten used to your new life and learned to adjust expectations

If I hadn't spent so much time on shadow-careers, I probably would've had a seat at that table. Unfortunately, it took a series of sidesteps, steps back, box steps, the movie *Step Up 2: The Streets,* and *sixteen* terrifying months of unemployment before I was in the correct field. It'd be greedy not to share the steps that got me here.

Step 1: Figure out where to direct your laser.

It's very easy to say, "My dream job is writing." Or cooking. Or colonoscopy captain to the stars! But there are thousands of mini-subcategories within each industry. Specificity is key to success. If you are able to verbalize exactly what you want, "A comedy writing job for a late-night unscripted television show," then you'll be surprised how many opportunities, even if they're peripheral, begin to present themselves.

Step 2: Apply.

This step seems incredibly obvious, but I found that a lot of people don't apply for jobs they think they're underqualified for. Imposter syndrome is alive and well within the neuroses of the working world, but that doesn't mean you shouldn't at least send in an application for a bomb-ass job. I've found that when companies put out an opening they describe their pie-in-the-sky ideal candidate. You can still be brought in for an interview even if you don't meet all of the requirements and it may result in a better-suited position later down the line.

For example, I applied to be a TV writer on *@midnight with Chris Hardwick,* a Comedy Central show. My résumé boasted zero prior TV experience *and* I'd been rejected for two lower-level positions on that same show. Either the executives were impressed with my persistence, or they took pity on me—regardless, they offered me a position as a researcher (five months after my initial failed interview). It was my very first job in Hollywood and I credit *@midnight* with saving me from self-destruction.

Step 3: Read your contracts.

Before you sign anything, whether it's for a freelance job or a job you've always wanted, make sure to read your contract. Since I began writing for myself I've read every line of every contract. I highlight things, and ask my smart lawyer friends what the legalese means. These contracts are often intentionally complicated, and thus not easy to understand, even for young and bright minds like you. It's very possible to sign something you don't understand and accidentally give away 100 percent ownership of your brilliant ideas—don't allow this to happen. Look out for "non-compete clauses"—they're poisonous to your growth. I've found that many contracts have standard language that can be adjusted to fit your specific desires. It's surprisingly simple to negotiate certain points if you're polite and patient.

Step 4: Adjust your expectations.

I used to think there were actual dream jobs, but as I fall further into my career in entertainment, it is becoming clear that there are only *ideal jobs.* An ideal job includes work that you're proud of, that you love, but that you also want to set on fire sometimes. It's perfectly normal to get a job you've been gunning toward your whole life, only to realize that it's less fulfilling and more stressful than you thought it would be. That's why it's important to adjust expectations. Don't look for a dream job, look for an ideal job.

If you can adjust your expectations, you'll be happier and more pleasant to work with—which will lead to promotions and better jobs in the future.

Step 5: Know your worth.

"Know your worth" sounds like something that should be scrawled across a sunset on an Instagram photo, but it's important to keep in mind when asking for a raise, working in a highly competitive job environment, or navigating the sticky power dynamics of the real world. Pursuing your ideal job turns your confidence into a pile of mush and opens you up to unexpected vulnerabilities. The slightest negative comment can derail your progress in a spectacular way. "They're not going to hire a first-time writer on a pilot," an executive once told me when trying to keep me on his show. This accepted wisdom scared me out of an interview for what would've been my first writing job. Instead, I accepted the executive's offer to promote me into a digital producer, later finding out that I *would've* gotten the writing job because my submission was that good. Sorry to brag, but it was.

I went straight back to that executive and asked for a 25 percent raise. I researched what other digital producers were making and told him I was grossly underpaid. He was impressed with my research, confidence, and aggressiveness and agreed to give me a 20 percent raise. Knowing your worth will help others know it too.

Step 6: Don't be afraid to demote yourself.

After three years in Los Angeles, and one missed opportunity to write on a show, it became clear that I was growing in the wrong direction. Working in digital production was fun (my team even won an Emmy), but it wasn't what I wanted to do.

Because I hadn't had any luck finding work as a TV writer, I quietly began looking for a job as a writers' assistant. Eventually, a new Comedy Central show created out of the pilot I'd passed up the previous year (it takes forever for a TV show to get made) was looking for a writers' assistant—and I was offered the job. When pursuing an ideal career, there is no room for pride, so I stepped down as a producer to take the job as an assistant. On the day of my twenty-ninth birthday, for the second time in three years, I started at the bottom again.

Step 7: Listen and learn.

I pride myself on being quick-witted and funny, but after entering an industry of literal comedians, it became clear that it's not the most useful trait in a room. A lot of people who start a new job are hungry to show off their goods, which often comes off as obnoxious. "He's too thirsty," a coworker once said about a researcher who was excellent at his job, but quick to speak up in the room. New-to-job people are always trying to prove themselves, whether it's with a fresh and interesting perspective or with their fresh and interesting personality. I quickly learned that it's much better to learn the personalities of those around you before injecting your own.

Step 8: Don't let them see you sweat.

At the last show I worked on, I became close friends with the host, comedian and all-around sweetie Guy Branum. Early on in my tenure as the writers' assistant, I forgot the boundaries of our relationship—he was my boss after all—and complained about a relatively minor work-related annoyance. Guy fanned out his palm, as he is known to do, and told me, "Oh, Marina, you're never supposed to let me see you sweat." It was one of the most useful things I've heard on a job.

No one likes working with a complain-y person.* In fact, I'd say it's probably the number-one killer of promising careers. When you feel frazzled or annoyed, take a deep breath and remember to never let them see you sweat.

Step 9: Enjoy the game of the pursuit.

Because you're stuck with it.

These steps are what have worked for me so far, but I'm no expert—just a gal who's happy with her current job. Everyone's success story is different, and mine is still in the development process.

The happiest ending to this chapter would be that I eventually moved up from writers' assistant to TV writer. My advice would hold more weight and I'd have a concrete response for the emails asking how to get to where I am. We could maybe all celebrate my long and winding journey at a hip party thrown by me, because I'd finally have more money than "just enough." But unfortunately, the entertainment industry doesn't let real life neatly fold inside a beautiful story box. It's messy and scary, never-ending and disappointing, but I'm okay with that because, thanks to Step 9, I've learned to enjoy the game of the pursuit.

---

* It helps to have *one* work confidant. Someone you can gossip with (I love to gossip!), and complain to, when things get hairy in the office. It's best to do all complaining offline and after hours, or at least use codenames so nothing can be traced back to you.

27

FLY FIRST CLASS

"I wish I was that man," my father longingly told me over Skype. He was referencing a viral news story about a Vietnamese-American doctor who was roughed up by airport police after refusing to give up his seat on an overbooked flight. Law enforcement officers broke his nose, knocked out his two front teeth, and gave him a concussion during the kerfuffle.

"Dad, he got hurt," I said.

"He only lost a few teeth," my father responded. Leave it to a Soviet to be jealous of someone who was "lightly" beaten by police. "He doesn't need the front ones to chew. Now he'll get free flights for life!"

My dad was right, the doctor won an unspecified financial settlement from United Airlines. My guess is that it's enough for him to have free flights for life, on his own airplane, to and from a small island that he also owns—plus a new set of teeth.

If he was really being honest with himself, I don't think my father would've given up two of his front teeth to fly for free. He is, after all, afraid of flying. Whenever we fly together, he shuts his eyes, grabs my hand, and doesn't let go until we've stopped ascending. "It's not natural," he tells me with his eyes still closed, "to be in the air this way."

I have a perfectly healthy relationship with flying. We're friends. As you know by now, the romanticism of airports is really what I'm after, but if I get to cap my trip to my favorite place with a flight, then throw that in too. Why not?

I treasured my flights to Asia. Long-ass flights allow me to act in a way that'd never be appropriate on the ground. I once watched five movies back to back. Five. Anywhere else, that'd be a warning sign of depression, but in the air there is nothing to do, which means you can do *anything.*

All the flight attendants on my flights to Taiwan had beautifully slender necks; their heads looked like they were balanced there, in midair. I especially loved when they dimmed the lights for "bedtime." It's like a big adult sleepover—except instead of listening to spooky stories told before bed, I just imagine all the ways my body could get sucked out of the cabin.

Some people are plane sleepers. I am not. My mother once handed me a tin of Altoids. "Here, try these," she said with a knowing look. Inside the tin was a variety of pills. "Don't take the blue ones and the white ones together," she instructed, "and don't drink if you take the ones that look like mints." I meant to write it down. I took two blue pills and washed them down with a couple glasses of wine. Nothing happened. A white one didn't do it for me either. I was wired for the whole flight. My first afternoon in Taiwan, though, was spent looking for a duck under my bed. Not sure if the pills and hallucinating a duck are related.

Because of my sleeplessness on flights, I often have to occupy myself with the passengers around me. I can spend hours imagining their lives. Coach is really the best place to do it—

the people are so vibrant and they have loud, open conversations, as if everyone around them is hard of hearing.

"Hey, Facebook," a woman on Spirit Airlines once spontaneously yelled at her phone. "I'm just here sitting pretty in the air. Facebook, what's *your* favorite airline?" I leaned in to see if Facebook had an answer. It didn't.

Another time I sat next to a couple who spent the first half of the flight kissing each other's palms, and the second half in a very complicated breakup. I hadn't started out in that seat: a very tall woman with dyed black hair politely asked to switch so that she could sit next to her teenage daughter. Switching seats with people inflates my ego. "Of course, no problem," I always say, unclasping my usually too-tight seatbelt. I refuse to loosen airplane seatbelts. *I'm just as small as whoever sat here last*, I tell myself. If the seatbelt is too tight, then I just sit there, not breathing.

Another time, on a four-hour flight to Chicago, a flight attendant had to explain to two teenage girls that they couldn't watch Snapchat without headphones. It was clear that someone had complained about them, and the flight attendant was trying to be civil. "Ugh, sor-ry, I didn't read that in the airplane *rules*," the girl next to me muttered. I blatantly rolled my eyes, hoping that maybe if I did it hard enough, the flight attendant wouldn't associate me with them. "Excuse me, ma'am," the other girl said before the flight attendant could escape, "can we get two pillows and blankets?"

"I'm sorry," she responded, keeping her cheery disposition, "we don't offer that in coach."

"But the people up front got them."

I could've grabbed her pretty teenage head and twisted it off her body. *Don't you know*, I wanted to say, *those people get pillows and blankets because they're better than us*.

The closest thing America has to a caste system can be seen on commercial airliners. Sure, there are societal injustices with invisible barriers, but commercial airplanes have unapologetic organizational systems which value the rich and punish the poor via nonexistent legroom, sobriety, and individuals with no volume control.

I'd never be a "First Class" person, due to my inability to make/spend* money, but goddammit did I want people to look at me the way I looked at the people sitting in first class, just to know what it felt like to be envied by strangers.

My cousin Polina got bumped up to first class once. "Bumped up," that's how she said it. Casually. She made it sound so easy, like when a table at your favorite restaurant opens up earlier than expected. *But she's not even married!* I thought. Only newlyweds, famous people, and white men get unexpected "bump ups."

It turns out that young ladies interviewing for impressive companies also get offers to fly first class. I learned this when a tech startup in Seattle was looking to fill a head writing position and offered to fly me out to "meet with the team."

I wasn't planning on accepting the offer, because I'd just gotten my first job in Los Angeles—which came with a self-promise not to move as soon as the mirage of a better life appeared. A-few-years-ago Marina would've been riddled with guilt about accepting a free trip for a job offer she wasn't going to take, but the Marina of today has been burned by so many powerful men at tech startups that she had no problem taking advantage of the opportunity.

I flew to Seattle and met the staff; a young, diverse set of creatives who liked to work almost as much as they liked to

---

* I hate spending money. One time, it took me fifty-five minutes to choose between two pregnancy tests—one for eight dollars and one for twenty-three dollars. I mean really, why the fifteen-dollar difference? Is one more accurate than the other? Does the twenty-three-dollar one come with a referral?

drink. The office had a lot of open space and difficult-to-understand communal couches. You know the ones where you're not sure where to sit because they are shaped like amoebas? Those.

On my last night in Seattle, I called Sam's cousins to come out and destroy the city with me. We started with drinks at my hotel, then went to an alcoholic slushy spot, a pirate bar, and a speakeasy—the night became a blur after that. Which made my early morning flight slightly inconvenient considering I wanted to die when I woke up. My hangover was so bad that I considered accepting the job offer to avoid getting on an airplane.

But a life goal is a life goal. I crawled onto the plane for my very first first-class flight* and slumped into my seat. It was so large that my feet were dangling off the edge, little-kid style. The flight attendant greeted me with a mimosa, the most decadent of breakfast drinks—orange juice and diamonds, really. The second my mouth touched the liquid, my stomach dropped. Whoever came up with the phrase "hair of the dog" probably died of cirrhosis.

As people loaded onto the airplane, many, many minutes after the flight attendants gently tucked me into my oversized seat, I did everything in my power to avoid eye contact with them. If they got a good look at my young, undeserving face, they'd immediately see that I was a fraud who had lied her way into first class.

When coach class was safely seated out of our first-class

---

* On the flight to Seattle, I sat in the row *behind* first class in something called premium economy (I'd never heard of it before). It turns out food and drink are also free in premium economy, but I was too much of a ding-dong to realize it. I declined all the flight attendant's kind attempts at wining and/or dining me—completely missing out on what would've been my introductory first*ish*-class flight. But whatever, you have to sit in front of the thin little curtain for it to count.

view, the show began; flight attendants walked through the aisles pretending we were important people who they cared for. They treated me nicer than any stranger has ever treated me. At one point, I accidentally dropped my napkin because I was hungover as all get out. I thought that if I stared at the napkin with enough intensity, I could will it back into my hands. Suddenly, it began to move. It floated up off the ground and into my opened palm. Like magic! Of course, there was a flight attendant attached to it, but still!

"I'm sorry, Miss Shifrin," she said, as if it were *her* fault that I dropped the napkin. Or maybe she truly felt bad for me. *"I'm sorry you're in first class,* Miss Shifrin*—it must be difficult, the pressure of maintaining this facade."*

"It's okay," I told her.

I ordered a Bloody Mary because my Uncle Alan once said that a shot of vodka would cure even the strongest of hangovers, but it didn't work. I was trapped in my own personal hangover hell. My tray looked like a science experiment in alcoholism. A sip of a mimosa, a sip of a black coffee, a sip of a Bloody Mary, and an untouched omelet. I looked around me. No one was talking to their Facebook, or fighting with the flight attendants, no one was breaking up or even memorable. I missed the people who would ask me to switch seats, or look over my shoulder to spoil flight magazine crossword answers, or divulge that they're from Ohio but had decided to visit their daughter in Los Angeles as a surprise. "She's an actress and she's very good." No one asked me out, or showed me pictures of their knee surgery. I wanted to go back to my coach people.

At a certain point on the flight, the airplane hit some turbulence and a wave of nausea washed over me. I sheepishly asked for some water. "Of course, Miss Shifrin," the flight attendant said, which made me uncomfortable. *Miss Shifrin, that's my future's name.* The water was there immediately.

I brought the glass (glass!) to my lips, hoping to quell some of my queasiness, but as the rim touched my mouth, the plane lurched again and caused me to smash my front teeth on the edge of the cup.

I unbuckled my (very loose) seatbelt and made my way to the bathroom, where I inspected my teeth in the mirror, tapping the front two to make sure they were in there securely. They were. My focus shifted to my face. My cheeks were saggy, my skin was gray, my eyes (one of which was still sporting the eyeliner from the night before) were puffy. I had no business being in first class. I splashed water on my face, pinched my cheeks, put my hair in a bun, and leaned in closer to the mirror to reinspect my teeth. Even if I only need my back teeth to chew, I was still glad to have the front ones in place.

28

BECOME A GOOD HOST

Sam says he's never seen me happier than when someone cancels on me. "Yes, because that means I can get into pajamas faster," I tell him. I've become somewhat of a misanthrope in my late twenties.

Every now and then, when I haven't bothered to see anyone in weeks, I worry that I'm catching some of my mom's agoraphobia. But mostly I happily sit in an oversized shirt watching old episodes of *Chopped* while heckling the dummy chefs in my empty apartment.

Whenever a loved one says they're coming to visit me, my instinctual reaction is to get angry. "Why me?" I yell at the ceiling. For someone who mapped her entire career around entertainment, I'm awful at entertaining. I haven't had a proper birthday party since I was about thirteen years old. I've had more root canals than I've had people over to my apartment. I don't understand those who enjoy hosting. What if you get sick? Or your visitors don't like your food? Or your toilet breaks? Or they're bored? It's too stressful. I take all this worry, ball it up, and throw it in the faces of my friends who are visiting.

Unfortunately, when you live in the middle of a tourist trap, friends from across the country will always want to come see you. It sucks. I love my friends, but I love my space even more. That being said, you do eventually get to an age when you have to own at least one extra set of clean sheets for visitors.

The first time I had visitors as an adult, I was twenty-two years old and had been in New York for four months. The poorest months in my life, and two bitches from college decide to visit me? Of course, because I lived in the Big City! Sure, they were two of my closest friends and they loved me and blah, blah, blah. But you do not visit your poor friend, during one of the biggest adjustments in her life, and say, "Why not, I'm on vacation!" to the second round of oyster shooters.

If I may address the visitor before the visitee for a moment, please follow a few rules:

- Do not visit for more than four days. I, myself, prefer three-day visits. If you need to stay longer, break up your stay among multiple friends or Airbnbs. Regardless of how kind and hospitable (unlike me) your friends are, regardless of how much they beg you to stay longer—everyone is relieved when their visitors leave and they can peacefully go back to their *30 Rock* marathons.

- Be sensitive to your host's financial situation. Maybe they just moved! Maybe they just switched jobs! Maybe they're saving up to buy a house or make a baby. Whatever it is, people always have weird money stuff going on, and it's none of your business. If they live next door to your dream five-star restaurant, maybe offer to take *them* out as a thank-you for a free stay.

- Pepper in some sightseeing options that your friend can politely bow out of. When you visit someone, they feel obligated to entertain you. That's why they're all like, "What do you want to do when you're here!?" "I'm down for whatever" or "I don't care! I just want to see you" is a very sweet sentiment that you can neatly fold up and put back inside your mouth. Being specific and direct with what you'd like to do when visiting a friend will help your friend with planning their days and yours.

- When entering a home, ask if you should take off your shoes. This might be hyper-specific to me, but I hate, hate, hate asking people to take off their shoes when they come into my house. It makes me feel like Larry David's worst nightmare. But between my Russian heritage and Sam's Asian heritage, we both grew up in strict shoes-off homes. Besides, shoes are so dirty and gross, why anyone would wear them inside their house is beyond me.

- Never come empty-handed. Russians would *never* enter someone else's home without a gift. Flowers. Alcohol. Soap. When you're visiting a home it's appropriate to bring something for your host(s). I like to bring something related to wherever I'm living. Maybe cheese or jam from a Los Angeles–based company . . . At the very least, I like to bring joke gifts—toilet paper (everyone needs it), a balloon animal–making kit, a head massager, a framed photo of Ted Danson—whatever. I simply refuse to show up empty-handed.

Now that we've gotten being a good visitor out of the way, you're ready to be a good host! Which I was *not* when my college friends came to visit. All I had in my fridge was a half-eaten jar of peanut butter, a canister of instant oatmeal, and some whole wheat tortillas. I didn't even have glasses for water. When my friends got to my apartment, they were shocked at the conditions I was living in. "You don't have any food," Meredith exclaimed. This was at a time when my office had a fully stocked fridge; my diet consisted of half a sandwich for lunch and the other half for dinner. Other nights, I stole fridge food from the family I was babysitting for. I spent about ten dollars a week on groceries and was proud of it.

I did not, at all, contemplate that I needed to buy food for my visitors. I was already putting them up, what more could they want? "Putting them up" of course meant that I let Meredith and Kate sleep in my bed while I slept on the couch, like a martyr—especially because it was hot and the living room did *not* have air conditioning.

Meredith had never been to New York before, and her first tourist activity was going to Associated Market on Fifth Avenue to buy me groceries. A weird way to start a visit to the Big Apple, if you ask me.

"You can't live like this," she told me while loading cereal into a shopping cart.

It wasn't until years later that I understood what it meant to be a good host. My video had just gone viral, and I had an unexpected opportunity to go on the *Today Show*. My pen-pal Amy, who single-handedly coached me through my twenty-fifth year of life, offered me a spot in her apartment. When I got there, she took me under her wing like the scared baby bird that I was. She had clean sheets, an extra razor, snacks, tea, dessert, and cold vodka in the fridge. After staying with her, I realized that being a good host is a learned skill that

THE 8 ITEMS YOU NEED TO BE A GOOD
Host
Snacks
TORTILLA CHIPS
Milk for their Coffee
* ask your visitor which milk they prefer
Extra Toiletries
Clean Bedding
Fresh Towels
Tidy Home
a List of Activities Ready
Ingriedients for their favorite Drink
MILK
OR
OLIVES
Vodka

needs cultivating. It's more than just letting someone sleep in your house, it's making them feel appreciated.

Having visitors is inevitable. Believe me, I've tried to avoid it—but people love you, or they love your city, or they love a combination of both, and they're going to want to come visit.

There's a way that you can prepare yourself and your home to not only show your visitors a good time, but also, just maybe, squeeze in a little fun yourself. Here are a few things I like to do to avoid getting all pouty and stressed when a friend comes to stay with me.

BECOME A TOURIST TOO!

Sam and I recently had friends visiting from Germany who were very frank about what they wanted to see. They sent us a list of desires and open-invited us to come to whatever tickled our fancy. One of the more exciting items on their list was touring Warner Bros. Studios. I love tours, regardless of what's being toured, and had never been (despite my three years in Los Angeles). So, one Saturday morning, we all piled into a car and made our way to the lot. I was just as excited to see the *Gilmore Girls* set as the next guy. Overall, it was a great experience that reminded me, *Hey, I live in a cool city with fun things to do.* I've since made a list of things I've been *meaning* to see (museums, tours, hikes, beaches, shows) for when guests are in town. That way, the experience becomes novel and exciting for me too.

SET YOUR FRIEND FREE FOR AN AFTERNOON (OR A DAY).

That same couple had Levi's shopping (foreigners love Levi's) on their list. I'm not much of a shopper, so I sent them off into the world (with directions of course) to find some jeans. A lot of my friends are independent people who don't mind exploring a city on their own. Obviously, don't leave them high and dry, but if you need an afternoon off from playing host, by all means get down with your bad self. Chances are it will give your guest much-needed break/alone time and you the reset needed to continue being a delightful host with a cheery demeanor (even if that's not your natural state of being).

SUGGEST AN IN-HOME MEAL.

The thing that stresses me out most about having visitors is that it's expensive. I hate spending money, but don't want my money habits to get in the way of a friend's trip. I tend to always say yes for drinks, eats, and entertainment, which can add up over a few days. I've found that cooking a meal at home is a great way to take a break from the exhaustion of running around—your guests are tired too, I promise—and a good way to cut down on the cost of having visitors. Plus, if your friends are as lovely or incredible as mine, they'll offer to cook, or at least clean.

IT'S OKAY TO SAY NO.

I once had a friend ask if she could crash for nine days while working on a project in LA. I knew that prolonged periods with visitors stress me out, but I said yes anyway. On her fourth day in Los Angeles, I came home to a thank-you note with a gift certificate to a local café. She said that she felt as though she'd overstayed her welcome and booked an Airbnb nearby. I was mortified. Instead of being up front and asking her to split up her visit between two spots, I made her feel uncomfortable in my home. She, a Queen-Goddess of Tact, picked up on my sour-face mood and salvaged our friendship by finding her own spot. I vowed to be up front with my guests from that day forward.

A few years ago, Meredith came to visit me in LA. Not to brag, but I had wine *and* a makeshift cutting board charcuterie plate waiting for her. "Where's the half-eaten jar of peanut butter?" she asked with a smile. My evolution was splayed out in the details of my snacks. Sure, I was worried about whether or not she'd have fun, but at least I was a little more refined, a little more stable, and a lot cleaner than I had been during those early months in New York.

I still get stressed when someone tells me they're coming to visit, but if a friend does decide to stop by I always have snacks at the ready and vodka chilling in the fridge.

29

VISIT RUSSIA

In the early hours of the late afternoon, James, a short boy with chipmunk cheeks and a White Sox hat, screamed "Communist!" at me until the veins in his neck began to bulge. The insult was as surprising as it was confusing. I'd heard many jabs in the twelve years I'd been alive, mostly from my parents, but none as topical as this one.

I was in sixth grade, months into my leather-jacket phase, an awkward anamorph trapped between girl and woman, and James just handed me yet another thing to add to my list of insecurities.

When it comes down to the bevy of pejoratives you can call an immigrant, *Communist* isn't all that bad. It even feels a little retro-punky. Still, I didn't like James or his tone, so I pulled my collar to my mouth and ordered a KGB operative to "visit" his house.*

Even if I'd *wanted* to serve up a worthy retort to his histori-

* A few weeks later a tree fell through James's roof. I'm not saying the two are related, but the timing is curious.

cally relevant affront, I had no concept of communism, or Russia in general. My parents' stories made it seem like everyone spent their free time standing in never-ending lines, waiting for nondescript goods, while icy rain shards cut up their cheeks. Our life before America was shrouded in mystery, almost like it never existed.

When it was time to leave Russia, Olga and Vladimir packed hundreds of photos into two boxes and shipped them to my Uncle Alan in Chicago. Photos of me as a newborn, of my parents when they were young, of my grandmothers who passed before I was born, and of my grandfathers who loved them. Each photo contained a little memento of my past, which made it particularly devastating when both boxes got lost in the mail.

So many questions disappeared with those boxes. What did my mom look like when she was pregnant? How did my dad wear his hair in his twenties? Did our apartment have carpet? Or rugs on the walls? Were there trees in our yard? Did I look like my grandmothers?

We only had a handful of pictures, all taken right before we immigrated. In one, everybody is ecstatically envisioning the promise of a better future, but that excitement is hidden under a stern layer of closed-mouth smiles. The sad eyes and straight lips are what I imagined all of the people in Russia looked like. A culture too somber to be happy. Too tough to grin.

"The post office people were jealous of us," my mom once told me. "They lost those photos on purpose."

This sour and suspicious tone coated all of my parents' anecdotes, the few that they shared. There was the time my mother's tonsils were removed without general anesthesia. "They put a metal pipe in my mouth so that I couldn't close it during the surgery," she casually told me in the ice cream aisle of the grocery store. We were buying Breyer's for my little brother who'd just had his tonsils out. Or the time

I am the young boy in the middle.

my twenty-seven-year-old dad watched paramedics load his mother into an ambulance. "Oh god, what if I don't survive this?" my grandmother said as they closed the door. She didn't.

My mom was even younger when her mother died. She returned from summer camp only to find out that her mother had unexpectedly passed away. My mom was thirteen. No one told her about her own mother's death because they "didn't want to ruin her summer vacation." Death was just a minor inconvenience when compared to its burdensome predecessor: life.

Despite all the negatives, I had a gnawing pull toward the mother country. A pull that turned into an all-out yank when the country became relevant again for the first time since the Cold War. Headlines of hacking, sanctions, golden showers, and other incendiary rumors circling the 2016 presidential election were bleeding into my daily life. I became an unwilling cultural ambassador to a country I hadn't been in since birth. Coworkers, friends, and casual acquaintances bombarded me with questions about Russia, questions I hadn't the first clue how to answer.

One morning, shortly after yet another news story of rising United States–Russia tensions broke, I bought a ticket to Moscow. Curiosity is the catalyst of growth. Minutes after sharing my news on Facebook, three friends requested that I not "get kidnapped." I couldn't figure out whether to be amused or offended.

I landed in Russia in the afternoon on a Friday in July. I wore a green flannel shirt, black jeans, dirty Vans, four pearl necklaces, and the unmistakable stench of someone who had been crammed inside a metallic cylinder filled with 402 bloated strangers for twelve hours.

It was odd wearing *four* pearl necklaces. Three necklaces are understandable, but the fourth made it feel like I should have a cocktail in one hand and a vacuum in the other. The necklaces were gifts from my father to his cousins. He insisted on keeping their price tags on so that "your aunts know how much they cost." I also had: Crest 3D white strips for my cousin who wanted "white teeth like an American," one of my dad's oil paintings, an iPhone 4S, a jump drive with footage of my grandpa and his brothers, some tank tops sporting the California bear, four hundred dollars in cash for my mom's sister, a purple tween purse filled with glow-in-the-dark stars, and Ghirardelli chocolates. When immigrants return to their birth country they become pack mules. Distant relatives and friends burst into their lives asking for various parcels to be delivered on their behalf. All sorts of odds and ends are methodically shoved inside belongings, until one doesn't even know what's in her suitcase anymore. Apologies, TSA.

I adjusted my pearls, as if arranging them neatly would make me less likely to incur an import tariff, and got in line for immigration. Greeting your birth nation for the first time is like tasting a long-forgotten dish your grandma used to cook. It's a little bit of déjà vu mixed with nostalgia for something you've never really known. My restless attention wandered to the other people in line: the old women with long earlobes—stretched from the strain of heavy jewelry; the little girls with hair in thick, perfect braids, their stern mothers hustling everybody along. Hearing strangers speak a language that I had previously only heard among family members made me feel a contrived sense of connection to everyone around me. Immediate guilt followed. It felt like I was disrespecting my parents by returning to the country that had stripped us of our birthright, citizenship, and family simply because we were Jewish. Olga and Vladimir had clawed their way out of Russia and here I was . . . on vacation.

When I got to the immigration window, the woman stared at me to make sure my face matched my passport. Her deep navy suit starkly contrasted her faded skin, and my entire body itched to smile at her, launch into the Russian I wasn't able to use in America. But instead I stared back, with a glare just as intense. I grew nervous. Should I greet her in English? Or maybe I should speak Russian?

My dad warned me against speaking Russian. "They don't like the people who got out," he told me shortly after I bought my ticket. "They'll hear your accent and arrest you."

"Keep your mouth shut," my mom yelled from the kitchen.

Worried that my sunny Midwestern disposition would make me stand out, I bought a small phrase book titled *Just Enough Russian: How to Get By and Be Easily Understood*. In the "Meeting People" section you learned how to offer a drink, a cigarette, and a cigar—all before learning how to introduce yourself.

Meeting people/17

Meeting people

[*See also 'Everyday expressions', p. 13*]

Can I offer you ...	**Хотите** khat*i*tye
a drink?	**что-нибудь выпить?** sht*o*-nibut' v*y*pit'
a cigarette?	**сигарету?** sigar*ye*tu
a cigar?	**сигару?** sig*a*ru
Are you staying long?	**Вы надолго приехали?** vy nad*o*lga pri*ye*khali

Name

What's your name?	**Как Вас зовут?** kak vas zav*u*t
My name is ...	**Меня зовут ...** min*ya* zav*u*t

When the colorless agent finished staring at my face she begrudgingly hit her computer keys and printed a small slip of paper. She shoved it toward me and made an X near a line. "Sign," she said in English. She made a second X. "Sign," she said again. That was the end of my first interaction with a Russian person on Russian soil. "Sign. Sign." I didn't even have a chance to offer her a drink.

There's an addictive rush to landing somewhere you haven't been before (or at least in twenty-seven years). Being on foreign land comes with new rules and customs. The social pressures typically towering over every interaction are lifted, giving you the freedom to act in innovative ways. "Oh, unapologetic camel toes are very trendy in Los Angeles," I'd say, tugging at my crotch. Traveling allows you to temporarily try on a new persona. It's invigorating.

Endorphins coursed through my body as I stepped out of customs. My second cousin, Ilya, was already waiting for me at baggage claim. Ilya, a short dude with a bouncy gait and a nervous laugh, carries himself with confidence and mischievous magnetism. He has some important job where he makes a lot of money charming rich people into giving him more money. His livelihood depends on his charisma and it shows in all of his interactions.

"Welcome home," he said, wrapping his arms around my waist and drawing me in for a kiss. I pursed my lips together in anticipation, but his kiss adeptly landed on my cheek. My childhood was strung together by an endless series of cheek kisses, but I'd fallen out of the habit after college. I had forgotten how adult and feminine it made me feel.

Before I realized what was happening, Ilya dove toward my luggage, ripping my bags from my hands. This was the first of many reminders that Russia is a heavily patriarchal society where women should never be burdened with the literal or metaphorical weight of life. Too tired to assert my independence, I peeled the pearl necklaces off my oily skin instead.

"Sis, do you mind if I smoke a cigarette?" Ilya asked. In Russian, the word *cousin* is translated as "secondary sister," which is usually shortened to "sister," or "sis." It instantly made me feel close to him.

We stepped outside and I was hit with a wave of swampy humidity that made my chest heavier than it already was. My thick flannel desperately clung to my body, making me regret the six sweaters and jackets I'd packed.

Ilya popped a cigarette into his mouth and tipped the pack toward me. "Do you want a cigarette?" he asked. He must've read the same phrase book as me. His pack had a close-up of a man's neck, with tubes protruding from a large hole. You could see a few rotting tooth stumps jutting out from the man's otherwise naked gums. The word *EMPHYSEMA* was stamped across the photo in big, Cyrillic letters. Ilya caught me staring. "We like to collect these," he said, tapping the warning label. "I have cancer in my car."

Ilya started up his second cigarette as we neared his brand-new BMW. Beads of sweat congregated underneath my boobs as the midday sun bore down on us. Over the next two weeks, I'd spend a lot of time standing next to cousins as they finished up cigarettes. Underneath trees, in alleyways, on balconies, in light rain, and unforgiving sun. Cigarettes were my closest companion and by the end of the trip I couldn't taste things in quite the same way.

I unbuttoned my flannel, exposing a sheer tank top underneath; no time for modesty in this weather. Every time I had imagined Russia it was in the context of cold and snow; heat was nowhere in my purview, and neither were German luxury vehicles. All of my parents' stories revolved around a shortage of food and products, and an abundance of sadness. It was clear my perception of Russia was about to get turned on its head.

Even though Ilya carried the small stature that comes

with Shifrin genetics, he refused to let me help him load my enormous suitcase into his car. I watched as he struggled, using a sort of humping motion to tip my baggage full of winter wear into the trunk.

"You ready?" he wheezed into the car. I was.

As we drove through the green outskirts toward Moscow, gargantuan apartment buildings began to crowd the road, not a single-family home in sight. It was clear that keeping up appearances was important to Russia, and the appearance it wanted to keep was "We can crush you."

"Aren't they beautiful?" Ilya asked while peeking up at the buildings.

No, I thought. "Big," I responded in my limited Russian. I could get my point across, but mostly sounded like an intelligent toddler. "Mmm . . . I love mushrooms. Mushrooms in soup. Mushrooms with potatoes. Mushroom pierogis. All mushrooms . . ." I prattled off at my first family dinner because the word was easy for me to pronounce. Every subsequent dish I ate during my trip had mushrooms in it.

Later in that same meal, my dad's cousin, a college professor, asked about my hobbies in America. "I like to pee," I enthusiastically told him. The whole table was quiet for a moment before bursting into laughter. (In Russian, *to pee* and *to write* are the same word with different emphases: писать vs. писать.) As the last traces of embarrassment left my face I thought about all the times I had laughed at my parents' own awkward pronunciations of American words: *Shit* for sheet. *Van* for when. *Bitch* for beach. *Zief* for thief. Fresh hues of shame colored my face.

Ilya's apartment was on the fourth floor of a pre–1917 Revolution building with walls as thick as my couch. It had the same sweetly stale rye smell as my grandfather's immigrant-run building in Chicago. *Do all large groups of Russians smell like rye bread?* I thought as we approached Ilya's comically small elevator. In order to fit inside, Ilya and I had to straddle my luggage and squeeze our bodies together. Normally, I'd be empathetically uncomfortable with this level of proximity, but I knew that Russians were used to living in small quarters, and didn't have issues with physical contact in the way that I, or my rigid American counterparts, did.

As soon as the elevator doors opened, Sophia, Ilya's mom, who couldn't have been over five feet tall, pushed him out of the way and leaped into my arms. She was the female version of my father, with the same delicate wrists and bullfrog shape. Her worn skin, large chest, and skinny legs looked like my future.

"Did you see any grizzly bears out there?" Sophia grinned, knowing that my dad had prepared me for the worst. Years of smoking turned her voice into a raspy whisper.

I introduced myself with a formal greeting and quickly learned that Aunt Sophia, who insisted I call her Sopha or the diminutive Sophka, didn't do anything according to formalities. I should've guessed when she greeted me in a neon-yellow nightie and nothing else. "Do you like it?" she asked, pointing her tiny brown leg out like an elderly ballerina. "I bought it just for your visit!" she cackled. Her laugh sounded like a deflating mattress, making it my main objective to make her laugh as much as possible.

As I dutifully slipped off my shoes at the entrance, Ilya's wife, Olga,* came out of the bedroom. I was taken with how beautiful she was. Her circular Uzbek face and fox-like features were complemented by her bottle-blond hair. She had a

* Yes, Olga is also my mother's name. In fact, I have another cousin on the same side of the family named Olga, also married to an Ilya. There are three Anyas, three Tanyas, a couple of Sanyas, and a handful of Borises in my family. Russian names must be paired with a possessive—*your Olga, my Boris, his Anya, her Vladimir*—so everyone will know who is actually being talked about.

tiny waist, a defined collarbone, and weightless breasts that sat atop her chest. Normally women with such beauty, especially Russian ones, would've intimidated me, but I was thrilled that the Shifrin gene pool was adding a model-esque blonde to the rotation. Still, I envied her elasticity.

Despite the fact that she didn't speak any English, Olga and I got very close during my trip, not only because she was tasked with entertaining me for much of it, but also because she was practicing for her beauty school finals. She'd spend an hour each day lightly correcting my pronunciation while staring into my dumb face, brushing different colors onto it, stepping back to observe her work before leaning back in—her nose nearly touching mine. It was quite intimate.

"I have a mustache!" I yelled the first time she got near my face.

She looked closer and furrowed her brow. "You do! Oh my god," she exclaimed. After her laughter subsided, Olga began to delicately pluck the hairs on my upper lip because "women cannot have mustaches."

The first time Olga did my makeup was for Ilya's work retreat in the Moscow countryside. The retreat was also my first time interacting with non-family Russians. They were mainly interested in homelessness and whether or not Americans *actually* thought Russian spies had tampered with the election.

Early in the evening, a man with sleeve tattoos, blue eyes, and a shirt that read "Carry On and Slap the Bitch" grilled me about homelessness in America.

"Is it true that your homeless are overweight?" he asked while swaying from side to side.

We had shown up to the retreat halfway through; many of the attendees were lobster-faced and wasted. He took two steps downwind of me and lit a cigarette.

Another of Ilya's coworkers, a nicer man with a gentler

energy, added to Slap the Bitch's inquiry. "My cousin was in San Francisco and he said that they all had cell phones." Slap the Bitch's mouth dropped open and he began to make a sound I could only describe as "drunken stoner chortle."

I looked out beyond the crew of tanked consultants (or maybe they were data engineers? I still couldn't quite figure out what it was that Ilya did) toward the beautiful lake. It was like the setting of a Nicholas Sparks novel. The muggy heat gave the edges of my vision a dreamy blur and the scene was lush with greenery. In the middle of the lake was an inflatable jungle gym infested with Russian men in speedos. They were climbing ropes, hanging on walls, jumping off platforms. It was a jubilant scene filled with the elated squeals of summer—a new contrast to what I had in my head for Russia. Everyone was sopping, sunburnt, yet completely ignorant about socio-economic dynamics.

The whole country felt liked a warped version of America in the seventies; there was no compassion for the complexities of homelessness, no one wore seatbelts, people were suspicious of the gays, men worked, women cooked, and everyone smoked two packs a day despite the warnings printed on the cartons. Sure, there weren't hour-long lines for bread rations anymore, but people were wearing shirts that said SLAP THE BITCH with no social ramifications.

I spent most of the trip teetering between relief that my family had left and sadness over my disconnect with the culture. The disconnect was painfully obvious when it came to my complete ignorance of the famous monuments that littered the city. On my first day, Ilya brought me to a pond near his home. "Do you know where we are?" he asked, barely able to contain his giddiness.

"Outside?" I wagered.

Ilya spread his arms. "We're at Patriarch's Ponds!" he gushed. His entire face dropped at my lack of reaction.

"Patriarch's Ponds?" he repeated. "Master and Margarita? It starts right here, right in this spot."

"Oh yes, I've been meaning to read it . . ." I lied. Russian literature is notorious for its distinctively flowery ability to dissect the human condition, but unfortunately, translated novels "are not like the real thing" as my dad always tells me, and "the nuances are lost on foreign-speakers." Ilya bought me a copy of *Master and Margarita* the next day, demanding that I read it. It's sitting under my coffee cup as I type. I'll get to it next, Ilya, I promise.

A disappointing result of having left Russia at such a young age was my stunted grasp of the language. Speaking Russian for two weeks was difficult—the words felt clunky in my mouth. I became a half-speed version of myself. Well-meaning people, too impatient to wait for me to find the right words—were constantly finishing my sentences. I longed for the sophisticated ease with which my cousins spoke.

Truthfully, I was jealous of Ilya. He grew up with a rich, historical, complicated culture at his fingertips, while I grew up with Maggiano's and making out in minivans. My parents left one of the most populous cities in Europe in exchange for a two-car garage and the boring stability of the suburbs—I couldn't help feeling like I'd missed out.

Sensing that I was in the middle of compiling an unintelligible retort to Slap the Bitch, Olga pulled me away for a walk. Although she was younger than me, she knew better than to get into a fight with a drunk man. She was cooler than that. "Let him think what he wants, you focus on yourself," she told me as we walked down a tree-lined path. I swallowed my annoyance.

Everything in my staunchly progressive bones tells me not to say this, but it was nice to take a break from being a disappointed feminist all the time. I got used to spending my days getting my makeup done, and my evenings being wined and dined by my cousin and his male friends. Toward the end of the trip, I stopped reaching for my wallet, knowing that it was a useless gesture. I didn't touch any doorknobs or pay for a single thing. Even souvenirs—after a lot of back and forth—were paid for by cousins. Male cousins who worked hard, drank harder, and were perpetually exhausted—I much preferred the laidback lives of their wives. At least during my two weeks there.

I forgot how fun it can be to be a girl. My struggle to succeed in a male-dominated industry had muted my desire to be seen as a woman—I tried, so hard, to be one of the boys. Entering the comedy world felt like I had to choose between being powerful or being feminine, but Russia presented me with a third option: both. The women taught me that I could have a face full of makeup *and* ambition beyond my femininity. It was okay to be strong, yet delicate. Russian women are the toughest broads out there, and I'm honored to be a part of the sisterhood.

I spent my last night in Russia at the Kremlin, where my parents spent their last night too. The pride of Moscow's past shines brightest at night and the Kremlin is the best place to take it all in. All the buildings are lit up like architectural Christmas trees—it's truly breathtaking.

We walked over to the exact spot where my parents took their final photo in Russia, only to find it was gated off. "Oh no," Olga gasped, knowing that I'd been wanting to replicate their photo since arriving.

Normally, I would've marinated in the disappointment of a symbolic opportunity ruined by bad timing. But I didn't much care. Either Olga's calm and collected nature had rubbed off on me, or I'm just getting older. Big problems of the past have shrunken to minor annoyances of today. I don't get as worked up when things don't go as planned.

The last photo my parents took in Russia. They are wasted.

Mainly because I'm done overexerting myself on the small stuff.

"Do you want a drink?" I asked Olga, no longer needing my phrase book to guide me.

We briefly debated whether or not to Uber,* but decided to take the train so that I could say goodbye to my beloved Metro. I could've spent the entire trip in the Moscow Metro. Each stop looked like its own magnificent museum; some with painted ceilings, others with bronze statues in every corner, all radiating the regal beauty of a different era. The Metro was where I finally understood the showy elegance of Moscow. Deep beneath the monstrous buildings, and even bigger egos, lay the desire to be beautiful, to be accepted and imitated by all. The Metro is where I began to relate to my birth country.

The Mayakovskaya Metro stop, where Sophka lived, had art deco columns, marbled walls, and large metallic arches at every entrance.

"I used to stand at one end of the arch and slide a ruble to my friend at the other end," my dad told me over FaceTime. "If I did it right, the ruble would slide across the entire arch and land in my friend's palm."

As we waited for the train, I took a ruble and slid it up the side of one of those metal arches. A flicker of familial connection tickled my soul. The steel blur flew up the wall, over my head, to the other side of the arch where it hit the marbled floor only to roll back to my feet. Olga and I cheered so loud that our yells reverberated off the ceiling mosaics.

This was the country I was taught to fear. Fear that was fueled by my parents and anchored by movies, media, and

---

* Yes, Russia has Uber too. It's exactly the same as it is in the US, except all the drivers are from the US and have thick American accents. Just kidding.

neighborhood bullies yelling "Communist!" But when you greet fear with open arms and laughter, the fear diminishes, first within yourself, and then within those around you. A week into my trip, my parents began to tell me lighter stories of their childhood, stories that had happiness hidden within their words. During one of our daily check-ins, my mom told me of the time her parents took her to Детский мир, the Russian equivalent of Toys 'R' Us. "It was the best day of my life," she said, the phone screen reflecting her glassy eyes. My heart folded in half at the thought of my mom as a rosy-cheeked eight-year-old standing in line at the toy store. Years before she got her tonsils ripped from her throat and her mother died, Olga had a day at Детский мир. I went there a few days later with my cousin's daughter, Anya, and bought everything she could carry. As I stood there between a stuffed gorilla and a *Frozen* display, my pilgrimage felt complete.

Russia gave me something I didn't know I needed: closure on my past. Answering where I came from helped me figure out where I'm going. Sharing a dinner table with people who had loved and held me as a baby was an incredible experience. It encouraged me to move forward with confidence, power, and security in the fact that I'd earned my tiny spot in the world.

I landed in Los Angeles on a Saturday afternoon in August. After a long and uneventful wait in the immigration line, a sterile machine checked my passport and scanned my face. "Can I offer you a cigarette?" I asked the machine. It did not answer.

30

WRITE A BOOK

Please flip to page one.

APPENDIX

A LIFE PLAN FOR TWO, FOLLOWED BY ONE

Modern Love

BY MARINA SHIFRIN

APRIL 4, 2013

Kevin was everything an overweight ten-year-old girl could ever hope for in a man. His hair was the color of Cheetos and he was an incredible speller. It was decided; I was in love.

"You live six houses down from me," he said, making my heart turn inside out. My family had just moved to Highland Park, Ill., from Skokie, Ill., and I didn't know anyone. Here was this magnificent boy who actually had taken the time to calculate how many houses stood between us. I started to wonder if the glow from my wedding dress would make him look washed-out.

Soon after, I began devising a plan in which Kevin and I would end up "2gether 4ever," as all my notebooks stated.

Months of morning strolls to the bus yielded a confession from Kevin: he had a crush on Caitlin, who was thin, blonde and cheery: my opposite. I didn't mind. I figured it would be healthy for us to see other people before we spent the rest of our lives together.

When he asked me whom I liked, I panicked. I wasn't ready to reveal my plan, so I made a promise: I'd tell him everyone I'd ever liked on my sixteenth birthday. It worked. He went back to lusting after Caitlin, and I went back to picking out names for our children.

On my sixteenth birthday, Kevin (who by then had moved on, crush-wise, to Haley) was waiting in my driveway. Admitting to your best friend that you have liked him for the entirety of your friendship is about as awkward as getting a bikini wax from your dentist.

I could have lied, but Kevin had developed this annoying habit of reading my thoughts. Finally, I worked up the courage to tell him the truth: I'd had a crush on him for a few years, but was totally over it. Totally.

He took the news as any scrawny, pale high-school boy would: by triumphantly leaning back in his chair like a champion. I began to worry about the plan and our future together, not knowing that a few months later we would encounter our largest obstacle yet.

Surprisingly, our relationship hadn't changed much after my confession. About four years earlier we had started a tradition where we would shoot hoops at one of our houses until it was time for dinner; very 1970s of us, even though it was really the late '90s. And one night, a few months after I had partly professed my love, we decided to just sit and talk, lamenting how high school was half over and neither of us had received our first kiss.

Ten minutes later I was wiping slobber from my double chin, shocked at how easy that was. The plan was progressing much faster than I had imagined.

A couple of months after our first kiss, Kevin asked me to come over because he had something to tell me. I grabbed my basketball and greased my lips with Lip Smacker's Dr Pepper flavor. As I passed the fourth house, my stomach sank. I realized Kevin was going to ask me out, and I was going to have to say no.

It was too early. I knew we had to wait until after college, so both of us could get good at sex. That's what college is for, right?

When I arrived, he was already shooting hoops. We threw the ball around until I was ready to explain why we had to wait before we became girlfriend-boyfriend.

"So, I have a girlfriend," Kevin said, interrupting my thoughts.

I was stunned. "That's so great!" I yelled over my shoulder. "My mom said I need to be home to help with dinner and clean my room. OK, bye!"

Their relationship went strong for the first year, even stronger for the second. I began to lose faith in the plan. Then Kevin's first girlfriend cheated on him during our senior-year spring break.

As soon as I heard the news, I skipped up his driveway with a basketball under my arm. It wasn't until I saw how devastated he was that I decided to focus my energy on putting him back together. Before I could even get excited about the possibility of taking her place, college entered the picture, and with it came our largest speed bump: I was moving to Missouri, and Kevin was staying in Illinois.

He came over the morning I was leaving for Missouri; I had promised him he would be the last person I said goodbye to before I left. He cried and I made fun of him, then we sat in my driveway dreading the fact that we wouldn't live six houses away from each other anymore.

Thanks to the wonders of twenty-first-century technology, we stayed close. But it wasn't until our junior year that the plan started up again. I was going through my latest breakup when

Kevin suggested I come visit him. Approximately five seconds after he suggested it, I hopped into my car and made the seven-hour trek to Chicago.

I remember scanning the disgusting walls of his frat house as I swirled the contents of my red Solo cup. Somewhere between the last drink and his morning alarm, Kevin and I moved into the final phases of my plan: we slept together. For some reason, though, it ended up feeling more like a goodbye than a hello.

The next morning, we gave each other a confused embrace before I walked to my car with what felt like one of the worst hangovers of my life. The cold Chicago air ripped tears from my eyes as I slammed my car door and checked my phone. A text from Kevin: "when do u want 2 talk about this?"

I wasn't hungover; I was heartbroken. I sat in my car and sobbed.

Later that week, Kevin told me he valued our friendship too much to take the "risk" of dating. I told him I totally agreed. Totally.

Yet I still wasn't quite ready to abandon the plan.

If I've learned anything during the approximately twenty-seven times I've watched "When Harry Met Sally," it's that you need to ignore your best friend for a month, and in that time he will realize he's in love with you and will come charging back into your life at the first available opportunity.

So I ignored Kevin's texts and calls, patiently waiting for him to realize we really were supposed to be together. When I was back home for New Year's I made sure every status advertised my whereabouts for the night. How else was he going to burst in at midnight to tell me he couldn't live without me? Spoiler alert: he didn't.

Subsequently, I decided to move to New York, where twentysomethings who no longer believe in love go to pursue more attainable goals, like being a stand-up comic. One day I awoke to an e-mail from my parents; the basketball hoop in my front yard had been knocked over during a storm and they decided to remove it completely.

I took this as a sign to officially abandon the plan. This time I cut Kevin out of my life completely and began to focus on more important things, like my blossoming waitressing career.

Years later, I was surprised to find myself sitting in a booth across from Kevin in Highland Park. He held my hands as I cried over all the time we'd lost while I was too busy ignoring his apologies and refusing his friendship. I asked if he could forgive me for trying to push him out of my life, and he responded with, "I'm just glad there isn't a redheaded two-year-old sitting next to you."

We were going to be OK. With that, I returned to the city where homeless dreamers rub elbows with the dreamers with homes, hopeful that our reunion would repair what had been lost. Slowly we began talking again and keeping track of each other's lives. Our conversations were different now that I had given up the self-consciousness that plagues girls who have fallen in love.

A couple of months ago I was crashing at my parents' house before moving out of the country. Kevin came over for a quick goodbye before heading to work. He got out of his car and gave me a hug.

"Why do you have to move so far away from me?" he asked as our chins wrapped around each other's shoulders. My heart, once again, turned inside out.

I am no longer in love with Kevin, but I love him. Two letters, big difference. I love him when he has girlfriends and when I have boyfriends. I love him when he makes me laugh and when he makes me cry. I love him when he says goodbye and when he says hello. I love him when he knows my thoughts and even when he doesn't. I know he will always be there no matter how hard I try to get rid of him.

The plan had totally worked. Totally.